D1570184

LINGUISTIC ANALYSIS
AND PHENOMENOLOGY

Also by Wolfe Mays

THE PHILOSOPHY OF WHITEHEAD
ÉTUDES D'ÉPISTÉMOLOGIE GÉNÉTIQUE,
vols I and IV (*with others*)

Also by S. C. Brown

DO RELIGIOUS CLAIMS MAKE SENSE?

LINGUISTIC ANALYSIS AND PHENOMENOLOGY

EDITED BY

WOLFE MAYS

*Reader in Philosophy at the University
of Manchester and Editor of 'The Journal
of the British Society for
Phenomenology'*

and

S. C. BROWN

*Lecturer in Philosophy at Birkbeck
College, London, and Assistant Director
of the Royal Institute of Philosophy*

LEWISBURG: BUCKNELL UNIVERSITY PRESS

ASSOCIATED UNIVERSITY PRESSES, INC.
CRANBURY, N.J. 08512

Library of Congress catalog card no. 70-165551

ISBN: 0-8387-1025-5

Printed in Great Britain

CONTENTS

Part Three: Aesthetics

Part Four: Body and Mind

Part Five: Good and Evil

Part Six: Philosophical Methodology

PREFACE

THE following is an edited record of the 'Philosophers into Europe' Conference held at the University of Southampton in 1969 under the auspices of the Royal Institute of Philosophy and the British Society for Phenomenology. The papers are published as they were then presented and reflect, therefore, the views of their authors at that time.

The title *Linguistic Analysis and Phenomenology* may suggest that the contributors to this volume write either as analytical philosophers or as phenomenologists. We recognise, however, that a number of the contributions do not strictly belong to either category and some indeed not at all. What emerged from the Conference was that there is a greater community of *interest* in Western philosophy than might be expected. In some symposia, indeed, an affinity rather than a diversity of *approach* is apparent.

The editors wish to record their gratitude to the following persons who have assisted in the preparation of this volume: to Miss Hephzibah Crane for compiling the index, to Mrs Olive Ayers for typing much of the manuscript, and to Mrs Mavis Brown for transcribing much of the discussion from the tapes.

W. M.
S. C. B.

1

INTRODUCTION

Wolfe Mays

Wolfe Mays

I. LOGICIANS AND LOTUS-EATERS

ONE increasingly finds in philosophical writings nowadays references
to the differences which exist between phenomenology and linguistic
analysis, and the difficulties of reconciling them. Even the journalist
has taken a hand here: some years ago in the American magazine
Time (7 January 1966) there appeared a 'write-up' of these two
schools: philosophers belonging to the latter school were referred to
as logicians, because of their interest in logic and language, whilst
those belonging to the former were referred to as lotus-eaters,
because of their concern with subjective experience. In such
discussions phenomenology is often referred to as Continental
philosophy, but it is far from being the dominant school on the
Continent. And although linguistic analysis tends to be identified
with British philosophy, there are still some philosophers in Britain
who do not accept its main tenets.

Kaufmann, commenting on this situation, thinks it to be one of the
saddest features of our age that we are faced with such an entirely
unnecessary dichotomy between those who are devoted to intellectual cleanliness and rigour, but who deal with small, and often
trivial, questions, and those who attempt to deal with the big and
interesting questions, but in such an obscure manner that positivist
critics argue that such attempts are doomed to failure[1]. Morton
White too believes that nothing could be more important than
reuniting these two contrasting elements in twentieth-century
philosophy: the analytic, pragmatic, linguistic concern of the recent
Anglo-American tradition needs to be supplemented by some of the
insights and the more humane cultivated concerns of the predomin-

antly Continental tradition.[2] Unfortunately, the encounter between
the Anglo-Saxon and French philosophers at Royaumont in the late
1950s, which was intended to produce some sort of *rapprochement*,
seems to have ended in mutual incomprehension.[3]

2. DIFFERENCES BETWEEN THE TWO SCHOOLS

Western philosophy has, however, always had a twofold character.
On the one hand, it has exhibited a more general interest in broader
questions having a humane and cultural significance. Many
Eastern philosophies are of this sort: Confucianism, for example,
largely consists of ethical precepts. On the other hand, there has also
been an interest in questions of a more specialised kind dealing, for
example, with epistemological and logical matters, which have
usually been a necessary preliminary to the discussion of these
broader issues. If two parties wish to arrive at some agreement as to
the nature of the good or justice, some initial definition of the term is
desirable, if they are to have a common starting-point and avoid
misunderstandings.

What seems to have happened increasingly in recent years, at
least among analytical philosophers, is that there has been a much
larger concern with questions of methodology than with questions
relating to the broader kinds of problem. For the analytical philosopher the main function of philosophy is not to answer the big
questions of life and the universe, but rather to clarify the language
in which we talk about them. When this is done we shall see, he
argues, that these problems largely arise from confusions as to our
use of language. He would deny that it was his task to give moral
advice or to make moral pronouncements: this, he would say, ought
to be left to the minister, priest or wise man. However, not all
philosophers would wish to separate off the wisdom aspect or
philosophy from the more methodological aspects. The former,
reflected in the study of value judgements of what is good, beautiful
and true, has from the time of Plato, at least, formed a very important part of the subject-matter of philosophy, and distinguished it
from such factual sciences as physics and biology.

The earlier analytical philosophers, such as G. E. Moore,[4] were
mainly concerned with the meaning of statements rather than the
study of facts, which they felt could be left to the scientist, and with
the analysis and clarification of common-sense beliefs. More recent
linguistic philosophy, following Wittgenstein, has argued that philosophy is concerned with 'use' rather than 'meaning'. Its task is to
note when a word is legitimately used and when not. On this view,
philosophical perplexity arises because some people abuse our

ordinary ways of speaking. For example, one might say that when we talk of survival after death, we are wrongly using the word survival. The only legitimate sense in which it can be used is in the sense it has in such a phrase as 'survival after a train accident', where survival means bodily survival. What is meant by legitimacy in such discussions is not always made clear, nor for that matter is 'normal usage' on which legitimacy seems to depend.

Husserl, who was the founder of the phenomenological school, tried, on the other hand, to get beyond not only language, but our everyday preconceptions involved in the common-sense approach to the world. He was concerned with examining and describing our individual experiences, in the hope that we could get back to our original primitive experience before it became overlaid by our everyday conceptions. Existentialist writers who have to some extent been influenced by Husserl have emphasised the study of our particular concrete lived experiences. For example, Heidegger and Sartre regard man as a decision-making creature having freedom of choice, and involved in extreme situations. Situations such as that of the member of the French Resistance subjected to torture by the Gestapo are not to be regarded as exceptional – since they reveal the true situation in which we are all the time.

This polarisation between phenomenology and linguistic analysis is, however, a considerable simplification. Some types of phenomenology have much more in common with logical studies: this is especially the case with the writings of Husserl, who was originally a mathematician by training. On the other hand, some of the more recent kinds of linguistic philosophy have an informal non-systematic character. In their search for the concrete and the particular they resemble the existentialists, although the latter direct themselves to subjective experience rather than language. But they differ in this essential respect that, as we have already seen, the existentialist believes that one can obtain an insight into man and the human situation by the study of extreme situations. The linguistic philosopher usually concentrates on the paradigm case, and takes ordinary linguistic usage as his standard and condemns divergent usages.

Thus if a linguistic philosopher wishes to explain what is meant by 'human freedom', he might proceed by analysing the different ways in which expressions like 'compelled', 'could have', 'chose to' and 'decide' are used. He would argue that knowing how to use these words is a condition of answering the question 'Are men free?' By the analysis of such words, it is claimed, we can discuss in an informal way the problems of value pervading our practical life. What seems to be assumed in this approach is that when we employ such a phrase as 'freedom of the will', it is in no way affected by the preconceptions, scientific, religious, etc., which are inherent in our language. Only if one takes up such a position can it be argued that ordinary language, in which our philosophical problems are to be expressed, is neutral.

Taylor has elaborated on the shortcomings of this approach by pointing out that the reason why most philosophical problems cannot be solved simply by the study of ordinary language is that they do not arise there: 'They arise within such bodies of doctrines as theology, metaphysics or science or on the borderline between these and ordinary fact. Each of these bodies of doctrine for instance has been responsible for a problem about the freedom of the will.'[5] For example, the findings of physiology and psychoanalysis have led to deterministic accounts of human nature. To this philosophers have contrasted our experience of the freedom of the will and our belief that we are responsible for our actions – a belief which certainly plays an important role in ethics, theology and law. In a court of law, for example, this may show itself in a conflict between the evidence of the psychiatrist as to the diminished responsibility of the prisoner, who may, say, have killed his wife, and the judge who refuses to accept this evidence and continues to assign full responsibility to the prisoner for his action.

If we really wish to understand the meaning of such words as 'free will', an appeal to ordinary usage is not always enough. In the case of 'freedom of the will', Taylor tells us, it is assumed that the theories which inhabit the infected terms, 'cause', 'freedom', 'physical', 'mental', etc., flee on being confronted with their ordinary selves, and this, he goes on, is simply a reaffirmation of the common-sense view of the world.[6] Consider the example we quoted earlier: if we analyse the notion of survival by reference to our everyday use of this word, as when we speak of survival after a train accident, we may prejudge the issue, as this comparison implicitly accepts the view that the only sort of survival is bodily survival. But the notion of survival has varied from age to age; for example, in the Middle Ages one burnt the bodies of heretics in order that their souls might survive.

The analyst's belief that we ought to express all philosophical concepts into those of ordinary language seems bound up with his view that in philosophy, unlike science, there is no need for a technical vocabulary, since the problems with which philosophers are or should be concerned arise in our common-sense world, and here ordinary language is supreme. Austin, for example, believed that everyday English had built into it all the subtle distinctions men had found it necessary to draw in the past. And as it has stood up to the test of time in all ordinary and reasonable practical matters, we ought not to interfere with it, unless we had good reasons for doing so.[7]

Although Austin is making a valid point against a too facile rectification of names, and the introduction of technical neologisms in philosophy, his argument could be taken as a justification not only of conservatism in thought, but also in ideas. There is no reason to believe that past linguistic practice is necessarily a good guide to future linguistic practice. Poets as well as scientists coin new vocabularies to express the kind of experience they are interested in. And further, as Austin himself clearly recognised, ordinary language is not unbiased and free from superstition.

A case could certainly be made out for accepting our ordinary language as a guide to the practical and moral questions of life, since most of our everyday problems are expressed in terms of it. But ordinary language runs into difficulties not only when we deal with technical scientific questions, but also when we concern ourselves with abnormal types of experience. Psychoanalysis has therefore had to coin a new vocabulary to express some of the concepts it has introduced in order to study such experience, for example such terms as the Id, Super Ego, Oedipus Complex, etc. If we took ordinary language as a guide here, it could be argued that since the personal pronoun 'I' was simple, so also is the structure of the self.

This does not mean that the linguistic approach to philosophy is not without its solid philosophical achievements. It has developed among its practitioners a great sensitivity to subtle differences in the use of words. In certain fields analysis is helpful as an antidote to woolly thinking. But it has been argued that its influence has been largely a negative one. By concentrating on analysis it has discouraged philosophers from having new ideas and led them to concentrate on making finer and finer distinctions, in diagnosing what we can already say in ordinary language. Knowing how to use our language will not, it is pointed out, answer our philosophical questions unless we arbitrarily assume that one specific language gives us a privileged insight into the nature of things, and some such assumption seems to underly a great deal of such philosophical thinking.

The claim of linguistic analysis, that its function is to teach and develop techniques which are neutral with respect to moral and social values, has been criticised on the ground that such an approach gives us no moral critique of present-day thought, and takes the moral rules and speech of society as it finds them. But these rules often reflect social standards of behaviour which are themselves up for discussion. A social reformer might regard at least some of them as pernicious and harmful and in need of change. The neutral role assigned to ethical inquiry by linguistic philosophers may be clearly seen if we compare, for example, their position with that of the French existentialists. The former tell us that the function of the moral philosopher is simply to analyse and clarify the language in which ethical problems are stated, although they stress the need to lay down general rules for the correct use of ethical statements. They argue that agreement on moral matters demands some moral rules accepted by us, and this attempt to find a moral justification for doing or choosing a particular course of action in a given situation always involves an appeal to a moral principle which is regarded as universalisable.

The existentialist, on the other hand, tends to emphasise individual differences and non-standard moral situations. For him the basis of ethics is to be found in intuitive decision-making rather than intellectual rule-following. It is not, he says, by the application of abstract moral rules that we can make decisions. Such abstract principles do not make any difference to our initial choices. They are only used to justify our decisions after they have been made. Our choices are therefore ontologically prior to any such justification. For Sartre, for example, it is just as fallacious to believe that the approval of another or of society can justify our actions, as it is to think that universally valid absolutes or objectives exist.

3. ATTEMPTS AT RECONCILIATION

Despite the apparent difference between ordinary-language philosophy and phenomenology, attempts have been made to bring these schools of thought closer together. It has been argued that the gulf between them is not as great as may seem at first sight, since they have a number of points in common. They are both concerned, it is held, with the pre-theoretical world of lived experience and language, rather than with the world posited by science. They are also opposed to dualism, refuse to treat mind as an occult process, and are against metaphysical speculation. Hence they would seem to be considering similar sorts of questions, but from different standpoints.[8]

In support of this position it is argued that phenomenologists such as Heidegger and Merleau-Ponty have a deep interest in language. In addition ordinary-language philosophy today has a fundamental concern in the active agent as the locus of meaning, and directs our attention to the context of actual use for an understanding of our words and expressions. It now emphasises the behavioural aspects of language and talks of speech acts rather than statements (e.g. Austin). Other recent forms of linguistic philosophy (e.g. Hampshire) emphasise freedom and choice, and in this sense they may be said to have an existential dimension.

Both phenomenology and linguistic analysis, it has been argued, are primarily concerned with conceptual analysis. Commenting on this claim, Edie points out that the concept is no longer a clear-cut distinct idea, but rather a behavioural, contextual, implicit 'meaning', which is laboriously discovered by means of investigations of linguistic usage, and never fully grasped in full self-reflexive clarity. Nevertheless, he goes on, 'the "concepts" which are the objects of linguistic analysis seem necessarily to be limited to the realm of fully reflexive categorial thought'.[9] He is, however, not entirely happy with this sort of attempt to reconcile the two schools; he notes that phenomenology is also concerned with the realm of pre-reflective awareness, and with the elucidation of the structures of experience which precede and condition thought about it, before they are expressed in linguistic terms. But he concedes that both linguistic analysis and phenomenology, although using very different kinds of data, seem to be interested in similar sorts of questions. Edie believes that we ought to play down the differences between their respective methods, and come rather to grips with the substantial philosophic problems with which they are both concerned. Although at the same time he warns us that this 'must not lead us too hastily to minimise the radically different means they use to establish these conclusions'.[10]

But not all writers would admit (1) that there are substantial points of agreement between these two schools, or even (2) that they deal with similar sorts of problems. Natanson,[11] for example, is of the opinion that the notion of 'intentionality', that is, the idea that all consciousness involves consciousness of an object, is missing from the analyst's account, since he is primarily concerned with linguistic usage. And this, Natanson tells us, leads to a very different account of meaning, one which ignores the fact that language is only meaningful to someone who speaks and listens and gives sounds a meaning. In addition, he argues, there is a range of experiences, within which meanings are grasped before they are expressed in linguistic terms. He regards the world of common-sense experience in which we as persons are involved, and the ordinary language we use to express the meanings located there, as dealing rather with surface phenomena, whose depth and structure the phenomenologist endeavours to uncover. He then agrees with Husserl that our common-sense picture of the world involves an abstract categorisation, which we must put on one side if we wish to give an adequate description of the immediate data of experience.

Natanson makes the following further criticisms of linguistic philosophy: (1) since the analytical philosopher is primarily an observer, he shares with the scientist a professional distrust of first-person reports and thus adopts a view of mind different from that of the phenomenologist and one more akin to behaviourism; (2) an element of the early therapeutism remains in analysis with its insistence on treating the metaphysician as a disturbed person. Both these objections need some qualification. In the case of (1), phenomenologists such as Merleau-Ponty are much concerned with the study of human behaviour, but they would regard our actions as 'meaningful', that is, directed to some purpose, and not merely as sets of physiological reflexes; in the case of (2), some analytical philosophers have recently elaborated what they have termed a 'descriptive metaphysics', which bears some resemblance to phenomenological description, although the dimension described is still largely a linguistic one. Natanson recognises this when he, for example, describes the philosophical approaches of Strawson and Hampshire as 'egological, descriptive, and in a sense . . . phenomenological'.[12]

Despite the commendable efforts of some writers, mainly in America, to show that phenomenologists and linguistic philosophers are not as far apart philosophically as may appear at first sight, and despite the interesting points of resemblance they have established, there is one essential difference between these two approaches. This is clearly to be seen in Husserl, who urges us to attempt to see the world as freed (*a*) from the categories imposed by our public common-sense world, and (*b*) from the explanatory schema of science, and to concentrate instead on the data and values of our immediate experience as a basis for philosophising. The linguistic philosopher, on the other hand, accepts the common-sense view of things, as reflected through the mesh of language, and, unlike the Husserlian, he does not react to the contemporary scientific world picture, and is indeed unconcerned with it in his analyses. Although the phenomenologist accepts the findings of science, and recognises the legitimacy of the physical, biological and psychological approaches in their own respective spheres, he would regard them as being essentially theoretical, since they are largely concerned with causal explanations of observed phenomena.

4. THE PROBLEM OF METHOD

I will not attempt to summarise and comment on the symposia which made up the 'Philosophers into Europe' Conference; the reader may turn to the symposia themselves and the edited records of the discussion elsewhere in this volume. I will merely mention two basic problems which came up in them, and to which linguistic philosophy and phenomenology have each in their own way contributed. These are (1) the problem of method, which we have already touched upon, and which I shall discuss at greater length in this section, and (2) the concept of the person, which I shall discuss in the next section.

In (1) I shall be primarily concerned with the remarks of Manser, the chairman of the symposium on method. Manser is concerned to assimilate Continental philosophy to the British style of philosophising. He thinks that some 'common market-place' or forum for English and European philosophy might be best achieved if English philosophers endeavoured to show their colleagues across the Channel 'that the kind of researches which we are engaged in in this country are in fact relevant, and importantly so, to what is being done in Europe'.[13] He believes that we ought to produce philosophy in our current idiom, and not in the idiom employed currently in Continental philosophy, and try to show how it is relevant to questions asked or problems raised by Husserl, Heidegger or Merleau-Ponty and their disciples and colleagues.

Manser recognises that Continental philosophers have something worth saying. He would therefore not dismiss such questions or problems, as some analytical philosophers have done in the past, as meaningless or irrelevant. There is certainly much to be said for his contention that these questions or problems might be better dealt with in the idiom of English analytical philosophy, and I agree with him that if the work of Continental philosophers were expressed in more homely language, some of the difficulties of this kind of writing would, if not vanish, at least decrease considerably.

Manser rejects Husserl's view that philosophy can be a strict or rigorous science, and points out that Husserl did not simply chronicle his eidetic intuitions but also attempted to convince other people. Manser goes on to suggest that Husserl's aim was to make philosophy like mathematics and physics.[14] However, whatever Husserl's aim may have been, he did think that he could only arrive at his philosophical concepts by something like a process of approximation, and that at the start of a philosophical inquiry all concepts or terms must remain fluid. We cannot, he says, begin philosophising with definitions of the type given in the exact sciences; we must always be prepared to refine the intuitions from which we start in our continuing investigations.'It is misleading and radically perverse to apply the formal and external standards of a logic of terminology to scientific work in the first stage of progressive effort.'[15] Clearness, he thinks, is quite compatible with a certain margin of indeterminacy. Phenomenology is therefore not to be thought of after the manner of an exact formal science, but has in some ways more the character of an empirical discipline.

Although most present-day phenomenologists would accept Husserl's emphasis on the description and clarification of our un-explicit knowledge of the structures inherent in experience, they would not all accept his view that philosophy should use the methodology of scientific inquiry, even if this is interpreted in a very liberal sense. Thus, Edie tells us, a certain flexibility is apparent within contemporary phenomenology. Phenomenologists do not now attempt to find a self-sufficient method applicable to all circumstances and to all phenomena. The categories of the early Husserlian phenomenology of reason have been found to be inadequate for the analysis of other realms of experience, for example, the aesthetic, religious, social and the pathological.[16] A considerable part of the philosophical writings of, for example, Sartre is concerned with descriptions of imaginative and emotional experience, which when compared with cognitive experience have a more fluid and imprecise character. And this, apart from the opaqueness of the language used, is one of the reasons why their writings often give the impression of being ambiguous and obscure. As Edie points out, from the frequent Anglo-American accusations of 'muddled logic' levelled against Sartre, one suspects that they are really distressed by so much empirical experience.[17]

Manser, following Wittgenstein, argues that there is not a philosophical method, but many methods, and quotes Wittgenstein's comparison of the methods of a philosopher with the tools of the carpenter. 'The "method" of carpentry, as it were, is to employ all the tools in the correct manner, appropriate to the job in hand.'[18] Although I would not wish to restrict philosophy solely to one method, one might find it difficult to find philosophical methods which correspond to the hammer, screwdriver, saw, etc., of the carpenter's tool-box. This appeal to the humble carpenter and his tool-box is reminiscent of Locke's comparison of himself to an underlabourer. In both cases there is an attempt to deflate the generalising activity of philosophers, by contrasting it with such down-to-earth concrete manual tasks. But if we concentrated on carpenters who were good at their job, instead of on their tools, then one's conception of the philosophical enterprise might be a very different one. Philosophy might have more the characteristics of an artistic or creative activity, and would then come much closer to the existentialist conception of it.

Tugendhat's approach to the problem of method was somewhat different from that of Manser, and certainly more in keeping with the traditional conception of philosophy as a study of general truths. Although critical of Husserl, whom he at one time followed, he is equally critical of some kinds of linguistic philosophy. If philosophy deals with the meaning of words, how are we to know, he asks, if philosophy is not to be trivial, which words are important ones?[19] To this Manser had answered, referring to Austin, that there was no *a priori* way of determining which words were the important ones.[20] Tugendhat, however, believes with Strawson that in philosophy the questions we discuss are of a certain level of generality, and he finds in the general structure of our linguistic understanding a criterion for distinguishing philosophically important words. For Tugendhat the subject-matter of philosophy is not conscious behaviour, but the un-explicit knowledge of the structure of our conscious behaviour.

Further, he believes that the structure which is being analysed (though linguistic) is not given in words at all. Philosophers, he tells us, have on the contrary 'to invent new words (or new meanings for old words) in order to describe the structural aspects they are interested in (e.g. 'reference', 'illocutionary act')'.[21] Tugendhat goes on, 'not only the connection between the primary elements of understanding may be non-linguistic, the primary elements themselves may be non-linguistic'. He illustrates this by pointing out that in the case of actions, 'The person who does something consciously understands and even knows what he is doing, yet neither he nor anybody else may be able to express in words what he is doing (making just this grimace, playing precisely that tune).'[22] For Tugendhat conscious lived behaviour would seem to be prior to its linguistic expression, and in this he is in agreement with most phenomenological writers, who make the existential dimension (even if in Tugendhat's case it is a conceptual one) prior to the linguistic one.[23]

Manser, however, is critical of Tugendhat's emphasis on the structure of conceptual behaviour and finds it difficult to accept as a basis for philosophising. He argues, 'If one starts an investigation with a belief in some underlying scheme, then one is liable to distort the facts to make them fit'.[24] He also finds unacceptable such generalisations as 'general features of human consciousness', 'the use

of words' and 'the structure of our conceptual apparatus' as these
emphasise general concepts at the expense of the particular case.
Manser's criticism of philosophy as a study of general concepts and
of the use of generalisation as a method, although deriving from
Wittgenstein, nevertheless resembles the sort of criticism Sartre
might make. Further, the linguistic philosopher's notion of poly-
morphism – that a concept has not one meaning, but refers to a
family of divergent although related meanings or uses – also bears
some resemblance to Sartre's emphasis on the concrete and particular case, and his rejection of abstract concepts as criteria for
understanding the human situation.

Because of this emphasis on the concrete and the particular, Sartre
is critical of the Cartesian attempt to identify consciousness with
knowledge, which presumably has for its object the abstract and the
general. Curiously enough, Ryle seems to make such an identification
in his earlier criticism of Husserl's doctrine of intentionality. On
Husserl's view, he tells us, knowing is with believing, guessing,
dreaming, wanting, etc., only a species or sub-species of 'consciousness of . . .'. He believes that Cook Wilson has shown in a strict
phenomenological manner that the whole assumption is vicious:
'Knowing is not one definable species of "consciousness of . . ."
among others, it is something anyhow partly in terms of which
believing, fancying, guessing, wanting and the rest have to be
defined';[25] and he continues, 'a phenomenology operating with this
modified notion of intentionality would not be obviously bound to
terminate in an egocentric metaphysic'.[26] But Husserl emphasised in
his philosophical writings the phenomenon of intersubjectivity – that
we are aware of other people, even if only by empathy, as sharing
with us similar sorts of experiences and meanings.[27]

Ryle's reinterpretation of intentionality does seem to assume that
philosophers can only speak meaningfully about mental acts which
can be expressed in cognitive terms. This comes out in Ryle's
statement that 'Belief *e.g.* is a state of mind involving *ignorance* of
such and such a *knowledge* of so and so: it involves more than that, but
at least it involves this double reference to knowledge'.[28] What Ryle
seems to be referring to here is rational belief, into which reflection
enters; but there are also so-called irrational beliefs which for the
subject have as much force as the beliefs entertained by a judicial
inquirer. Indeed 'rational belief' like rational subjective probability
seems to be a largely normative concept to which we endeavour to
attain in our more judicial moments, a calculated balance of
ignorance and knowledge.

Ryle's early position may be contrasted with that of Sartre, who argues that our consciousness of things is by no means limited to our knowledge of them. My knowledge of the tree, he tells us, is only one of my possible forms of consciousness of it. I can also, he says, love it, hate it, etc. – these are merely ways of discovering the world.[29] Similarly Van Breda points out, in criticism of Strawson, that the reality we wish to understand is not conceptual reality but the world in which we live in all its complexity. Apprehending the world through the use of concepts is not the only way – others are love, religion and emotion.[30]

As against the claim that philosophy concerns itself with the conceptual structures of consciousness, which form its subject-matter, Manser agrees with Wittgenstein that philosophy is not a subject to be learned. What philosophers have to do, he tells us, is to philosophise, to get on with the job in detail. He goes on, 'it is the problems which are primary, which determine what is to be described and what sort of description is necessary'.[31] We cannot decide *a priori* how to deal with any problem, nor even what problems will arise.

However, admirable as this delineation of the function and purpose of philosophy and the philosopher is, one may question (*a*) whether our philosophical descriptions always have to be connected with a problem, and (*b*) its corollary that the task of philosophy is simply to solve philosophical problems. Underlying the approach is the assumption that if philosophical problems can be stated in clear-cut terms, we will be able to get clear-cut solutions to them. But even in science the precise problem one is trying to solve is not always clear: often a solution may be arrived at by trial and error and inspired guesses. One may then find that one has solved a very different kind of problem from the one started with.

This view that if we could only state our position precisely, then we could obtain an agreed answer, has been vigorously championed by analytical philosophers. Unfortunately, after nearly half a century of analytical philosophy, most of the classical problems still remain with us. It does not, however, seem to be the case that the solution of philosophical problems has been the sole preoccupation of philosophers in the past. There are other types of philosophical activity, such as describing and analysing our experienced behaviour and language, which philosophers have engaged in, primarily because of their desire to understand our experience of human values. An existentialist might claim that an understanding of the manner and circumstances in which an individual makes a critical decision is just as important philosophically as, for example, solving the paradox of the liar.

Ayer has argued that description by itself, whether it is said to be of essences or of the ordinary or extraordinary use of words, is unlikely to be of philosophical interest. Description needs, he believes, 'to be undertaken in the service of some theory or with the aim of elucidating some philosophical puzzle; otherwise it soon turns out to be a bore'.[32] The first part of this remark seems to make philosophical inquiry resemble a scientific one, and the latter a logical one. But despite the reference to theory, Ayer does assume that the method of philosophy is discursive, and that its data are largely of a cognitive sort. On such an approach one tends to neglect those aspects which deal with our immediate aesthetic apprehension of things, and our intuitive ways of coming to terms with ourselves and other persons. On the other hand, if it takes note of such activities, it tends to assimilate them to a critical examination of the language in which they are expressed, and thereby makes the whole undertaking a purely cognitive inquiry.

Manser would seem to agree with the analyst that philosophy is in some ways a neutral inquiry, and that it is wrong for philosophers to tamper with ordinary usage. As Wittgenstein puts it, 'Philosophy may in no way interfere with the use of language; it can in the end only describe it . . . It leaves everything as it is'.[33] Wittgenstein assumes that philosophical problems are radically different from empirical problems, and are to be solved by looking into the workings of our language. But since our outlook upon the world and our language alter with social and scientific progress, philosophers, in order to take account of these changes, may, as we have already seen, have to coin new kinds of expression before ordinary language catches up, as it were. Further, the point also made that philosophical problems often occur in the no-man's-land between empirical inquiries, is highly relevant here. It is not possible to solve such problems merely by redefining ordinary language, which then, in any case, ceases to be ordinary. There has to be some reference to the empirical background, social or otherwise, against which these changes occur.

We have also seen that psychoanalysis, in order to describe and explain our abnormal behaviour, has had to go beyond ordinary language, and invent a new terminology. This has not gone unnoted by Austin, who tells us that in, for example, psychiatry, some extraordinary varieties of behaviour are noticed and clarified by means of concepts which have no equivalent expressions in ordinary speech: as examples he gives compulsive behaviour and displacement behaviour.[34] Although presumably they would have been given such expression if they had been of more practical importance. Analytical philosophers have tried to bring such concepts down to earth, as it were, by assimilating them to those of ordinary language. But if we try to reduce the Freudian concepts in this way, we overlook that they were initially brought in to deal with aspects of behaviour of which common-sense had not taken adequate account.

Further, Freudian theory endeavours to explain not only abnormal behaviour, but every kind of behaviour, normal or otherwise. As against the linguistic philosopher's acceptance of the paradigm case as a criterion of philosophical verisimilitude, a Freudian would claim that a study of abnormal experience enables us to obtain a better understanding of our so-called normal experience. In this the Freudian would be joined by the existentialist, with his belief that extreme situations give us a greater insight into human reality than the more mundane examples catalogued by the linguistic philosopher. And although Existentialism rejects the Freudian unconscious as an explanatory scheme, it has had to introduce the related distinction between pre-reflective and reflective consciousness.

5. THE PROBLEM OF THE PERSON

Another topic in which contemporary British philosophy is showing increasing interest is that of the person, and it is also one with which Continental philosophy has been much concerned. Of the two symposia on the person, one dealt with the general concept of a person and its relation to the mind – body problem, and the other with the concrete person as he finds himself in a particular ethical situation.

At least two different strands may be distinguished in past thinking about the person. There is (*a*) the legal sense in which there is an emphasis on the part a man plays in legal transactions. For all practical and legal purposes, despite all the changes a person may undergo, we still say he is one and the same person. Bodily continuity or identity plays an important part in this conception, and so also does the social aspect of a person.

And there is (*b*) the sense of self-consciousness, in which one is aware of oneself as having perceptions, feelings, thoughts, desires, aspirations, etc. The view that a person must necessarily have bodily attributes, i.e. that he is essentially embodied, does not seem to have troubled some classical philosophers who saw no inconsistency in persons existing without their bodies, which they regarded as disposable furniture of this vale of tears. On the other hand, a feature of more recent philosophical accounts of the person is to make bodily attributes an essential element in the definition of a person.

In recent years British analytical philosophers have interested themselves more in the logical concept of a person than in giving what might be called an ontological account of it, as an existentialist might. Thus for Strawson (the chairman of the '*Body and Mind*' symposium), the concept of a person is logically prior to one's experience of an individual mind or body.

In part Miss Ishiguro seems to agree with this approach. She believes that the primacy of the concept of the person, to which bodily and mental predicates are ascribable, is needed not merely to solve the 'other minds' problem, but in order to state it.[35] However, it might be argued that the problem only arises when one doubts one's immediate intuitive awareness of other persons, and proceeds to look for a justification of how we come to know their existence. The question is then shifted from the plane of immediate intuitive awareness (i.e. from an ontological level) on to that of formal knowledge (i.e. a logical one). It is only on the latter level that a logical justification for the existence of others becomes necessary.

Miss Ishiguro's position is a more complex one than that postulated by the analytical philosopher. In her approach to the concept of a person, she also accepts the view of Sartre and Heidegger, that a man's relationships with his future states are essential to our understanding of what a person is: the person is aware from within, as it were, of his intentions and projects. These projects and intentions are for Miss Ishiguro grasped in the causal physical world in which we discover ourselves as agents.[36] Spicker considers Miss Ishiguro's example of the way in which our whole body is involved when we write with a pen, by pointing out that for her 'the living, acting hand and the pen with which the whole person, i.e. the whole body, writes are "bodies" in the sense of "physical objects".'[37] A Sartrean would argue against Miss Ishiguro's position that it is the lived not the animal body through which we act, and further we do not act within the causal physical world but within the lived experienced world. It is this which makes our actions much more than sets of bodily movements, and gives them a meaningful character.

Spicker also notes that Miss Ishiguro uses the term 'future' equivocally: in some cases it refers to one's bodily continuity in the future, in others to one's intentions towards the future which are implicit in our understanding of ourselves as agents. In the former, she would seem to be accepting a purely third-person account of the body: bodily continuity in the future being conceived as occurring within the framework of public physical time. On the other hand, when we talk about our intentions or projects towards the future, these are bound up with time-consciousness – with our memories and expectations. It is on this level of our projects that we experience freedom, and can give cogent reasons why we undertake certain tasks.

Although, as van Peursen points out, Miss Ishiguro has attempted to bring together in her account of the person British conceptual analysis and European Existentialism,[38] it is doubtful whether she has been entirely successful in this enterprise. There would seem to be a tension between Miss Ishiguro's acceptance of the concept of the person having physical bodily attributes predicated of it, and her belief that a person has also the characteristics of a Sartrean 'for itself' taken up with its future projects. As Strawson points out, 'Miss Ishiguro undertakes to argue in favour of the primacy of the concept of a person from the nature of intentional action'.[39] For Sartre, however, the concept of a person has no logical priority but only an ontological one. Further, for him the person is not something self-contained in itself, but is dependent for its very existence upon its relationships with others. Our experience of others is a precondition of our being aware, not only of others, but also of ourselves as persons. He gives the example of someone looking through a keyhole, who when caught in the act manifests shame, and through his shame becomes conscious of himself as a person.

Miss Ishiguro regards the possession of bodily attributes as essential and not contingent attributes of a person. But there have been philosophers who have believed otherwise, that minds could exist without their earthly trappings. Findlay, for example, in the discussion on this symposium argued that a person could be a spirit, which, though requiring a body in this world, did not require his present particular elaborate investment. The statement that a person is essentially and not contingently embodied then involves a specific theory of the body – mind relationship. There is nothing inconsistent in the assumption that the concept of a person does not necessarily include bodily attributes – disembodied minds might exist.

Miss Ishiguro is critical of those British philosophers who accept rule-following as a criterion for understanding action, and for taking up moral attitudes, and who argue that rules can serve as patterns for analysing human intentional behaviour. She would agree with Sartre that our actions have to be understood in terms of our particular intentions and projects; she points out, 'When I do something with an aim, I know my aim without observation, but I do not always know what I do'. And she goes on, 'The awareness I have of following a rule is, as Melden says, not an observational one; I am not always *aware* of following a rule when I act'.[40] Sartre makes a similar point when he quotes Piaget's findings that children who are able to make an addition spontaneously cannot subsequently explain how they came about it.[41] Further, Miss Ishiguro points out that in the case of certain practices which she understands, 'I might not even know what would count as following the relevant rules', and she quotes as examples, setting out to paint or to annoy someone.[42]

On the other hand, a philosopher such as Peters, who accepts the rule-following model of human behaviour, and who believes that man is a rule-following animal, tells us that 'Man in society is like a chess-player writ large'.[43] Nevertheless, it is recognised that we are more than rule-following animals, since the subject identifies himself as someone who can follow or not follow rules. But not only can we decide whether or not to follow rules, we can also decide which rules to apply in specific situations, and we are also able to make up the rules as we go along. As we have seen, a Sartrean existentialist would argue that we do not make moral decisions simply by the application of abstract moral principles. Hence to compare our decision-making in society with that of a player in a game of chess is not particularly enlightening, especially as a good deal of one's behaviour is on a pre-reflective level and not clearly thought out.

The criticism that we cannot understand our behaviour, moral or otherwise, by a conscious reference to rules, has been met by the problem being shifted on to a different level. It would be argued that all behaviour is rule-motivated, whether we are consciously aware of these rules or not. For example, we are told by Peters that 'general standards or rules are implicit in the concept of an action'.[44] On this view rules seem to be built into our dispositions, capacities and skills in the form of an infrastructure which determines our behavioural activities, and are not simply contemplated by us on an intellectual level, for example, as principles for our moral arguments. But, if we do not know which rules we are applying and if we are motivated by them largely in an unconscious manner, in what way is our behaviour different from that of a machine, which applies rules without 'understanding' them?

One may contrast Miss Ishiguro's partly conceptualist approach to the person with that of Frings (in 'The Person' symposium). Frings wishes to make sense of the phenomenon of the person, and seeks its unity in what he terms the self-value of the person, that is, in one's ethical existence. In contrast to persons, he points out, things do not have self-value. Frings, for his part, draws a radical distinction between the animal body and the 'lived' body of experience. He brings out this difference by referring to the blush of shame and its expression in the blushing face: these, he tells us, are one and not to be separated in fact, as it is only a lived body which can be ashamed. Further, Frings believes that the self-value of the person must be distinguished from the values which are deliberatēly attached to man by way of societal legislation and religious doctrines or philosophical ideas of man.[45]

For Frings the unity of the person is an essentially dynamic and lived one, and has to be sought in our immediate non-theoretical acted-out experience with another, with whom we share our every-day world. But any observed data, he tells us, for instance of the other's lived body, his language and gestures, etc., will give an objective analysis of a person; the real person recedes into the background, and becomes something like an object of judgement. We deal instead with the abstract concept of a person divorced from its network of existential relationships.

What Frings considers to be fundamental is then not the logical concept of a person, which we can only attain in abstract thought, but our intuitive awareness of another, which seems to exhibit itself in something like an 'I–Thou' relationship. We seem to have an immediate intuitive awareness of others as persons, and the logical concept would seem to be parasitic on this experience. This immediate awareness of others as persons seems to be present even in children. It is well brought out in the story of the little girl who was ill, and said to her mother after the doctor's visit: 'I don't like that doctor, mummy, she doesn't treat you like a person, she treats you like an "it".'

6. THE PHILOSOPHERS INTO EUROPE CONFERENCE

Phenomenology as a subject has not been much cultivated in Britain in the past. There were Husserl's somewhat abortive London lectures in 1922; a symposium in 1932, in which Ryle, Hodges and Acton took part; and another symposium in 1959, in which Taylor and Ayer were symposiasts. The 1932 symposium reads as if the phenomenological movement had come to a dead end: as if the symposiasts were discussing a piece of intellectual history. They could, of course, not have had any foreknowledge of the later developments of phenomenology, especially its influence on philosophical thought in France and Germany in the years after the Second World War.

Over the last decade, however, there has been a growing interest in Britain in both phenomenology and existential philosophy, partly as a result of the writings of Sartre and Merleau-Ponty, which have been read and discussed by specialists in the field of French studies, as well as by philosophers. Indeed, in more than one university department of philosophy, students have pressed their teachers for courses on Sartre! Merleau-Ponty was invited to Manchester in 1961, where he delivered a lecture criticising Wittgenstein's theory of language, which does not seem to have been published. As a consequence of this increased interest in existentialism and phenomenology, some philosophers began to turn to the writings of Husserl and Heidegger upon which Merleau-Ponty's work was based. The work of the Polish philosopher Ingarden, a pupil of Husserl, also struck a note of sympathy in Britain, and he too visited Manchester and gave a lecture on aesthetics.

Despite all that has been written about the different styles of British and Continental ways of thinking, British philosophy has always had links with that of the Continent, even although at times it looked as if they were not only divorced but radically opposed to each other. At the end of the last century and the early part of this one, Hegel's prestige stood high; both Moore and Russell were Hegelians in their early years. The reputation of Kant has not fared so badly as that of Hegel in Britain, and he has retained the esteem of analytical philosophers. As far as more recent philosophy is concerned, the teachings of the Vienna Circle have not been without supporters in Britain. And turning to Wittgenstein himself, one should remember his Continental background: his early reading included Schopenhauer and Kierkegaard, and both have not been without effect on his thought.

Taking note of the increased interest in phenomenology, the Royal Institute of Philosophy and the British Society for Phenomenology decided to organise a conference with the aim of bringing about an interchange of views between, on the one hand, a number of younger British philosophers interested in Continental philosophy and, on the other, Continental philosophers who had some acquaintance with analytical modes of thinking. To emphasise the need for some community of thought between British and European philosophers, the conference was called 'Philosophers into Europe'. This title did come in for some criticism. It was argued that if the model for the conference was to be the European Economic Community, not everyone thought that it would be a good thing for Britain to enter the Common Market. But it was not entirely a misnomer, as the conference was also concerned with the way European philosophers were trying to come to terms with British analytical philosophy. What the organisers did wish to avoid was a repetition of the Royaumont Colloquium, in which there was little or no *rapport* between the Anglo-American and

Continental philosophers taking part. Hence in planning the conference an attempt was made to see that even if the contributors did not agree, they would at least communicate with and understand each other.

The conference was held at the University of Southampton, 26-29 September, 1969, and about 120 people attended. The proceedings of the six symposia organised are included in this volume, together with the chairmen's remarks, and an edited record of the discussion. Unfortunately, Professor Ricœur, who had agreed to take part in the 'Doing Good and Suffering Evil' symposium, was unable to attend, and so in 'The Person' symposium was Dr Moore, who, however, presented a paper and a reply to Professor Frings. In the event, the former symposium turned into an interesting debate between Professor Winch and Mr Daly.

What did the conference achieve and did it come up to the expectations of the organisers? It was clear at least from the informal discussion which went on after the symposia, at meals, etc., that the conference had been a success, if only in bringing together people with similar interests. But more than this, it led to a genuine interchange of ideas between British and Continental philosophers, and thereby to a greater appreciation of each other's points of view. An attempt was made, especially in the informal discussions, to translate some of the obscurer doctrines of phenomenology into the more homely language of British philosophy.

It must, of course, be remembered that many of the people attending the conference were already interested in phenomenology and existential philosophy. This interchange of views was helped by the fact that the Continental philosophers present were as much at home in English as in their own language, and were also sympathetic at least to some of the contributions of analytical philosophy. It was interesting to see how frequently Husserl's philosophical views came up in the symposia. Was it, one may ask, because Husserl's position fitted in more with contemporary British interests in logic and analysis than, say, Heidegger's? One must not, of course, overlook that Husserl had been appreciative of the tradition of British empiricism from Locke to Mill and indeed claimed that in his phenomenology he was putting forward a radical empiricism. What the conference, then, did show was that the concepts of phenomenology and existentialism were being assimilated, if only slowly, into British analytical modes of thinking.

NOTES

1 Walter Kaufmann (ed.), *Existentialism from Dostoevsky to Sartre* (Cleveland and New York: Meridian Books, 1965) p. 51.

2 Morton White (ed.), *The Age of Analysis* (New York: Mentor Books, 1955) p. 242.

3 Quatrième Colloque de Royaumont, published as *La Philosophie analytique* (Paris, 1962).

4 See the discussion of these two schools in the *Time* magazine article, New York, 7 Jan. 1966.

5 Charles Taylor, 'Phenomenology and Linguistic Analysis', *Proceedings of the Aristotelian Society* supp. vol. XXXIII (1959) 107.

6 Ibid., p. 108.

7 J. L. Austin, 'A plea for Excuses', *Proceedings of the Aristotelian Society*, LVII (1956-7) 11, reprinted in *Philosophy and linguistics*, ed. Colin Lyas (London: Macmillan, 1971) pp. 79-101.

8 Eugene TeHeneppe, 'The Life-World and the World of Ordinary Language', in *An Invitation to Phenomenology*, ed. James M. Edie (Chicago: Quadrangle Books, 1965) pp. 132-46.

9 James M. Edie, 'Recent Work in Phenomenology', *American Philosophical Quarterly*, 1 2 (Apr. 1964) 125.

10 Ibid.

11 Maurice Natanson, 'Phenomenology and the Natural Attitude', in *Literature, Philosophy and the Social Sciences* (The Hague: Martinus Nijhoff, 1962) pp. 34-43.

12 Ibid., p. 41.

13 Anthony Manser, 'On Phenomenology as the Method of Philosophy', p. 273 below.

14 Ibid., p. 274 below.

15 Edmund Husserl, *Ideas* (London: Allen & Unwin, 1967) p. 245.

16 Cf. Edie, 'Recent Work in Phenomenology', loc. cit., p. 118.

17 Paul Thévenaz, in *What is Phenomenology?* ed. James M. Edie (London: Merlin Press, 1962) p. 167, n. 11.

18 Manser, loc. cit., p. 278 below.

19 E. Tugendhat, 'Description as the Method of Philosophy: A Reply to Mr Pettit', p. 259 below.

20 Manser, loc. cit., p. 276 below.

21 Tugendhat, loc. cit., p. 260 below.

22 Ibid., p. 260-1 below.

23 In addition there is some evidence that conceptual knowledge is not necessarily linguistic. H. G. Furth, *Thinking without Language* (Glencoe, Ill.: The Free Press; London: Collier-Macmillan, 1966) has shown with large numbers of deaf children and adults that many advanced forms of thinking may show little impairment, even though the thinker has a minute vocabulary and syntax. This would seem to indicate that the models of thought and language set up by linguistic philosophers are not entirely in accord with the empirical evidence.

24 Manser, loc. cit., p. 277 below.

25 G. Ryle, 'Phenomenology', *Proceedings of the Aristotelian Society*, supp. vol. XI (1932) 80.

26 Ibid., p. 81.

27 On the question of solipsism, see Husserl's letter to Dawes Hicks, 15 Mar. 1930 (quoted with permission of Professor H. L. Van Breda from *Jahrbuch für Philosophie und Phänomenologische Forschung*, p. 3) where he comments on Gilbert Ryle's 1929 *Mind* critical notice of Heidegger's *Sein und Zeit*:
'Mr Ryle is incidentally very much in the wrong in thinking that phenomenological idealism is solipsism. He has underestimated the full significance of the phenomenological reduction, and this through my own fault, since the *Ideas* have remained a fragment. It was only the second part that was to deal with the phenomenology of intersubjectivity' (our translation).

28 Ryle, loc. cit., p. 80.

[29] Cf. 'Intentionality: A Fundamental Idea of Husserl's Phenomenology', trans. J. P. Fell, *Journal of the British Society for Phenomenology*, i 2 (May 1970).

[30] Richard Rorty (ed.), *The Linguistic Turn: Recent Essays in Philosophical Method* (Chicago: University of Chicago Press, 1967) 25b, Father H. L. Van Breda, 'Discussion of Strawson's "Analysis, Science and Metaphysics" ', pp. 326–7.

[31] Manser, loc. cit., p. 279 below.

[32] A. J. Ayer, 'Phenomenology and Linguistic Analysis', *Proceedings of the Aristotelian Society*, supp. vol. (1959) 124.

[33] L. Wittgenstein, *Philosophical Investigations*, trans. G. E. Anscombe (Oxford: Blackwell, 1953) sect. 124, p. 49e.

[34] Austin, loc. cit., p. 30.

[35] Hide Ishiguro, 'A Person's Future and the Mind–Body Problem', p. 163 below.

[36] Ibid., p. 178 below.

[37] Stuart Spicker, 'The "Philosophers into Europe" Conference', *Journal of the British Society for Phenomenology*, i 3 (Oct. 1970) 23; also pp. 199–200 below.

[38] C. A. van Peursen, 'A reply to "A Person's Future and the Mind–Body Problem" ', p. 179 below.

[39] P. F. Strawson, 'Chairman's Remarks' on 'A Person's Future and the Mind–Body Problem', p. 186 below.

[40] Ishiguro, loc. cit., p. 172 below.

[41] Jean-Paul Sartre, *Being and Nothingness*, trans. Hazel E. Barnes (New York: Philosophical Library, 1956) p. liii.

[42] Ishiguro, loc. cit., p. 172 below.

[43] R. S. Peters, *The Concept of Motivation* (London: Routledge & Kegan Paul, 1958) p. 7.

[44] Ibid., p. 14.

[45] See Manfred S. Frings's contribution to the discussion in the symposium 'The Person', pp. 97–8; also p. 75 below.

PART ONE
FREEDOM AND DETERMINISM

B

2

FREEDOM AND DETERMINISM

Catherine Berry

I WISH to discuss the following statement by Maine de Biran, which I think represents quite fairly his position on freedom:

> Liberty or the idea of liberty, taken at its real source is nothing other than the feeling of our activity or power to act, to create the effort which constitutes the *self*.[1]

For Maine de Biran our inner sense (which he calls *sens interne* or *sens intime*) gives us our idea of liberty. We have from inside a certain feeling of ourselves as cause of certain actions, and this awareness of our power to act is our ground for holding that such actions are free. He further maintains that this experience contrasts with the feeling of undergoing something passively, being caused, or necessitated. He wants to disprove any claim that all our actions in one way or another are passive or necessitated.

Biran tries to do this by showing that all actions could not be determined because we have the experience of freedom and without it we would have no understanding of the contrasting experience of necessity. Furthermore, to question liberty would be to question our own existence, for, if liberty is defined as the feeling of ourselves as cause of actions and of effort, and this effort constitutes the self, to question the experience of effort is to question the existence of the self. The same fact of inner sense establishes both at once. And since the feeling of effort gives the awareness of my *self* through the feeling of my power to act, liberty must be logically prior to necessity. The

[1] *Essai sur les fondements de la psychologie*, ed. Tisserand, t. VIII, p. 250.

experience of passivity could not be primary because the subject of that experience would not be aware of himself as subject.

Is Maine de Biran's appeal to the feeling of freedom to refute determinism any more effectual than Dr Johnson's kicking a stone to refute Berkeley's idealism?

Spinoza alerts us to the danger of relying on our inner feeling of freedom in his *Note* to Proposition II, in Part III of the *Ethics*:

> Thus an infant thinks that it freely desires milk, an angry child thinks that it freely desires vengeance, or a timid child thinks it freely chooses flight. Again, a drunken man thinks that he speaks from the free will of the mind, those things which, were he sober, he would keep to himself . . . when we dream that we speak, we think that we speak from the free decision of the mind, yet we do not speak, or if we do, it is due to a spontaneous motion of the body.

In such cases a person other than the agent would not call these actions free, the testimony of the agent is overridden by other criteria. The presence of a feeling of freedom is no guarantee that the action it accompanies is correctly designated as free.

It could also be alleged, on the other hand, that people sometimes act freely without any characteristic free feeling. Just as we can act intentionally without having formed an intention to do what we do, I do not see that we must always feel ourselves to be the cause of our actions in order to be acting freely. And if it is said, 'You always have the feeling but you may not be aware of it', we could start to question whether it is a fact of experience that is being invoked, or an *a priori* principle. Or, if it is maintained that the self is cause whether or not we experience ourselves causing something, then it looks as if that notion does not rely exclusively on inner sense as its witness.

But supposing we do accept for a moment that all people always have a characteristic feeling of power to act whenever they are said to be acting freely, how are we to identify this feeling? It might be claimed that we could identify the feeling of effort as always accompanying our acting in a certain typical kind of way which we call acting freely. 'What certain typical kind of way?' If we succeed in describing this, haven't we succeeded in describing a free action without recourse to the feeling? At which point the feeling becomes merely an epiphenomenal accompaniment to free action, of greater or lesser interest to a psychologist, maybe, but of no heuristic value to a philosopher interested in knowing what a free action is.

Would it be open to a defender of Maine de Biran to retort that he is not interested in proving any ultimate ontological doctrine that men are free – after all Kant warns us that such a thing is not a

possible object of knowledge[1] – nor in offering a way for discovering
that a given action was free; but rather in giving a purely psychological account of freedom as an experience? If he went on to establish
that the only sphere in which talk of freedom is proper is in psychology, then he would be giving a reductionist account. For to say an
action is free because I feel myself to be cause of it and not compelled
or constrained in doing it, nor that it simply happened like a hiccup,
would be to give the statement the status of an avowal. The agent
would be the sole authority on whether or not it felt free, which
would be the only way of knowing that it was free. And that would
be to say that judgements about freedom are not possible, only
avowals are possible.

Certain difficulties attend this view. The possibility of an observer
attributing responsibility to a person on the basis of a judgement
concerning his freedom is ruled out. Either the notion of responsibility is private too, or, if public, is attributed independently of
freedom. But it is normally held that the concept of responsibility is
used publicly and that it is conceptually related to freedom. A good
deal of social and legal reform would have to take place if this were
not so, as well as the linguistic reform consequent to the position that
statements of freedom are avowals about private states. For these
reasons it would seem to me not open for Biran or anyone else to
defend his position along these lines.

To concentrate on freedom purely as an experience excludes not
only all use for it as a way of evaluating conduct, but also makes
nonsense of the idea of freedom as some kind of capacity. Some
philosophers have spoken, for instance, as if it made sense to extend
the scope of freedom. This would be consonant with the idea of self
as cause, but not with the way Biran presents the notion. To extend
one's freedom would be to make oneself cause of one's actions more
often. To see it this way is what I meant by freedom as a capacity.
One can extend one's capacities of knowing a foreign language by
becoming proficient in all the linguistic skills: not only reading and
understanding, for instance, but also pronunciation, fluency in
speaking and writing the language. I imagine that to increase one's
freedom might be something like this, for example, not only freedom
in choosing moral principles, but freedom to implement them
instead of giving in passively to resisting forces. If Biran insists that
power and will are coextensive,[2] such ideas are frivolous.

Why? Because if the feeling of power is just that feeling we get
when we act and are not passive, the will cannot anticipate or go
ahead of the power to do something. But sometimes I only find out I

---

[1] *Antinomy of Pure Reason*, A532/B560–A558/B586.   [2] Op. cit., p. 256.

am able to do something by succeeding in doing it. In other words I think that the notion of trying is required for the extension of freedom, and Biran leaves no room for trying.

Now this is extremely odd, since the central notion of effort in Biran's philosophy would appear to give trying pride of place. I have argued that this cannot be so as he holds that 'Will is concentrated in the same limits as power and does not extend beyond; desire begins on the contrary where power ends and embraces the whole field of our passivity'.[1] So if we will to do more than we know ourselves capable of we are really only desiring vainly to do something which is outside our control, governed by fate. If I am wrong to conclude that the notion of trying is eliminated by this, I think it could only be due to a misunderstanding of his term 'power' (*pouvoir*). The ambiguities latent in this term, as well as in 'feeling' and 'reality', are evident in the following statement of his:

> I conclude . . . that liberty, considered as the feeling of a power being used (*en exercice*), supposes the reality of that power, just as the inner feeling of our existence proves to us its reality.[2]

He claims that this is as evident as Descartes's *cogito ergo sum*, and that one can say, '*Je me sens libre, donc je le suis*'.[3] Both of these statements taken in one way would be incorrigible and in another way would be corrigible. Let us distinguish these by the terms 'feeling a power' and 'having a power'. If I feel I am exercising the power to move mountains, nobody can question or doubt this. But if I say I have the power to move mountains anybody can judge this by seeing whether I move mountains or not. If the 'reality' of the power is assessed by my feelings, then we might call this a 'psychological reality' of power. If the 'reality' of the power is assessed by my actions, then we could call this an 'existential reality'. Now, when he says that 'the feeling of a power being used supposes the reality of that power', it should only mean what I have called 'psychological reality', but I suspect that he wants to make this into a synthetic existential statement. This suspicion is supported by the further remark, 'I feel myself to be free, therefore I am free'. It could be that he is trying to show that I must be free, have power, if I feel this, that, although he has made this true by definition, it is not an idle definition, but one based on experience.

At all events I think it is true that his chief concern here is to establish that it is really I who exercises the power and not some outside force or being. He is not bothered by the problem of whether having a power to do something means I can do that thing. That is,

[1] Ibid.   [2] Op. cit., p. 257.   [3] Ibid., pp. 257–8.

he is not looking at the action end of the process, but at the *self* end of it. However, the way he expresses this plays on ambiguities, which, were they exploited in the direction of corrigibility, would lead to the conclusion of the truth he is wanting to establish (that I am free) not being a logical truth. If we take his statements in the incorrigible sense, then he is making analytic the truth he would seem to wish was a synthetic *a priori* truth.

In various ways I have tried to point out difficulties in the position held by Maine de Biran on freedom. This raises a problem. For it seems to me that his account is a possible phenomenological account of freedom. He has succeeded in describing his experience, and has managed to give it philosophical status in his doctrine based on the disctinction between activity and passivity. Any reader of his journals will note that this was his experience without doubt, a constant conflict between passive and active forces. Any reader of his *Essai sur les fondements de la psychologie* and other philosophical works would agree that this is his philosophy, that the feeling of effort or fact of inner sense, as he calls it, was prized by him as his discovery and contribution to philosophical problems. To this extent he has fulfilled admirably the requirements set for phenomenology by Merleau-Ponty, and he has been hailed as a forerunner of phenomenology by at least two philosophers: Raymond Vancourt and Michel Henry. So my problem is, if this is a phenomenological account of freedom, it is certainly not a satisfactory philosophical account of freedom.

At this point I ask myself, can there be a phenomenology of freedom? Is freedom a phenomenon of experience? Is it an object of consciousness which could be described as such? I am inclined to say no to these questions.

In his book, *Le volontaire et l'involontaire*, Paul Ricœur criticises Maine de Biran for trying to derive a theory of perception and knowledge from a philosophy of effort and will. For Biran everything is conceived on the model of effort being deployed against resistance. Ricœur wants to give a place to spontaneity and docility, for these notions provide him with an image of one of the limit concepts of liberty he considers at the very end of the book:

I further understand the limit concept of an incarnate freedom as man's freedom, but one whose body would be absolutely docile: a *gracious* freedom whose bodily spontaneity would be allied with the initiative which moves it without resistance. The athlete and the dancer perhaps sometimes give me a vision of it and a longing for it.[1]

Through his eidetic description of voluntary action Ricœur gives us some glimpses of a phenomenological account of freedom, but in the context of the description of essences.

Sartre denies that liberty has an essence. All he sees as possible is an understanding or comprehension of liberty.[2] It is the stuff of my being, he says, echoing a sentiment of Maine de Biran; however, unlike Biran, he looks for the understanding of liberty via its significance. A phenomenological critique of Biran would involve showing how he has disregarded the meaning of freedom, what it means to be free for us, to what freedom is directed. The Biranian account does not look further than freedom as a content of consciousness, it has not considered the ends we create which display certain values. Indeed freedom only acquires its significance in the way it directs us out of consciousness, in action, towards the world and other people.

I confess I find it most difficult most of the time to decide what one is talking about in talking of freedom. But it does seem evident that it must be something more than voluntary action, and I do not see that Biran has shown how it differs from this. His insistence on the notion of self as cause is important to my mind, although I think one can know or believe one is the cause of an action without experiencing it as a feeling. This can be shown along the lines of what Ricœur calls pre-reflexive imputation of myself.[3] But it is only a prerequisite for speaking of freedom since it is a feature of voluntary action.

Both Ricœur and Sartre have shown that phenomenological studies can reveal many more features of free action, through a description of voluntary action and related concepts such as decision, choice, intention, projects, responsibility. This can lay the foundation, but the reason that I balk at calling it a phenomenology of freedom is because I think the point of talking about freedom at all is a moral point, and that cannot be accounted for purely in phenomenological terms.

[1] (*Freedom and Nature: The Voluntary and the Involuntary*, trans. Erazim Kohak (Evanston, Ill.: Northwestern University Press, 1966) p. 485.

[2] *L'Être et le Néant*, pp. 513–14.   [3] Op. cit., pp. 58–62.

3

REPLY TO
MISS BERRY'S PAPER

Klaus Hartmann

In her paper, Miss Berry takes Maine de Biran's account of free will as her main topic. However, while we seem to be concerned with a monograph on Biran, her point is that Biran's position somehow stands for a wider philosophical persuasion, viz., that of phenomenology. If this understanding is correct it may be advisable first to look briefly into her criticism of Biran and next into the relevance of this criticism to phenomenology. Finally, we should attend to what amounts to little more than a suggestion on Miss Berry's part as to what is required for a satisfactory account of freedom.

I

The main point of criticism brought against Biran seems to be the following. If freedom (rather than 'liberty', which is a political concept) is vouched for by a special *feeling*, then such a feeling is no more than an 'epiphenomenal accompaniment to free action'. The argument against this is that we 'do not see that we must always feel ourselves to be the cause of our actions in order to be acting freely', or, that a description of the feeling would be a description of a free action 'without recourse to the feeling'. While the latter argument seems somewhat artificial, weight attaches to the former point, viz., that we do not understand the relation between feeling and freedom and thus have no reason to make the one vouch for the other. No epiphenomenon can as such assure us of anything other than itself both as to its That and its What.

The next argument is that freedom would be the subject of *avowal* only; a judgement concerning the freedom of the person claiming it is ruled out. Miss Berry thinks that in this way the common notion of responsibility is also ruled out. However, there is difficulty in her treatment of this problem since she thinks that what is wrong about avowal is that it is merely private while 'the concept of responsibility is used publicly'. This disjunction of 'private' and 'public' is an epistemological one, and if we follow Miss Berry's suggestion, then, to be acceptable, freedom would have to be available to public inspection. The current use of the concept of responsibility does, of course, imply nothing of the sort, it does not rest on an epistemological impossibility. (Incidentally, if an epistemological stance is to be adhered to, one might suggest Husserl's intersubjectivity theory, a device which does avoid the disjunction of 'private' and 'public' and yet achieves an interpersonal account of subjectivity.)

Another criticism points up a deficiency in Biran in so far as he seems to rule out freedom as a capacity (in the sense of an 'extension of freedom'). Or, with a slightly different slant, trying is ruled out because only to the extent that power is *'en exercice'* does the feeling testifying to it occur. On the other hand, the notion of power in Biran seems to point, however vaguely, to potentiality since 'power and will are coextensive'. In this respect, however, Biran 'is not looking at the action end of the process but at the *self* end of it'. If power and will are coextensive and if my feeling guarantees the reality of my freedom or power, then potentiality and actuality of freedom are tied in a knot. Freedom prior to encountering resistance, and thus exhibiting no feeling, cannot be consistently related to freedom in the course of its accomplishment. Miss Berry, rather than pressing the ambiguity of such a notion of power, settles for a logical criticism: either feeling and power are coextensive (whatever 'power' means precisely), and then we have no more than a *definition* such that freedom is the case when I have that feeling; or the truth claimed is not a 'logical truth'. The idea seems to be that, on the second reading, we are given an account of an unknown That ('that I am free'), a truth which, if I understand Miss Berry, would not be 'logical' inasmuch as it does not concern the What of freedom.

II

Biran having been disposed of, Miss Berry proceeds to give him another lease of life inasmuch as she sees in his position an early instance of a type of philosophy which may claim better credentials, phenomenology. One would suppose that if there is similarity between Biran and phenomenology, criticism brought against the former would *pro tanto* devolve on the latter. In fact, Miss Berry shifts her ground in a subtle manner, for she cannot be unaware of the fact that phenomenology rejects major stances of Biran's such as the psychological setting of the problem or the epiphenomenal relation between an indicator feeling and the matter indicated. Or, Biran himself would have to feature doctrines not mentioned in her criticism which would bring him closer to phenomenology.[1] In any case, Miss Berry reopens Biran's account in giving phenomenology credit. In the work of one of phenomenology's exponents, Paul Ricœur, she sees a partly successful attempt at offering description of liberty or, as we would once again prefer, of freedom. But, alas, it is eidetic description, description 'in the context of essence'. Now, how would that affect the success of such an undertaking? There seems to be mere nominalistic suspicion that eidetic description will not do. But could there be any other? Miss Berry accepts Ricœur's view that freedom can be known without a feeling, through 'pre-reflexive imputation of myself'. But, so she thinks, this would be only a 'prerequisite for speaking of freedom since it is a feature of voluntary action'. Somehow, voluntary action is not sufficient. But why? Would the will constitute too restrictive a content?

The reserve seems to be occasioned by an inspection of Sartre's *L'Être et le Néant* where Miss Berry finds an attention not just to the 'self end', as in Biran, but to that to which freedom 'is directed' and to its 'significance'. Then, so it may seem to her, freedom cannot be discussed as 'voluntary action' if that stands for the 'self end' as well as for a restricted psychological content.

Before we return to the approach to freedom instanced in Sartre's work, let us ask whether phenomenology is or is not committed to viewing freedom from the 'self end'. Leaving aside Ricœur's phenomenology of the will, what shall we say of the classical analyses of phenomenology? Could not phenomenology study the essence of the relation between the *cogito* and its object and thus, on the level of the will, the relation between the voluntative act and its meaningful objective? What bothers Miss Berry about phenomenology, however, seems to be something else. She answers 'no' to the question, 'Is freedom a phenomenon of experience?' (Incidentally, this question comes before her discussion of Ricœur and Sartre.) Would description of a phenomenon of freedom miss the point of freedom, or commit us to a one-sided attention to the 'self end' of freedom only? And would this be a commitment to the will as a mere prerequisite of freedom? Are these points bound up with one another? Let us take up the question.

If phenomenology could describe freedom, then freedom would be a phenomenon of experience (granted certain safeguards against

[1] For material on this line, see G. Funke, *Maine de Biran* (Bonn, 1947).

psychologism, summed up in the phenomenological reduction). For Miss Berry, a phenomenon of freedom will not do. She does not really tell us why, but, of course, there is ample precedent in her favour, precedent which takes the question out of the range of phenomenology. As for phenomenology, it seems that Husserl, although he gives little attention to our problem, would have thought that phenomenology can describe and clarify consciousness, including voluntative consciousness. Admittedly, there is disagreement as to whether phenomenological intuition does or does not objectify, in the sense of solidify, its givens and so must miss the point at issue. (We may recall M. Scheler's scruples in this matter.) Husserl, on the other hand, is quite confident that a falsifying solidification does not occur when he says, 'Let us then place ourselves within a living *cogito* ∴ . .'.[1] He would think that the phenomenological reduction avoids what would be a concomitant of the 'natural attitude'. Phenomenology, we may submit, will prove unable to settle the issue as long as it attaches itself to intuitional description.

The other aspect of the question as to whether description of freedom as a phenomenon would restrict it to the 'self end' and thus perhaps to the will or a voluntative faculty, would, for Husserl, be answered in terms of the noetic – noematic structures which assure us that the referent, too, is inspectable. But here one may hold that phenomenological reduction makes a difference since it cuts us off from existence claims in connection with referents. Then, so it may seem, the description is back to the 'self end'. Miss Berry, who does not mention phenomenological reduction, may think of description without such safeguards and thus retain of phenomenological description no more than the idea that its stance is subjective, though not transcendentally subjective. Accordingly, so it seems, its given would be a merely voluntative, psychic subject, without inclusion of its referent.

Another moot point, and this may be even more important, is whether phenomenology could handle the dimension of potentiality and actuality or, as Miss Berry with analytic caution would prefer, that of 'trying'. Doubts in this connection may be the reason why she sympathises with Sartre's analysis where she finds recourse to objective testimony to freedom and a wider notion of freedom generally. But this means in fact that she favours an ontological analysis rather than an epistemological one.

To lead over from epistemological to ontological analysis, let us return to the question as to what would be wrong about making

[1] *Ideas*, I, trans. W. Boyce Gibson (New York: Collier Books, 1962) p. 336.

freedom a phenomenon, now to be taken in the sense of 'object'. We all know the Kantian answer to which Miss Berry alludes, if in another context, viz., that freedom would thus be subjected to the laws of thought operative in the domain of appearance or nature and therefore be something conditioned rather than something unconditioned. In more general terms, objectification of freedom would miss freedom, not so much because of a dualism of lawfulness (nature, morality) but because it would make freedom a surd while what we mean by freedom is precisely that centre of thinking and acting which gives unto itself objects – a feat objects cannot perform although, as given to that centre, they themselves cease to be surds. We establish, as it were, a disjunction between subject and object and thus cannot accept the subject as an object, and certainly not the object account of a subject as the truth about the subject. However, objects, having ceased to be surds, can figure as a mediation for the subject to be itself in terms of a dialectical notion of freedom. Such a notion first occurs, in a practical context, in Kant's autonomy principle of the will according to which reason is the referent of finite reason. Even the tension of potentiality and actuality can be accommodated in this model.

III

Thus the stage is set for an altogether different account of freedom, the ontological one. It would be an account in which we *think* freedom in *a priori* terms rather than describe it epistemologically. Now we might say that to think freedom is, again, tantamount to objectifying it. But this would clearly not constitute an objectification in the incriminated sense, since everybody would grant that we at least *think* the non-objectified, however poorly and abstractly, just as thought escapes the relativity of intentionality when it thinks the non-relativity of, say, the thing-in-itself. The account of freedom in terms of thought (which Miss Berry mentions in the form of Ricœur's 'pre-reflexive imputation of myself') has, however, much wider possibilities, possibilities beyond the conflation of phenomenological and ontological thought as it occurs in Ricœur's work.[1] Miss Berry hints at such possibilities when she says that 'the point of talking about freedom at all is a moral point'. Maybe what she means is that freedom would have to be seen in conjunction with objectives and, at the same time, in a normative fashion. That is, certain deliverances of freedom would have to qualify for normative predicates in which the subject and its deliverances are recognised as successful units of a totality to be called freedom.

[1] For a treatment of this point, see my article, 'Phenomenology, Ontology, and Metaphysics' in *Review of Metaphysics*, XXII 1 (1968).

I am not clear as to whether Miss Berry would want to go that far; she may merely wish to object to phenomenological or psychological objectification and to the onesidedness of the epistemological approach, much as she practises it herself. When she sympathises with Sartre, she may just approve of his extension of the problem of freedom to objective testimony and not recognise the ontological status of his analysis which, incidentally, can handle the problem of potentiality *v*. actuality. (See Sartre's analysis of *pour-soi* and *valeur*.) Or she may not realise that it is due to Sartre's formalism that his ontological account of freedom does not reach moral content.

If, however, we pursue Miss Berry's suggestion on more original, classical, ground, we find, first, Kant's proposal that, in order to make ethics possible, we have to define ourselves as reasonable beings under the moral law. Freedom would be an implicate of our awareness of the moral law. The unwelcome concomitant is that there will have to be two notions of the will, free rational will and unfree inclination, a state of affairs which encumbers the potentiality *v*. actuality issue of freedom.

Next we find Hegel's proposal. It can be called a generalisation of Kant's notion of the rational will. Hegel's solution is to make freedom *categorially* explicable: there are realities involving freedom (subjective spirit, or knowledge and will, objective spirit, or family, society and State) which merit a unifying categorial predicate, asserting the reality in question to be a free reality. While any subjective inspection would miss freedom (through objectification or, as we may now say, through undialectical separation of it from its total domain which includes its opposite, its referent), categorial thought would be entitled to assert it if, that is, a logical construction of it in a dialectical theory can be given. (In Hegel, such a theory is the objective of Part III of the *Encyclopedia* and of the *Philosophy of Right*.) Hegel does objectify freedom, but only categorially. That is, he determines it not through descriptive content, nor through essences, but in terms of a concept expressing the relation of appropriation extended by the subject towards its referent. Freedom has to refer to its other to be what it is. That such a claim is meaningful also in the sense that freedom is the solution of the tension between project and accomplishment, the living solution of the problem of potentiality *v*. actuality, finds it expression in the fact that there is a category of unaccomplished freedom, such as subjective spirit, and a category for its accomplishment, such as objective spirit. The distance of the former stance from the resultative stance is a logical account of freedom in its potential and actual aspects. Sartre tries to use this Hegelian analysis (we may note, again, his use of categories like *pour-soi* and *valeur*, which exhibit a similar tension in that they constitute, in conjunction, an ontological account of the subject on its way to self-realisation), but he cannot, on the terms of his formal dialectic, give these categories content. Thus there is to be 'significance' to our freedom, but what significance cannot be stated.

Again, we do not know whether Miss Berry would want to follow us that far. We rather doubt it if only because in her treatment of the problem of freedom she attends mainly to the question of our factual consciousness that we are free, or, in theoretical terms, to an impracticable epistemological approach to the problem of freedom. The very choice of Maine de Biran as her guiding precedent shows this. It seems, however, that we may be driven that far if we do not wish to be trapped in stances inapplicable to freedom, such as positions in terms of verification, public inspection, descriptive objectification, positivism in general. As for phenomenology, the undialectical character of the intentionality relation makes it unlikely that the potentiality *v.* actuality problem can be solved, whatever we think of solidification in inspection (or an escape from it under phenomenological reduction), or of the availability of the referent of consciousness. However, if we adopt the suggested stance, we would at least be offered an answer as to *what* freedom is. Incidentally, this seems to be Miss Berry's concern too; she does not doubt for a minute that there is such a thing as freedom, she does not consider determinism a serious alternative, all she wants to know is from which position we can find out what it is. For that, however, she would have had to transcend her epistemological stance and write an ontological paper. The problem would have to be broached afresh on the categorial level. Her paper can be read as a *reductio ad absurdum* of freedom theory in epistemology, undertaken on the basis of a historical precedent that may not be quite a fair example of the possibilities inherent in epistemology.

Understandably, Miss Berry shies away from ontology, she would like to hold on to methodological nominalism, to inspection, to factuality, to logical and linguistic analysis. True enough, the ontological account is the opposite of all that, and the theoretical shift may be too alien to what Miss Berry is after to meet with her approval. Conversely, with her outlook, with her attention to verification and inspection, an account of freedom may be impossible. To the extent that she does realise that freedom cannot be experienced as a phenomenon, her own epistemological outlook is called in question, but she hesitates to make the drastic revision that may be needed.

4

CHAIRMAN'S OPENING REMARKS

Alasdair MacIntyre

It is characteristic of philosophical disagreements that they are often – in part at least – disagreements about where the disagreements lie. I myself am unclear as to whether Professor Hartmann really disagrees with Miss Berry at all, except on marginal points and in philosophical and literary style, although it may well be the case that Miss Berry disagrees with large parts of Professor Hartmann's paper which are independent of our discussion. Professor Hartmann certainly gives the impression that he believes that he disagrees profoundly with Miss Berry. He calls her a 'nominalist', not once but twice. And I judge that, in Professor Hartmann's circles, this is not very friendly. He even accuses her of an interest in verification and factuality. Now it may well be that in private life Miss Berry has a reputation as a nominalist and is perhaps notorious for her love of facts. But I find no trace of these vices – if they are in fact vices – in her paper.

I hope the symposiasts will forgive me if I proceed by listing what seem to me some crucial agreements which they have. I shall then be able to open up item by item a quarrel precisely with that on which I think the symposiasts agree as well as one or two quarrels with each of the symposiasts separately.

They first of all agree in rejecting as inadequate in a more or less radical way either an epistemological or a phenomenological account of freedom. Before I even glance at the grounds for this objection I want to state an initial unease of my own. The phrase 'knowledge of freedom', used by Professor Hartmann, may mean our own knowledge that we are in some sense 'free'. Here we may want to distinguish the basis of my knowledge that *I* am free from the basis of my knowledge that *you* are free, or we may not. But both Miss Berry and Professor Hartmann seem to assume too readily that any epistemological account of freedom will be one from a first-person standpoint. This knowledge that we as agents are free is to be distinguished from the knowledge of what it is to be free, of the concept and conditions of freedom. Now a writer like Maine de Biran does conflate these two questions precisely by his assimilation of '*Je me sens libre*' with the *cogito*. This enables us, in rebutting him, to treat the so-called appeal to the *feeling* of freedom too cavalierly.

Let me give two reasons for believing this. The first is that the notion of experience or of feeling as a ground for judgement is far from clear. Miss Berry asserts that if I feel that I am exercising the power to move mountains nobody can question or doubt this. But is this true? Consider the following case. Someone claims that he is exercising the power to move mountains and claims, on the basis of this feeling, that he is indeed exercising this power. Something very like this does indeed happen in cases of incipient schizophrenia, as well as in religion. Presently he discovers that he was deluded as to the possession of this power. He may now withdraw not only his second claim, but also his first, saying, 'What I took to be the feeling that I had a power I now perceive to have been something quite other. I still have the *same* feeling, but I now characterise it differently.' Of course the agent need not withdraw in this way. He may have another course open to him. He may say, 'I now see that I only *felt* that . . .' or 'I felt as if it were the case that . . .'. But note how our ordinary vocabulary of feeling and experience yields no clear guidance. In the face of this unclarity the right way to cope with the situation is surely not to follow de Biran (and in this instance, curiously, Miss Berry). For this would conceal from us the way in which experiences are cited – and rightly cited – as grounds for judgement and even judgements about our freedom. We do in certain instances learn to use what we feel as a guide to what we are. The inductive policies we use in such learning have largely escaped study because of the tradition that runs from the Cartesians of treating feeling-claims as incorrigible.

But now it may be said, 'Yes, we certainly do connect in various ways feeling hungry and being hungry, feeling fit and being fit, feeling angry and being angry, and so on'. But what about feeling free and being free? Miss Berry says – and all of us who have written on the subject would have to agree – 'I confess I find it most difficult most of the time to decide what one is talking about when talking about freedom'. Part of the answer surely is that we are talking, not about *one* thing, but about several. The unity of the concept of freedom is itself problematic, although writers like Ricœur and also Miss Berry and Professor Hartmann treat responsibility, creativity and the like as all being aspects of freedom. But are all these aspects of the one thing? Are these writers justified in this kind of treatment? I am strongly inclined to assert that the unity of the concept of freedom appears only in the realisation that all these aspects of human agency – and very different they are – are equally put in question both by certain theological doctrines and by certain truths of phsyical science. If everything that happens happens by the will of God or if it is the case that every physical movement is to be explained as arising from some prior state in accordance with the laws of mechanics, then we have to ask why we should treat those happenings or those episodes of physical movement which are coextensive in time and space with human action as points at which causal agency operates in some way or in some sense different from that in which it operates elsewhere. But in the course of attempts to answer this question, traits like creativity and spontaneity perhaps raise rather different issues from those raised by ascriptions of responsibility. And the way in which this is so may be illustrated by an example of the condition I have already mentioned – incipient schizophrenia.

Let me remark in passing how difficult I find it to grapple with the contentions of Miss Berry and Professor Hartmann because of their frugality and asceticism with examples. The case I have in mind is a true case history of a student who became convinced on the basis of feeling a sense of power that he could in fact perform various great athletic feats. He proceeded to try and failed in the most humiliating way. Because of this he came to be convinced that a power of evil was thwarting him and set about trying to identify this power. His initial hypothesis was, that his belief that he had this power in normal circumstances was indeed true and warranted by his feeling that he had it; only now some abnormal circumstance was thwarting him. He then went through a series of experiences as a result of which he abandoned this hypothesis, concluding quite rightly that the feelings in question were an alien invasion of his personality. He himself reported his condition to a psychiatrist. He came, that is, to distinguish between some of his feeling states which were genuinely part of his identity and for which he could take responsibility, and other feeling states which belonged to him only as a stomach-ache might have belonged to him. He did this by connecting these feeling states with the evidence they afforded him as to what he could do. Such judgements *are* made and it is not unimportant that

Miss Berry has abstracted her account of Maine de Biran's view of freedom from its context in de Biran's work as an empirical psychologist, in which he was actually concerned with these questions. For de Biran's attempt to distinguish active and passive is precisely an attempt to distinguish those parts of our personality which belong to our identity as persons and for which we are in a variety of ways accountable and those which are mere things which happen to us. Miss Berry seems to me to be mistaken in saying that if de Biran was right in his kind of analysis of freedom, the ascription of responsibility would thereby be ruled out. For this would only be true if it was also true that to ascribe feelings was to refer to some private inaccessible world. What Miss Berry may mean is that if we take it, as de Biran did, that freedom just is the feeling of freedom, then the whole notion of responsibility and its ascription would collapse. And if so, then she is quite right about this part of de Biran's doctrine. But this absurd thesis of de Biran's must not be confused with the thesis that we do need a psychological account of our knowledge of freedom. Miss Berry may well reply to this that she meant something quite other by 'a purely psychological account of freedom and its experience', for she does indeed contrast such an account with what she calls a way of discovering that a given action is free. But my whole point is that we cannot have the latter without the fomer. If Maine de Biran failed to carry through his epistemological project because of his Cartesianism, none the less the project seems to me to have been not entirely a disreputable one. We do need some sort of epistemological account at this point for these purposes. But if, of course, all that Miss Berry and Professor Hartmann mean is that such an account must wait upon some prior inquiry as to the character of the concept of freedom, they may well be right.

The second major head on which the symposiasts seem to agree is in their refusal to allow that the natural sciences have as yet happened – or at least that the natural sciences are important or relevant enough to be mentioned in their papers. I suspect this is because they assume too easily that Kant's argument, that there can be no well-founded doctrine that men are free, leaves it open to evade the problem raised by the natural sciences by adopting something like Kant's own doctrine in some version or other, perhaps as Hegel developed it. Kant and Hegel both evade the key difficulty, which may be stated as follows. Nothing can occur contrary to the laws of physics. The true outcome of the Kantian doctrine of the noumenal will (realised at one moment at least by Kant himself, but never fully spelt out by him) is that, if by coincidence things are already determined to occur in the phenomenal world on account of the laws being what they are and the initial conditions what they are in accordance with the maxims determining the good will, then and only then will the maxims be embodied in the world of physical movement. Or, as we might more truly say, whether what occurs in the world accords with what the good will wills or not, the will is never a causal agency in the phenomenal, and that is for practical purposes to say in the real world. The price of rescuing the will from being in certain respects an effect is to prevent it from being in precisely those respects a cause. And this will always be the price of rescuing the will from being an effect.

It may not be so obvious that Hegel paid this price as that Kant does. But the Hegelian method of treating freedom in terms of constraint and the overcoming of constraints imposed by particular types of institution and ways of life classed under the heading 'objec-ive spirit' presupposes that the contrast freedom/unfreedom can be founded and the criteria for the application of the predicate 'free' can be given independently of the relation of the individuals who are concerned to their natural make-up and environment and to each other as natural objects. It is a Hegelian assumption that subject *qua* subject can somehow thereby transcend his being *qua* object. This is an assumption which we have every reason not to make. The danger is that we make this assumption by adopting a whole way of speaking in relation to the problem of freedom which presupposes a certain solution to that problem and then triumphantly present it as a solution. Hegel falls victim to this and I am not at all sure that Professor Hartmann does not, together with those other followers of Kant who mistakenly suppose that from the Kantian dictum that the freedom of the rational will must be presupposed in morality (or, in Hegelian terms, if the histories of the subjective and objective spirit are to be intelligible) it follows that the freedom of the rational will must be presupposed. What in fact follows is *either* this *or* that morality as Kant understood it (or the history of the subjective and objective spirit as Hegel understood them) are not finally intelligible in the required sense. Perhaps Professor Hartmann here presupposes what he has to show.

But what would have to be shown? The fact that talk about freedom must have a moral point or the desire to exhibit history as an intelligible progress in freedom – neither of these alter the question of whether some concept of freedom has application or not. I take it that the minimal concept required to vindicate these projects is a concept of the human being as possessing and as able to expand rational autonomy, in the sense that his rational self-criticism and his rational exchanges with others can be distinguished as causal agencies from other causal agencies which operate on him and which he brings into operation. To make this distinction, we would have to extablish certain factual and scientific theses as well as certain conceptual ones. Studies of artificial intelligence, experimental psychology and neuro-physiology are all relevant disciplines here, even though their relevance is all too easy to misunderstand.

Let me finally put the kind of point I have been trying to make about the papers in a more general perspective. The family of problems which constitute the free-will/determinism issue are at the stage where we need to continue work on a wide range of different details. Block solutions are out. In recent years Anglo-Saxon philosophers may have for the first time in a long time been in danger of over-reacting against what their Continental colleagues always saw as the botanising tendencies of the British – the collection of distinctions for their own sake, the tendency to assert that truth is important, but that importance is not. Yet the realisation that importance is important too may itself be dangerous to philosophy in so far as it leads us to become over-interested in premature synthesis. This is a time when philosophy cannot aspire to be synthetic, not because philosophy can only be done in a detailed piecemeal way, but because it cannot yet be done in any other way. Too much work remains undone, and this I think is the true moral to be drawn from the symposiasts' papers.

DISCUSSION

Miss Berry: Is a phenomenology of freedom possible? Such should have been the title for my paper. For I started with the assumption that some British philosophers might understand a phenomenological account of freedom to be an account of the experience of freedom, with or without a stronger thesis that freedom is an experience only.

For this reason I chose to discuss the view of Maine de Biran. Now, he does not describe the experience of freedom beyond saying it is the feeling of the power to act or be the cause of one's actions. He does not go into details about the accompanying states of mind – perhaps a 'free as air' feeling, or 'the world is my footstool' kind of feeling, or again, a sensation of exhilaration, of lightness, exuberance, perhaps a tingling excitement and an 'all's well with the world' kind of happiness – he doesn't go in for anything like that. He takes it for granted that we know what it's like to feel free, but he does say that freedom is nothing but this feeling. It is this stronger thesis that I have argued against. (I shall discuss the details of the reply to these arguments later.)

The difficulties in the position suggested it was untenable. If this is right, we were left to conclude either that Biran's account is not a phenomenological account properly speaking, or that a phenomenological account was wrong.

There would appear to be good reasons for saying that Biran's thoughts of freedom do not constitute a phenomenology of freedom. For a start, other phenomenologists approach the topic differently, in my view more constructively. Dr Hartmann appears to agree on this and has helped to bring out the views of some phenomenologists on the question of freedom.

But I do still wonder whether a phenomenology of freedom is possible. (A more fundamental question than whether a particular phenomenological account is right, or how it could be improved to become so.) This is because I do not think that freedom is the name of an experience, nor of a phenomenon. It seems to me more like a notion we use in evaluating conduct, in appraising people's actions and their capacities for action. This is to say that its realm is the praxis and not experience or reflection. Of course we can think about the praxis, but if freedom only gets in at that stage, then I don't see what is gained by calling it a phenomenon of experience. I suggest that to do that is to use the term in such a wide sense that it loses its useful force.

An even more general problem now arises, how can phenomenology treat the field of practical action and morality? My misgivings here include the problem of 'pure description'. How can it yield, let alone wield, moral terms? To the extent that the term 'free', like good, points to a supervenient quality of an action, a 'pure description' of an action would appear to be necessarily prior to any description which uses moral terms. If there is any truth in the claim that freedom is something concerned with practical action and morality, then at the very least phenomenology cannot tell the whole story, and at worst it stops short where talk of freedom begins.

There are just a few specific comments I feel I must make about Dr Hartmann's reply, and one general remark I feel I would like to make.

1. On p. 33, where Dr Hartmann refers to one of my objections to a definition of freedom in terms of a feeling of freedom: '. . . a description of the feeling would be a description of a free action "without recourse to the feeling" ', I would ask that it be made to read: 'a description of the kind of action that a free feeling accompanies would be . . . etc.', otherwise it doesn't make sense. Perhaps this is why he finds the argument 'artificial'. But really it is a perfectly standard and unexceptionable point. If I don't know what A is and someone undertakes to explain it as that which is accompanied by B, this will not help unless I am clear about what B is. If I am not sure what B is, and am told, B is that which accompanies A, I'm not any better off. However, if someone is able to get me to understand what A is, which in these circumstances he must do without making use of B, then I have come to know what A is and the whole business about B falls out as superfluous, unnecessary and irrelevant to my understanding of A, even if it remains true that B in fact always happens to accompany A and only A.

2. Next, on p. 34, Dr Hartmann states confidently that to ask for freedom and responsibility to be available for public inspection is to ask for an epistemological impossibility. I would simply like to note that I do not understand what he has in mind here. I am not particularly interested in having my 'stance' pigeonholed according to methodological classifications. For an account of freedom to be satisfactory, I believe it needs to enable us to know when a given action is a free action, and how we are to know it is free – what there is about it that makes us say it is free. But how could this requirement

commit me to holding that freedom is situated in epistemology, or that it is an epistemological concept or problem or however one is to characterise 'an epistemological stance'?

3. At the end of section 1 on p. 34, Dr Hartmann tries to lend a sense to the term 'logical truth' which I don't understand. I say it is not a logical truth because it would be a synthetic contingent actual empirical truth. I don't see that I'm begging any questions in the tricky area of the analytic/synthetic distinction, but if there is a problem here, it would be interesting to know of it.

4. I am called on to justify why I could think that voluntary action and free action are not the same thing. True, I have assumed they are separable notions, without giving any grounds for this assumption, which would be a long story, but I think the onus would be on anyone to defend the more controversial thesis that free action and voluntary action could not be distinguished, so I just toss this one back.

I will leave many other points to the discussion, with a general prefatory remark to the effect that I am interested in the issue at stake, and not so interested in the metaphilosophical questions which Dr Hartmann finds so important. I have not made the issue at stake a general freedom/determinism dispute, partly because I usually find it unfruitful, and partly because I think we have first to get clear about what free action is in order to know what a determinist is denying, and partly because in the context of this conference it seemed appropriate to discuss whether phenomenology could help us understand more about what it is to be free.

Professor Hartmann: Let me briefly reply to Miss Berry's comments on my paper. To begin with, she questions whether I am right to say that 'freedom', if it is to be a public concept, must be open to public inspection – which is absurd. Now I wonder whether Miss Berry has this in mind, that avowal is ruled out because only the person making it can know or be assured that he is right. What are we asking for here? Public inspection? Avowals are contrasted, not only as private to public judgements, but also with judgements in which some kind of truth claim is made. But what is at stake here seems to be the primacy of the avowal. To this the opposite is inspectability.

Another point concerns my 'pigeonholing' Miss Berry by my use, for instance, of the term 'epistemology'. I think that she is concerned with the *criteria* for saying that one is 'free', with *criteria* for one's feeling of freedom being correct, or however one puts it: 'criterion-riddenness' is another way of saying 'epistemological'. If one asks for a criterion for an avowal being correct, one is asking an *epistemological* question. That is all I meant.

I now pass to some more general remarks. Professor MacIntyre mentioned a distinction between two kinds of cause: rational causes, due to the self, impinging upon the world, and other causes, not issuing from the self. If we did not study the problem of freedom in causal terms the Kantian problem would not arise. This is the crucial issue and it may be that here my 'Continental' side shows. For I think that the questions which are asked in such causal inquiries are pre-empted by categorial analysis. A causal study cannot provide us with an account of the self, for there is a distinction between the categories applicable to things like causes and to things like selves. Categorial analysis may be old-fashioned, but it does make intelligible to us what we should look for. It makes no sense to look for a solution to the problem of freedom in causal terms. In categorial analysis, we understand the meaning of freedom in terms other than causal ones. Better still, we understand the categorial difference of freedom and causality in a unitary categorial scheme.

There are certain difficulties in epistemological talk. For in such talk we are prone to apply standards of what would count as a criterion. But these standards are reductionist standards. They are standards, for instance, of what Husserl called 'the natural attitude' or they are causal standards. Such standards are clearly inapplicable. So the criterion-mindedness of epistemological studies does not really help here. There are also difficulties in an ontological approach. For the question arises as to how these ontological 'findings' are arrived at in the first place. There is a circle here – a dependence of epistemology on ontology and vice versa – which many authors have argued for. This is a matter on which I am pessimistic. I think that all we can do is to *prescribe*, to set up prescriptive predicates about what we think can be said of the world. Such prescriptive predicates have – since Aristotle – normally been called 'categories'. We posit certain entities as intelligible in terms of such categories. Freedom, I suggest, should be understood in categorial terms.

The epistemologist may say, 'How do you make sense of a category?' To this I would answer that a rational account can be given for a category. It is set over against other categories so that, for instance, the difference between being and being for itself becomes apparent. If categorial reflection has to take precedence, then, I suggest, causal discussions of freedom have to lapse. I agree that in this way we will never find out what God, I suppose, will know, how it is possible for the self to be a causal agent. In the same way we will not know how a person learns because this, too, will be a transition between one categorial predicate and another. This is where I am pessimistic. I do not think that philosophers can solve the kind of problem that Professor MacIntyre has in mind. For this is pre-empted by categorial analysis.

Finally I would like to say something about the question whether a phenomenology of freedom is possible, whether Husserl would have been able to give a better account than Maine de Biran did. As this question may not interest others, I did not enlarge on it in my paper. But I think that, in the light of Husserl's later writings (for instance, his posthumous *Theory of Phenomenological Reduction*), more could be said. It would appear that the starting-point for a phenomenology of freedom would be a study of time-consciousness. Here Husserl has provided certain notions, supposed descriptions of habitualities, of an ego which is at the bottom of it all. I myself would make the objection that the description Husserl offered in his later writings is vitiated by a categorial apparatus which is not suitable. What is an ego, categorially? It is a surd. In description you will never make that surd rational. The further point in Husserl is that the ego is a limiting case, always eluding description. So even if we add this area of the late Husserlian phenomenology, I do not think we would get very far. Such accounts would again be pre-empted by proper categorial analysis; they can be seen to be vitiated by impossibilities of which Husserl was not aware.

Mr Philip Pettit (Dublin): Would Professor Hartmann give a definition of the terms 'ontology' and 'epistemology', as he uses them?

Professor Hartmann: I do not think anybody has ever succeeded in giving a definition that would satisfy an English audience. It is clear that epistemology is a study of knowledge, of how knowledge is attained. If this is taken genetically I would reject it. But if it is taken in terms of criteria it is, I think, clear enough that epistemology is the study of knowledge in the light of possible criteria for obtaining it. Ontology, on the other hand, is the study of being. It tries to develop predicates. When we are assured that we can award these predicates rightly we call them 'categories'. Does this satisfy you?

Pettit: Yes, that is quite clear. But you suggest in your paper that there is a different *method* involved in each study, that each has a different status. In epistemology, you suggest, we speak of terms which have a descriptive content. But you seem to suggest that, in ontology, a term like '*freedom*' would not have a descriptive content.

Hartmann: You are quite right. I can express my pessimism about an epistemological approach by saying that I do not think we could avoid legislating prior to finding our criteria.

Pettit: If you regard freedom as an ontological category, how do you intend to define it?

Hartmann: It is defined in the context of an explanatory scheme of categories. There is a precedent for this in the Kantian table of categories. That is an attempt to give a definition by context or architectonic.

Pettit: I would agree with you. You have, then, a set of categories which, in a sense, tend to define one another. But what does one do with these categories?

Hartmann: We use them to learn what things are.

Professor Ernst Tugendhat (Heidelberg): I would propose the following explanation of what these terms 'epistemology' and 'ontology' mean. An 'ontological' account is one which says what something *is*. An 'epistemological' account says *how it is known*. It is quite incomprehensible to me why Professor Hartmann should want to oppose these two aspects. How could one say something about what something *is* without being clear how one can have knowledge of it?

Hartmann: My point is not that it should not be possible to come to know categories in order to set them up but rather that, once epistemology gets into full swing, what one has is sense-data analysis and then you do not get categories. In the last analysis, categories rest on a reconstruction of what is granted. It is granted that you know what a person is, what freedom is, what being is, and so on, and one tries to give a reconstruction. Is the problem about *how* this is done an epistemological one? I would say 'no'. It is not an epistemological question how thought goes about reconstructing categories. To answer the question one would have to see how reconstruction is proposed by an author engaged in reconstruction, see what are the rules pertaining to categories, what is their regularity or their 'dialectic' – and so on. So one grants the reconstruction on systemic grounds – that is the answer.

Dr S. Raschid London): You seem to be glossing over a very big problem here by invoking the name of Husserl. In the Husserlian perspective one cannot make such a distinction between ontology and epistemology without first discussing the scope of the phenomenological reduction. This is why some people, Professor Ricœur for instance, have argued that it is a completely dis-ontologised philosophy. In the Husserlian perspective, it can at least be argued that ontology is subsumed in epistemology.

Professor J. N. Findlay (Yale): I think Miss Berry has raised an issue of the utmost importance, namely, the question as to whether any experience of something or other can really *give* you the thing of which you are said to be having the experience. This is the real issue that the discussion has brought out and which also came out in this last remark about Husserlian epistemology taking the lead over ontology. It is clear that there is a use of 'experience' – an experience of something – in which it makes no sense to treat what you have experiences *of* as being some object which could be called in question. For example, in the experience of time, it may be that we have to apprehend the objects with which we deal as following upon one another. But our own experiences are not, as it were, strung together because they *appear* to us as coming one after the other. In the case of experiences it must, it seems, be said that you have experience of succession which is the succession itself. There is not just a succession and some sort of awareness directed upon the succession – you actually live through the succession.

This concept has been used by many people and I think it is a valid one. If you make use of it, you will accept that there are phenomena which are also things-in-themselves. And this was the early view of Husserl – before he was seduced by Idealism – when he wrote the great work *Logische Untersuchungen*. He then thought that there was a limiting case of *Selbstgegebenheit* when the thing that appeared was the thing itself.

The question is, whether there can be an experience of such a thing as freedom. Maine de Biran has shown that there is a great phenomenological, as well as ontological, distinction between doing things and undergoing them. That white screen is impinging on me in a manner which I would be ready to describe as 'undergoing', whereas the words which I am now uttering have – in part at least – the character of 'doing'. There are cases where a phenomenology is also an ontology. There are, of course, other problems which arise here, since there are undoubtedly cases where one thinks one's experience is of a certain character which it has not got, and so on. And these are very difficult questions. But I think one has to concede that they only exist because there are limiting cases where things are given *as they are* and where it does not make sense to suppose that they might be otherwise. The epistemology cannot be opposed to the ontology. The notion of freedom is one of the key notions where this is the case. There are, that is to say, certain cases in which we do both *feel* freedom and the feeling of freedom is not just a feeling but is freedom itself, emphasised and brought home to the free person.

Professor H. D. Lewis (London): Miss Berry seems to me to be worried about this point, that if our freedom is to be made some basis for the ascription of responsibility, then this raises a difficulty at once if we are to ascribe responsibility to other people. Her answer seems to be that I can ascribe freedom to myself if it is established on the basis of something we call a 'feeling' of freedom or some internal appearance of my freedom. Then we ascribe responsibility to other people, talk about it in a legal context, and so forth. How can we do this unless there is some objective criterion? Now this does not seem to me to be a real difficulty at all for the reason that, while I can only directly be conscious of freedom in my own case, I can, *by analogy*, ascribe it to other people in the situations where I have reason to believe that they are purposing in the same way as I am when I act freely. So, unless there is some insurmountable difficulty about knowing other persons, there seems to be every possibility of ascribing responsibility to other people on the basis of that freedom, provided that I am convinced – and *properly* convinced – about it in my own case.

Miss Berry: I think that responsibility is a public notion, despite what Professor Hartmann has said, in the sense that it is something we all understand when we use it. I do not believe we understand it by analogy. When I say 'public' what I mean is that the concept is at our disposal, that we can use it.

Professor P. G. Winch (London): There seems to be a general assumption – made, for instance, by Professor Hartmann – that if you mention publicity you are mentioning something which is a matter of – to use Professor Findlay's phrase – 'sensuous observation' and which Professor Hartmann would also say was now a matter for causal explanation, something I did not understand in his remarks at all.

I think that the point that Miss Berry was really making here is that we do use notions like 'freedom' and 'responsibility' and a whole lot of other notions in the context of certain kinds of discussion about our actions and other people's actions – in the context of certain situations in which certain sorts of question are raised. This is what is *public* about these notions. It is in that context, I should have thought – to come to Professor Lewis's point – that I understand and am in a position to raise questions about my own actions, whether I am free in what I do in certain respects. It is not because I am, as it were, applying to myself some objective, possibly causal, relation I have observed in the world, but because I have learnt to discuss my actions as well as other people's actions. I would not be able to make the sense I do of my own actions nor would I be able to raise the question whether or not I was free in a certain situation unless I was familiar with that kind of discussion. That kind of discussion involves, of course, my familiarity with the kind of situations which can arise between myself and other people and between them in the context of the lives we lead. *That*, it seems to me, is where the notion of publicity should be located rather than via an insistence on some distinction between 'inner experience' and 'sensuous observation'.

Professor Tymieniecka (*Washington*) : I would like to come back to one of the initial questions, namely, whether phenomenology is capable of clarifying the idea of 'freedom'. There are at least two points of view from which this issue should be considered. One of them bears on the question whether there is just one concept of freedom. It may in fact be suggested that there are so many different ways in which we use the word 'freedom' that such a phenomenon as freedom itself does not exist. Here I would like to point out that phenomenology has done some work, not precisely in the field of freedom, but in other fields, in which such a situation has been clarified. I would like to draw attention to the work of Max Scheler concerning the concept of love. Max Scheler has first analysed the fundamental ways in which we use the word 'love', then he came to distinguish the fundamental forms of what appears then as the one phenomenon of love. It seems to me that something like this might be undertaken in connection with the concept of freedom.

How would a phenomenologist approach such an undertaking? In connection with Professor Hartmann's mentioning of 'categories', we could view – as Husserl would say, 'directly', 'intuitively' – the content of the idea of freedom. That is, after an extensive analysis of its variations in different types of freedom (which would demand a thorough knowledge of psychology, sociology, and so on), perhaps we could arrive at the 'phenomenon' or the 'essence' of freedom. That would, more or less, be a categorial analysis.

But there is another approach possible which would be, I think, much more fundamental. This refers indeed not only to the view of Husserl but of the development of transcendental philosophy till the present time. Husserl engaged – as is known – in a very minute, subtle and comprehensive analysis of human consciousness. In doing so he moved in two opposite directions. Firstly, going from the more complex consciousness that developed Western man has to the very rudimentary acts of consciousness from which it has genetically developed, Husserl tried regressively to reach the point at which consciousness is embodied. In the 'embodied consciousness' phenomenology has claimed to have overcome the mind – body problem namely, to reconcile the opposition between thinking and action, between intention and its fulfilment. Husserl, and Merleau-Ponty after him, tried to establish analytically how conscious acts are embodied in rudiments of bodily movement. Thus we could have a bridge between our thinking and our acting in the world. It could be that along similar lines a bridge may also be found between volition and its accomplishment. We would have to enter into an extensive inquiry of the vast net of relations, between the *feeling* of freedom, on the one hand, and the types of actual conditions within the human being as within his lived world, upon which the passage to the concrete realisation in action, on the other hand, relies. This is a possible project for phenomenology.

Chairman's concluding remarks

It may not be in the nature of *things* that philosophical discussions like this tend to be inconclusive, but it is certainly in the nature of *persons* that they are. It is, I think, possible for a discussion to be inconclusive in a rather barren way or inconclusive in a more fruitful way. And it might be worth while to note finally three reasons why this discussion has involved a certain lack of communication. There seem to me to be at least three points at which communication has not gone on.

Firstly, Miss Berry's original problem is a very particular problem. She takes it up by tackling a particular view of the necessary approach to the problem. But her question is about the role which experiences may or may not play in the judgements that we make about our own freedom and perhaps about that of other people. It seems to me that there is a fairly crucial problem here and that answering it involves understanding the notion of experience in a way very different from that in which, for instance, empiricists have understood it. But there is no way of saying whether any particular solution offered is correct or not outside the context of a more general treatment of freedom. Experiences have a role in our discoveries about our own freedom or our lack of it – and I think there are very important experiences connected with discoveries of lack of freedom here. But it is impossible to assess how we should take these, apart from a notion about how judgements of freedom are to be taken in a more general way. And this, I think, is the first trouble – to try to discuss Miss Berry's thesis independently of supplying such a context.

The second block in the discussion arises out of Professor Hartmann's remarks. Quite clearly, if you are going to say both that freedom is to be understood in terms of certain ultimate categorial distinctions and that there are no public criteria of application for the predicate 'free', then there is going to be some difficulty in knowing how we are to assess the success or otherwise of your categorial analyses. And there is in general this problem, that in discussion we may miss each other because in fact it is not clear what a speaker is trying to do in putting forward a particular analysis. And I have to confess that I – at least, and, I suspect, in common with a number of other people – was at a certain point puzzled to know what would count as a success or failure of a certain kind of argumentation in Professor Hartmann's discussion.

Both these previous points may perhaps be applicable to future discussions. The third point applies more particularly to the concept of freedom. It is quite clear that both in those uses which have interested philosophers and in ordinary-language uses, the 'free' is bound up with notions of causal agency. If we are to show that the concept of freedom (or variety of concepts which appear to have been brought under this label) *do* have application, this will involve us in discussing the relationship of human agency to other agencies. But we cannot avoid this by taking it as a surd problem. I take Professor Findlay's point here to be extremely important. But it is important for spirits in a world of physical objects that very often their fate is represented by that of the man who fell out of the top storey of a forty-storey skyscraper – who, as he went past the thirty-fifth storey, was heard to say, 'So far, so good'. What we want to know is precisely why, in a world where there are physical laws of this kind, our avowals and imputations of freedom stand differently from his utterance.

PART TWO
THE PERSON

5

THE TWO PERSONS

F. C. T. Moore

DESCARTES'S classical statement of the view that the human person consists of two individual substances, the body and the soul, has often been attacked, and has been attacked from various points of view. Many of these attacks, however, so far from rejecting what is usually known as Cartesian dualism, have merely launched the same doctrine under a new rig. They have distinguished between mental and physical objects, processes and cognitions (between ideas and material things, sensation and introspection, and so forth); they have distinguished mental from physical language by the application of one criterion of *intentionality* or another; they have distinguished reasons from causes; they have distinguished the body as an object in the world from the body as an embodied subject.

I advert here summarily to a range of philosophical traditions and positions since they all seem to me to have this in common – that by making a firm distinction between mental and bodily facts, between psychological and physical descriptions, and so forth, they come under severe strain in face of an intermediary class of phenomena of which the following are instances: dreams, unconscious motives, subliminal perceptions or impressions. A symptom of the positions which I am grouping together is that they commonly deny the existence of any such intermediary class. We may no longer speak of experiences undergone while asleep: what a man says when he wakes provides the only criterion for talk about dreaming. Similarly, all mention of the unconscious, of unconscious sensations, motives, impressions or emotions is interpreted as a complex way of speaking of a man's conscious behaviour, and of his conscious utterances. Moreover, where the normal criteria of consciousness are absent altogether, no mental terms should be applied at all. They may not be applied, except by analogy, to animals; children, before they have begun to learn language, cannot properly be granted any of the attributes of consciousness.

Views of this sort are common, both in the Anglo-Saxon and in the phenomenological traditions. It seems to me that they are in this respect both misleading and implausible. I shall argue that we ought to continue to apply mental predicates in these intermediary cases, that they are in fact intermediary cases, and that one way of describing what marks off these from the normal instances is to say that they are unconscious mental phenomena.

The question then arises by what criteria any 'phenomena' (the word itself is paradoxical in this context) can be described. And the first criterion is *reflective*. For we sometimes become aware of previously unconscious sensations, motives, emotions or, more obviously, of dreams. This awareness may be evinced in such expressions as the following: 'I realised that I was dreaming', 'I realised that I had a headache', 'I realised that my real motive for complaining was jealousy', 'I thought that it was a trump, although nothing went through my head at the time', 'I must have seen the fly that would have flown into my eye had I not blinked', 'In the middle of taking disciplinary action, I realised that I was really rather amused by the incident'.

Now it seems that all these claims entail the further claim that some mental predicate was already applicable to the speaker, although he was not conscious of the corresponding mental state or action before. If I say 'I realised that I had a headache', I am also saying that I had the headache before I became aware of it – and certainly not saying that the headache came into existence when I became conscious of it: that is a quite different sort of case which we describe by saying 'A headache suddenly came on'. If I say 'I realized that my real motive for complaining was jealousy', I am claiming that I did have the motive at the time of the complaint, though the motive need not have come out in anything I did or said, and though, *ex hypothesi*, I was not conscious of it. When I say 'I must have seen the fly that would have flown into my eye had I not blinked', I am claiming that I had a visual experience of which I was not conscious.

Now two objections might be made here. One is that these further claims are not in fact entailed by such assertions. The second is that if there is any such entailment, it is misleading, and we should modify the concepts which give rise to it.

The first point is as follows, that the very characteristic of these past-tense applications of mental predicates is that they do *not* entail the corresponding present-tense application. Whereas an assertion made now of the sentence 'I learnt algebra' is the assertion of a proposition which does entail that the present-tense proposition that I am learning algebra was true at an earlier time, an assertion, on the other hand, like 'I thought that there was another step to go down' made by a man who has just stumbled on the stairs does not entail that the corresponding present-tense proposition was true when he was about to stumble, that at that moment he was thinking that there was another step. But this is, of course, precisely what I wish to maintain, that nothing goes through the man's head at that time, but that nevertheless in some sense he *is* thinking 'There is another step'. That is why he stumbles, and he becomes aware of the thought when he stumbles. The first objection, then, lacks force.

The second objection admits that we speak in this way – that according to our ordinary ways of thinking of such cases, some such corresponding present-tense propositions as those instanced are indeed entailed. But it claims that this is a quite misleading way of thinking of such cases. For the notion of an unconscious mental phenomenon is a monster. It carries the contradiction on its face: a 'phenomenon' which does not 'appear', something *mental* which is not *conscious*. The past-tense assertions mentioned appear to tolerate the intrusion of this monster, but we should not let them. All that should be said is that sometimes we are just inclined to make such past-tense assertions. We do speak so, but what is the point of bringing out a suppositious entailment, of making the extra claim: 'But there is an inner reality too – an unconscious thought'?

Now such assertions certainly do have a function. For example, there is a difference between the case of a headache coming on, and the case of a headache coming to consciousness: the difference that in the one case something happens of which we are aware, while in the other we become aware of something which we realise, in becoming aware of it, to have been going on already.

Even the proponents of the neo-Cartesian view which I am attacking are forced into some concessions at this point. Malcolm, for example, in his book *Dreaming*, describes dream-telling as 'relating stories in the past tense under the influence of an impression'. But what is the *impression* by which Malcolm claims dream-tellers to be influenced? There are two possibilities. First, it could be the dream itself (the impression which a man experienced while asleep). But this cannot be what Malcolm means, for he wishes to deny the occurrence of mental events of such a kind. Thus the impression must be the impression of having had a certain experience during sleep. But if p cannot be conceived, could we understand what it would mean to speak of the impression that p? When we speak of the impression of having had a certain experience during sleep we are thereby making the conceptual extension by which unconscious mental phenomena are admitted. But Malcolm wishes to reject such an extension. If he does, he is left with no way of accounting for dreaming.

This somewhat cavalier discussion has been intended to elucidate what I called the reflective criterion for applying mental predicates in the case of an intermediary class of phenomena of which some examples have been enumerated. The claim was made that such phenomena sometimes came to consciousness, and that this was reflected in certain ways of speaking of them – characteristically with a past – or continuous-tensed mental predicate subordinate to some expression like 'became aware' or 'realised'. The question was raised whether such uses did in fact entail the truth of the corresponding present-tense propositions. And it seemed that to deny this led to artificiality, or at worst to inconsistency. Here then is a point of strain for the Cartesian position.

It may be observed that even if this criterion is admitted, the application of these mental predicates in the case of 'unconscious mental phenomena' will be possible only *ex post facto*. Now it is, of course, true that the full range of criteria for judging whether a person is in such and such an emotional state, or is having such and such an experience, or is acting with such and such intentions, or has any other type of mental predicate applicable to him, is lacking in the case of these unconscious occurrences. We cannot ask him at the time, nor can he speak to us of the matter at the time. Or rather, if we do ask him, he will not be able to give a suitable answer, unless the question provokes in him the awareness of the phenomenon in himself. However, it should not be concluded that *post hoc* judgements of the kind we have discussed at length are the only available criteria. On the contrary, the normal range of behavioural criteria for determining the applicability of mental predicates is available, though they are of course less secure. We may, however, speak without absurdity of a person's unconscious motives after watching his actions; we may speak without metaphor of a dog's dream when we see it stir, in sleep, twitching its paws, and producing relatively sub-vocal barks. It becomes possible in fact, with proper caution, and always remembering the priority of the reflective criterion, to speak of a whole mental underworld, whose existence is established reflectively, but whose extent and geography may be mapped by other means.

Now if it be granted that sense can be attached to talk of unconscious mental phenomena, the question still remains whether there is an advantage in so doing. Certainly, if it is true that there are such phenomena, this is enough reason for arguing the point, and something substantial will have been said about what constitutes a person. But yet the question remains how the notion of unconscious mental phenomena behaves in use, and it is to this question that I now turn, taking two examples: first, how the notion enables us to deal with one of a traditional cluster of philosophical problems which I dub 'Rousseau's paradox', and secondly, by discussing a particular psychological phenomenon, and showing how the notion may apply there. I shall treat these examples fairly cursorily, since I intend merely to show the concept at work, before coming back once more to attack it.

First, then, what is Rousseau's problem? I refer by this label to the puzzle which he poses as follows: language is a series of conventions; now how can these conventions have been set up without an already existing language in which to explain them? This is a general form of argument which seems to show in its application to the historical origin of language that language could never have been instituted, but must have existed always. It can also be applied with suitable modifications to three other cases: to Quine's 'translation situation' (discussed in *Word and Object*), where it seems to show that two language users ignorant of each other's language could never come to learn one the language of the other unless they already had some language in common by which attempted translations could be shown to be right or wrong; to the case of learning language from scratch by a child, where it seems to show that the child could never come to learn a language unless it already had one; to the case of changes in a language, where it seems to show that a new idea could never find formulation in words unless there were already words for it.

It is a vast range of problems which I mention; one could add in an equally cavalier way the vast range of solutions, by pointing out that for some philosophers these 'prelinguistic languages', as we might call them, did exist, as acquaintance with transcendent forms, dimly remembered, as innate ideas, and so forth. But it is of little profit to pursue the question at this level of generality. I ask this: How can the notion of unconscious mental phenomena in any way help to sort out Rousseau's paradox?

The answer is that there is a form of the paradox concerning the origin of the *person*. Suppose we take (after Maine de Biran) a first deliberate action as a paradigm of the birth of a personality – let us say, the movement of an arm. We may then ask whether someone could move his arm deliberately without knowing that he had an arm to move. The answer is, clearly, that he could not. But we may then ask how he came to have the knowledge that he had an arm; and the answer would naturally be that it was by the experience of moving it. The paradox has now taken this form: if a man deliberately moves his arm, then he already has knowledge of his arm; but if he has knowledge of his arm, he can have gained that knowledge only by moving the arm.

Thus, if we take a view like that of Maine de Biran, that willed action is constitutive of the human person, and that a first act of will is the first appearance in a human baby of a human person, we seem to be faced with another, and equally intolerable, form of Rousseau's paradox. It is at this point that the notion of unconscious mental phenomena disposes easily, but perhaps too easily, of our difficulties. For we may answer simply that the first act of will is indeed preceded by knowledge of its object, but by unconscious knowledge. We might put it another way by saying that we can think of this first deliberate action as one in which mental materials already present first come to the light of consciousness.

Let us turn from this very abridged account of Rousseau's paradox and the way in which the notion of unconscious mental phenomena can help to resolve one form of it, and consider a concrete psychological phenomenon.

Consider the case of a homosexual undergoing aversive therapy. He is regularly shown erotic photographs of men, which he finds pleasurable and stimulating. But injections of apomorphine are so administered that each time he sees the photographs he suffers a fit of nausea. Conversely, during his periods of comfort and rest, he is surrounded by erotic photographs of women. After a period of concentrated conditioning, he returns to his life with a complete reorientation of his sexual desires.

We might try to give an account of this case in terms of stimulus and response, with the claim that there is no need to refer to extra inner events, mental occurrences of which the patient is unaware. Here might be such an attempt: there is stimulus-group A (homosexual stimuli), and stimulus-group B (heterosexual stimuli); and there is reaction-group C (reactions of sexual excitation); in addition, there is a convenient means of artificially producing nausea (N), and, by contrast, of providing relief (R).

For the patient, the following pattern holds: $A \rightarrow B$, $B \rightarrow$ not $- C$. Under artificial conditions, the following pattern is made to hold: $A \rightarrow C + N$, $B \rightarrow$ not $- C + R$. As a result of the treatment, the following pattern subsequently holds: $A \rightarrow$ not $- C$, $B \rightarrow C$.

Now this may be a clear way of describing the cure. But it explains nothing, and it raises many problems. It would of course be pointless to give a detailed critique of this gross formulation of a stimulus/response account of the cure. The interest of the formulation is that it displays two fundamental difficulties of any such account (I do not mean to suggest that such difficulties are insuperable).

First, how can such stimulus groups be identified? Consider the suggested formulae. It is clear that in the case of the first pair, for a given subject, not all the circumstances that would fall under *A* or *B* do actually produce the relevant response. Satiation, an exclusive devotion to one person, a powerful diversion of fear or anxiety, even climatic conditions, may all severely restrict the number of circumstances which may be designated by *A* or *B*. Moreover, in the case of the second pair of formulae, *A* and *B* represent an artificially small selection from the range of cases ordinarily covered by *A* and *B* of the first pair – or, indeed, perhaps not a selection from them at all.

We may ask why an induced aversion to certain homosexually erotic photographs should eradicate all homosexual desires. It is natural to say here that this is how the patient *interprets* the photographs, though such interpretation need not be conscious. For him, the photographs are not merely a particular stimulus, but representative of a whole class of stimuli. Indeed, their effectiveness as particular stimuli depends on their association with that class. How else could patterns of silver bromide on paper induce sexual excitation? It is natural (and in a certain idiom proper) to speak here of unconscious mental activities of association and interpretation.

Consider further why *N* plays its role. In the case of a successful treatment the man resists a stimulus *A*, we might say, because he does not like being sick. But why should it not instead lead him to resist the efforts of his psychotherapists whom he knows to be responsible for his nausea? Why might he not even welcome the nausea out of a desire to be punished for a *continuing* perversity? And so forth. Here too it is natural to say that the patient is in some way prepared to make the relevant associations, to co-operate with the psychotherapist in manipulating the underworld of his own existence.

It is argued, then, that an attempt to give an account of particular cases like this in terms of stimulus and response does not in fact dispense us from referring to conscious and unconscious mental processes and postures.

I have argued as follows. Cartesianism has presented us with two persons, the physical and the mental. Some of the most radical attacks on Descartes have maintained this dualism, though adopting quite different idioms to express it. All these positions come under strain in face of what it is after all natural to call unconscious mental phenomena. It has been urged that the proper way to relieve this strain is to readmit an intermediary class of phenomena under that label, and to allow their presence to be established by appeal to physical as well as to reflective criteria.

But a radical objection may be made to my 'solution'. For the dualistic positions which I have briefly mentioned typically exclude a third term. Consider, for instance, the search for criteria of *intentionality*, where intentionality is treated not merely as a logical feature of certain propositions, but as a distinguishing mark of psychological propositions.

To take a more specific example, it is sometimes held that we ought to distinguish 'I am looking for a cow', where this entails 'There is a cow for which I am looking', from 'I am looking for a cow' where any cow will do, and the entailment does not hold, by saying that the second is an *intentional* expression – the criterion being the occurrence in the proposition of a term such that the truth of the proposition does not entail the existence of anything denoted by the term. Now by this criterion 'My car needs a new tyre' would be intentional. And this is sometimes cited as a *counter-example* to this criterion of intentionality. Such appeal shows that what is being sought is not a logical feature alone of such expressions, but some feature which will mark off psychological from other propositions. Now, given the success of this programme (a weighty hypothesis), we whould have a criterion by which we could test any proposition to ascertain whether it is intentional. And then, it is reasonable to suggest, any tested proposition will either be intentional or not. There will be no third term – no intermediary. Thus, the form of argument by which I have held that all 'dualistic' positions (of which the present one was cited as a recent instance) must be modified to allow for intermediary cases seems to come to grief. In the case of descriptions of dreams, unconscious motives, and so on, they either will or will not be intentional (and in fact probably will be: 'I dreamt of Pauline' is likely to come out as intentional under any criteria).

It seems, then, that not only does the distinction between intentional and non-intentional expressions (a form of 'dualism' if you will) require no modification in face of so-called unconscious mental phenomena, but (always hypothesising the success of the programme) it is perfectly able to accommodate them.

In reply to this objection, we must point out once more how two ways are open to students of the notion of intentionality. They may either concern themselves with the logical peculiarities of certain expressions delimited by certain related criteria, or they may, in accepting or rejecting such criteria, make appeal to an *already assumed* distinction between psychological and non-psychological propositions.

But it is this distinction which gives rise to our initial difficulty. For as soon as any such distinction is accepted, the unconscious poses its problem once more, requiring, as it seems to, a phenomenon (I continue to use this word, for want of a better) to be both mental and not mental, both physical and not physical.

Yet by whatever criteria this distinction is now established, it seems that a third term is not permitted, that an intermediary is unthinkable. Thus we must be led either, like Descartes, to maintain that dreams and so forth are straightforwardly admissible as mental phenomena, that '*l'âme pense toujours*', or to hold that such phenomena are not admissible at all, like Malcolm, Sartre or MacIntyre, to cite some diverse contemporary examples. However, neither of these positions is a satisfactory way of dealing with the facts – facts which seem to compel us ineluctably to bend our concepts.

The suggestion now emerges that the solution originally presented in the present argument is no more than a rationalisation of existing usage and ways of thinking about such cases. What at first appeared as a solution should in fact be taken as a *reductio ad absurdum* of our Cartesian concepts, or the 'two persons' view. For if we accept this view we are forced either to close our eyes to an important class of facts, or, in attempting to give an account of them, to contradict ourselves, or, at best, generate anomalies.

The present argument, then, amounts to no more than a weary repetition of the anti-Cartesian slogan: *not two persons, but one*. Here is not the place to pursue the problems consequent upon such repetition, which have been recently aired in works of Paul Ricœur, P. F. Strawson and Charles Taylor, to give a few instances. But perhaps the preliminary task was worth performing again. It bears repeating that there are not two persons, but one. We are therefore left with the important question: What then is the one person?

6

TOWARDS THE
CONSTITUTION OF
THE UNITY OF THE PERSON

Manfred S. Frings

READING Dr F. C. T. Moore's paper 'The Two Persons' I cannot escape the impression that for him any acceptable explanation of the unity of the human person still depends upon overcoming the Cartesian dualism of two heteronomous substances, namely, the dualism of mind and body as *modi extensionis* and *cogitationis*.

True, Dr Moore is himself critical of many attempts that have been made to overcome this dualism. He states, for instance, that many of these 'have merely launched the same doctrine under a new rig'. He submits to us an alternative according to which it is 'urged that the proper way to relieve this strain (of unconscious mental phenomena) is to readmit an intermediary class of phenomena under that label, and to allow their presence to be established by appeal to physical as well as to reflective criteria'. Having Cartesian dualism in mind, however, it is quite natural that at the end of his presentation Dr Moore asks the only question one can raise within the context of his argumentation: 'What then is the one person?'.

It is the formulation of this question, i.e. asking about the 'what' of the 'one' person, which interested me most while reading Dr Moore's essay. For asking about the whatness of the 'one' person underlies Dr Moore's entire paper. This becomes especially obvious in his cursory treatment of 'Rousseau's paradox'. According to Dr Moore this paradox states that language, for instance, is a series of conventions that must have been set up on the basis of an already existing language. This implies that the origin of language has not been instituted by men, but rather must have always already existed. In other words: we can never learn a language unless we already have one to learn. Such argumentation is Platonic and Gottfried Martin has appropriately referred to it as 'Plato's fundamental argument', saying that, for instance, in order to be able to recognise two equal pieces of wood we must know in advance what equality (as such) is. We must already have at out disposal the whatness of equality in order to know two pieces of wood to *be* equal, for their equality does not lie in the wood of the two perceivable pieces.

Now, asking about the unity of the person, with or versus Descartes's dualism, has always suggested a taking into account of the possibility of intermediaries so that we can better grasp the unity of the human person. But no matter if we think in Cartesian or 'anti-Cartesian' terms as to this unity, the presupposition of two substances in the explication of the unity of the person remains: either we accept them or strive to overcome them. It is not surprising, therefore, that at the end Dr Moore writes:

> What at first appeared as a solution should in fact be taken as a *reductio ad absurdum* of our Cartesian concepts, or the 'two persons' view. For if we accept this view, we are forced, either to close our eyes to an important class of facts, or in attempting to give an account of them, to contradict ourselves, or, at best, generate anomalies. The present argument, then, amounts to no more than a weary repetition of the anti-Cartesian slogan: *not two persons, but one.*

In what follows I shall not take up as a starting-point a position for or against Descartes, as Dr Moore at least implicitly chose to do. Rather, I intend to continue where Dr Moore left off. However, my basic thrust will not be to search for the direction in which one might discover an answer to Dr Moore's significant question 'What then is the one person?' Rather, I wish to propose an explication of the unity of the person in terms of a different question, viz., '*How* is "one" person?'

Such an approach might enable us to avoid a frequent presupposition found in the field of personalism, viz., to link the concept of person with that of a 'substance' altogether, or to conceive the person's unity as a static one, composed of mind and body. It is my contention that the human person is not subject to any composition of elements, be they substances or *modi*, unconscious or subconscious acts, inner and outer perceptions, volitional deeds or kinematic impulses, psychic or physical experiences, etc. The unity of what we

call 'person' is an *essentially dynamic and lived unity* equally defying
composite elements, linguistic-analytic explanations and logical
definitions. I shall submit four existential modes of how the human
person *presences* as 'one' person in order to back up my claim. In so
doing I neither claim that these four kinds of the presencing of the
person are treated exhaustively nor that they are the only kinds of
personal presencing.

In our everyday life and in our immediate experience of them the
persons we happen to meet in no way reveal themselves to us as
compositions of substances with or without intermediaries, no matter
how such intermediaries may theoretically be justified or rejected as
groundless. Persons reveal themselves first in our *plain lived experience
with* them, which is a very different experience from that which we
have in dealing with thing-objects. The human person already
appears as defying objective descriptions like those we make in
regard to things. True, we can refer to a person in descriptive and
explanatory terms when, for instance, we speak of a 'good' person, a
'modest' person, a 'complicated' person, an 'attractive' person. But
such descriptive usages are already encompassed and guided by a
previous initial experience we had with another person. We also
rightly attribute to the person a 'will', 'character', 'behaviour', even
something like a 'personality', and certain reactions in given
situations. Indeed, we can describe a sequence of deeds of a person
(e.g. of a criminal) and may even trace a certain 'X' characteristic
for the kind and scope of deeds this or that particular person has been
acting out. Moreover, we may be able to 'analyse' his deeds by
making statements and an inventory of them in order to determine
if such statements fulfil some plausible explanatory progression of a
person's actions. But despite all this, who would assert that in these
descriptive data of a person a definitive whatness of his unity can be
attained? If we are to seek this unity of the person it should be
sought in a primordial *acted-out* experience *with* and *of* the person
with whom we share our everyday 'World'. Hence, I refer to what
by the phenomenologist is called the Life-World, as the 'naïve' and
pre-logical and self-evidential facticity of the 'World' in which we live
out daily lives and in which things and people are 'with' us in terms
of a 'given' familiarity as long as we live, i.e. they are as beings
'there' for us in a pre-logical and pre-theoretical way. This is the
World as an experienced ground where the sun 'rises' and 'sets' in
the beautiful horizon of the seas and is not yet for us a fixed star
radiating energy. This primordial World, so often described and
explicated in phenomenological studies, is 'there' just as long as we
continue to be. It is a horizon for any and all possible activities,

including those of logic and science. It is the World into which we wake *up* in the morning and from which we *fall* to fall asleep at night; it is the World *into* which we are born and *from* which we will depart.

Phenomenologists and existentialists are not agreed on the primary character of this Life-World which we appear to take for granted in our theoretical reflections and in our daily lives. For Husserl, the Life-World is experienced in terms of a doxic-theoretic character; for Max Scheler, in terms of an emotively-felt primordial value-experience; for Heidegger, it is first the World of practical engagement with things around us relating to equipmental manifolds manifest in the use of things. In each case of the explication of man's primordial World, we find a different designation for it. Husserl called it *die Lebenswelt*. Long before Husserl appears to have seen the significance of the Life-World, Max Scheler referred to it as *die natürliche Weltanschauung* (the natural view of looking at the World), and Heidegger refers in this context to *Alltäglichkeit* (Everydayness) in *Being and Time*. In each case, too, we are concerned with a particular phase of the phenomenological reduction into the World of our immediate, natural experience, its structure and the ground of the passively and plainly received givenness of the Life-World, i.e. as prior to theoretical, logical and scientific objective determinations and abstractions. In this Life-World, 'World' and 'Self' do not appear to have an epistemological object – subject relation. Rather, Self and World are inseparably co-related and experienced. As Scheler put it: 'To every person there belongs a world. To every world there belongs a person.'

In attempting to explicate the unity of the person as the 'one' person, I suggest that we do not remain within a conceptual framework of past metaphysics. Valuable though this may be, it is also necessary to regress into the a-logical, non-metaphysical plain lived experience of the Life-World where we truly 'meet' the person in immediate, non-theoretical experience. We must attempt to regress into the basic characters of our With-World through which the 'World' is shared and co-experienced with the other. Such a primordially given and shared World is first manifest in the family into which we were born, the first with-experience in the family (Husserl's *erste Normalität*) with its passively and freely accepted World-about: its home, surrounding garden, trees, fields, sky and earth. It is here where we find the locus of our first experienced encounter with a 'thou', the 'other' person as someone different from us – different not in terms of a different body 'and' mind, but different in terms of an unfolding *individuality* which begins to set itself off in the distanciality experienced in this being-together-with-others.

One reason why Cartesian dualism (with and without intermediaries) cannot account for the unity of the person is precisely because of the fact that it cannot account for the particuliarity of human individuality. True, each person has a body and mind (we may even grant this in the sense of Cartesian *modi*), but the individuality of the person does not come about in such having a (qualitatively) different body 'and' mind. Rather, a person's individuality must be sought in his unique way of *acting out his existence*. It must be sought in his body-movements, etc., in all of which different *acts* the person reveals (as Scheler puts it) a 'qualitative direction' of his own that is peculiar for this and that person and is at the same time experienced by others in pre-reflective fashion.

It is within this Life-World that I submit some explications of the 'how' of the unity of the person, thereby providing an alternative basis for the discussion. Inasmuch as both my starting-point (the Life-World) and my objective (the 'how' of the one person) are different from Dr Moore's, the following is not to be taken as a criticism of what Dr Moore has told us. Instead, I prefer to see my effort as a juxtaposition to Dr Moore's and in part a complement to some of his arguments.

In speaking of the lived experience among persons I used the term 'plain'. By 'plain' I mean that in persons' experiencing one another in the Life-World, there is no initial objectivation of the other as another person; rather, when we meet other persons in our natural attitude, their personal being is *immediately co*-experienced, i.e. not in a conscious or volitional fashion. A person is *before* us. Hence also the reciprocally natural 'understanding' among persons is a fact in the Life-World which in its facticity is taken for granted in the sense that we passively accept it in interpersonal experience. This immediate experience must be distinguished from subsequent objective thinking 'about' the person. In meeting other persons, we do not bring to our consciousness that they are endowed with 'will', 'intellect', 'language', etc. Such qualities of the person – as they no doubt *also* belong to the person inclusive of the person's being always an embodied person – remain initially quite hidden in the immediate experience of the *person*. If, for example, I unexpectedly meet a person who is unknown to me, the initial co-experience of this person is not affected if he begins to speak in a language other than my own or if I subsequently realise that he limps. It is only when we begin to make observations such as these, namely when we observe the sounds of his language or his body-movements and gestures, that we can make such observed data 'fit' in the initial presence of his person.

Subsequently observed data may fulfil or disagree with the initial 'picture' of the person. But it is precisely in the moment of initial presencing of the person that the peculiar one-ness of the person is a lived facticity. Any observed data, for instance of his body, language, gestures, etc., diminish his person and, indeed, make his person disappear into their background. His person may be lost in objective analyses and become something like an object of judgement and statements which the person in the initial, lived co-experience definitely was not.

This leads me to the kernel of my presentation, viz., to bring into focus the aforementioned four modes of the presencing of the person in the Life-World which I consider to be a fourfold constitution of the lived unity of the person. In attempting to sketch this manifold of the givenness of the 'one' person in plain life-experience, a brief note on matters phenomenological may be added. The reader of this paper must bear in mind that he is not 'in' an interpersonal experience while reading this paper. Rather, he is in an act of reflecting on the contents of this paper which he might have already begun to evaluate negatively, positively or neutrally. This attitude of consciousness, however, modifies and hides the phenomenon under discussion: the unity of the person in plain lived co-experience. It follows from this that the contents of my outline take on in the reader's mind (and, indeed, in my own while I am writing) an objectifying variation of the phenomenon. In order partially to remove this variation of consciousness from the immediate lived experience with and of another person, it might be helpful to recall a lived experience with another person which took place in the normal stream of daily life. In this fashion one may check the text along this or that recalled interpersonal experience. Yet, in doing this, the initial, lived co-experience as recalled will only become approximately present since it is 'past' in the 'present' act of recalling. Such recalling, then, would again modify the phenomenon under discussion to a certain degree.

Keeping this in mind, let us first take up the point of objectifying a person. I can pay special attention to his or her body, volitional attitudes, language or moving about. In such an attitude, however, the person begins to withdraw into a background of the now observed data, which, in turn, have moved into the foreground of my experiencing the person. For example, if I observe how a person walks, it is the walking which I may find typical or not typical *for* his person. Again, if I have kept correspondence with a person I never met, or if I hear him speak over the telephone, my picture of his person may or may not correspond with the person should I subsequently meet him in lived experience. In short, what we call 'person' is subject to a coming to the fore or a withdrawing in lived experience, depending on the intensities of observational attitudes in *regard* to the person. These attitudes may fall into two groups: (1) I may observe the person after my initial co-experience. In this case my observations may comply, or be forced by me to comply, or may not comply with my initial picture of his person. (2) My observations may be prior to my meeting the person as in the above case, viz., when I listen to his voice over the telephone. Here, there may also set in a disappointment or disagreement or fulfilment of my picture of him when I will meet him face to face. In each case, however, the person presences himself to me in some varying degree which appears to be dependent upon the intensities of observation. To put it more succinctly, the more I observe him the more his person appears to recede into a background of my deliberate, close observation.

There are also cases when the person begins to disappear in a specific kind of co-experience. This is the case when we find ourselves amidst a raging mass of people. In such a mass-experience the individuality of the person begins to dissolve in the mass such that the 'other' becomes an unknown X in the psychic contagion prevailing throughout the neutralised co-experience in a raging mass. We shall take up this point later.

By calling to mind such well-known instances of intersubjective experience, let me emphasise that by no means is the immediacy of the givenness of the person a static fact throughout the Life-World. That which we call the 'person' is given already in such common cases within a mode of presencing which I call the 'mode of depth' and which, upon closer investigation, appears to span two extreme poles: the immediate and full presence of a person on the one hand and his being reduced 'as' a person to the anonymity of a mass-X of the other. It is this dynamic span of the givenness of the person, ranging from anonymity to the full presence and experienced nearness of the person which shows a certain 'psycho-physical independence' of the 'sphere' of the person (to borrow two terms of Max Scheler's employed in a different context). Now, an initial, full and total presence of the person is by no means a common happening in the Life-World. It seems that personal presencing happens mostly in between these two extreme poles during our lives. A total and full presence of the sphere of the person may be seen in the event of genuine love at 'first' sight. For in the unforeseen split moment of lived reciprocal personal presencing it is neither race, deeds, language nor any other quality of the persons concerned – let alone their bodies 'and' minds – that unites the unknown into the unexpected event: it is the value of the *person* in the very absence of observation, objectivation and language. For at first such fully lived person-al co-presence is one of *silence* which 'speaks' of the unique one-ness of the *value* of the person. But it is not the purpose of our discussion to enlarge upon the details of the silence of person-al being which is even more manifest in the extremely rare presencing of genuine sainthood in history (e.g. Buddha, Jesus, Francis). The reason why I draw the reader's attention to this example of the mode of depth is to show that the givenness of the human person and its unity must not be divorced from the immediate value-experience which in all possible degrees of intensities is felt in intersubjective being.

This leads me to the next mode of how the person presences – a mode to which Dr Moore also referred within his own context. Let this mode be called 'mode of growth'. It remains highly problematic when we can justifiably speak of a human being as a person in his lifetime. Dr Moore seems to be in agreement with Maine de Biran that 'a first deliberate action' may be 'a paradigm of the birth of a personality'. But Dr Moore sees a first willed action as a possible constituent of the being of the person within the framework of 'Rousseau's paradox', and hence a version of the Platonic argument: 'If a man deliberately moves his arm, then he already has knowledge of his arm, but if he has knowledge of his arm, he can have gained that knowledge only by moving the arm'.

As far as the 'birth' of the human person in his lifetime is concerned (and as far as we can justifiably apply the word 'person' to a human being), I contend that this genetic mode of the presence of a person must include a consideration of the *ethical existence* of the person. For already the mere application of the term 'person' implies a *self*-value, i.e. a value which is radically distinct from so-called 'attached' values, namely, of things to which we attach a price-tag indicating their value. The self-value of the person must also be distinguished from those values which are deliberately attached to man by way of societal legislation, religious doctrines or philosophical ideas of man. The human person experiences *his* self-value amidst other beings. But this is the case only when a human being is *able* to differentiate himself from the other and *lets* himself be differentiated from and by the other, i.e. if he has intuitive insight into his own acts and those different from his. If a human being becomes aware of the difference of the feeling, willing, thinking and all acting of other persons (perhaps at the age of two), such that he no longer unconsciously imitates and follows other persons' wills and deeds in the form of emotive identification and infection (mother – baby relation), and if such a difference is experienced in terms of an early 'understanding' of the other so that the human being lives his own being-able-to-do, it is then that the term 'person' obtains a justified application. In other words: if a human being experiences his existence in the aforementioned *distanciality* from his member-persons in the Life-World, we may then speak of him as a person. Only then is he only able to do 'right' or 'wrong' and more importantly able to *be* 'good', or other than good, in regard to others. In everyday language this state of affairs is well expressed when we say that he or she grows *into* a person, by which we tacitly imply that, on the one hand, he or she is not yet a full person, but, on the other, is on the way to becoming that person into which he or she grows. It may be an ambiguous way of speaking of the 'birth' of a personality at an early time of one's life. For we saw that the sphere of the person can both be fully present to us as well as become anonymously absent, which mode would certainly, if it is accepted, also pertain to the growing person. It also may be that the 'birth' of person comes close to a secondary judgement of ours after we have already experienced him as something *like* a person (although we are still unable to tell which person the child is growing into). The experience of a growing child is, however, an immediate one since he is in the *act* of becoming a person, which act I co-experience through his growing individuality which is already set off from me. True, a very small child to whom we do not apply the term 'person' is also set off from others, but this is because it is we who as persons have set him off. The very small child, by himself, is certainly not capable of being *able* to differentiate himself from others. He is *un*able to be on his own as a person with regard to other persons around him.

This mode of the growth of the person, then, is intrinsically connected with the experience of interpersonal distanciality. It is throughout the growth of a human being 'into' a person that the givenness of the person in the Life-World varies in degrees from early immature childhood to the distanced individuality of a fully grown-up person.

It was stated above that the individuality of the person disappears in the psychic contagion of a mass. The 'other' loses his individuality if the person is swept away by the movement of a mass. This implies that in mass-experiences, such as emotionally charged revolts, the person begins to lose his felt relation *to* the other. The ontological state of being-with-others is reduced to a minimum in favour of a state of neutral 'alongsidedness' of anonymous anyones. The anonymised person is, therefore, in a state of being thrust 'forward' to the psychic goal which hovers over and moves on the mass, seemingly uniting it. This experience of being-alongside, rather than 'with' others, finds a typical expression in Japanese mass-demonstrations where the mass-elements form into a snake-like motion such that they are at each other's anonymous side. This anonymous alongside-experience allows of their being directed 'forward' with the progressing motion of the mass. 'Anyone' *is* at one's side in a mass. This experienced anonymity in the mass may well account for the fact that (in extreme cases) one or the other mass-element is trampled to 'anyone's' death, but not as someone's.

The only temporary anonymous presencing of the person in mass-experiences, however, can hardly be regarded as a basic mode of personal presencing. This is because of the transient nature of all mass phenomena. The 'mode of anonymity' must be seen in the constant fact that the person is always within an anonymous field of persons-around. This pertains to the anonymous persons-around in regard to me as well as vice versa: I, too, belong to this field for any other member of the persons-around.

Parenthetically, I would like to make a brief reference to Heidegger's explication of the 'the They-around' (*das Man*) which he treats in the fourth chapter of *Being and Time*. Although Heidegger never takes into consideration the self-value of the human person and its ontological relevance, 'the They-around' helps us to focus on the anonymous mode of personal presence. While reading this paper, for instance, we had been surrounded not only by things given in the background of the act of reading and perceiving this paper, but also by persons-around. But we were not genuinely with this or that particular person; rather, we were 'with' others as not distinguished in their individuality, with the They-around-one as an irreducible with-experience. On the one hand, and although we take it for granted in the Life-World, this pure with-experience is intrinsically tied up with things ready-at-hand (Heidegger); on the other hand, it is not tied up with things and is the 'fundamental existential category of human thinking' (Scheler). Heidegger emphasises the first aspect of the With-World although he also agrees to the second one. He tells us that if we come across a boat (thing) anchored at the shore of a lake, the boat 'points' to someone who made it or wants to use it.[1] The boat, then, 'relates' to my With-World. The equipmentality (*Zuhandenheit*) of the boat, and the other, are met 'in one' (*in eins*).[2] But the other is not 'with' me, with reference to the equipmental order and destinations of things

[1] M. Heidegger, *Sein und Zeit*, p. 118.   [2] Ibid., p. 123.

ready-at-hand alone, a point which Heidegger seems to de-emphasise in its significance. The communal with-experience is equally, if not primordially, manifest in the absence of things. Max Scheler stresses this aspect of the With-World throughout his works, saying that, for example, in the case of an absolutely isolated Robinson Crusoe, the experience of the absence of the other is as much of a fundamental experience in Robinson Crusoe's conscious-ness as is the consciousness of his own self:

> It belongs to the *eternal and ideal essence* of the mature person that his entire conscious being and acting is as much one of conscious-ness of self, of self-responsible, individual reality as it is one of conscious co-responsibly experienced membership of a communal form of togetherness . . . Our proposition holds that the intentional experience of 'belonging' to a community at all, and to be a 'member' of it, was also the case with a Robinson Crusoe – i.e. it was as originally given as his individual ego and self. Our proposition further holds that this consciousness of membership also belongs to the essence of such persons who live in isolation and that communal *intentionality* exists totally independent of the fortuitous sense experience we have of other people, of their looks, etc., of the number and kinds of people which might fulfil this experiencing membership or not.[1]

Both Scheler and Heidegger drew special attention to this twofold around-experience of the other, who is both met 'in one' with the instrumentality of things, and as 'one' in my With-World only. In our context it is an experienced field of anonymity from which the one-ness of the human person may *emerge*. In this anonymous field of persons-around, strictly speaking, there does not exist simply 'one' person; rather, the They-around is in itself a unity of pure being-with-others-experience. Nevertheless, it must be considered as different in value from the mere equipmentality of things lying around and before us in their matrixes of relations, destinations and serviceabilities. The emergence of the person from its mode of anonymity shows that the one-ness of the person is not a problematic of the individual person with a body 'and' a mind only but also and especially a problematic of the ontological facticity of the anonymous one-ness of persons-around as distinct in value from that of the equipmentality of things.

From these brief considerations of the 'They-around' two points may be inferred: (1) that an explication of the 'how' of the unity of

[1] M. Scheler, *Vom Ewigen im Menschen*, in *Gesammelte Werke*, 5th ed. (Bern and Munich, 1966) Band 5, pp. 371 and 372.

the person must take into consideration the ontological one-ness of the anonymous field of persons-around, and (2) that one-ness here again appears to be a dynamic conception in that it is ontologically interwoven with the anonymous 'one' of the They-around *from which* the sphere of the person may come to the fore in any mode of embodied and individual presencing and *into which* it may recede and disappear into anonymity.

In the above three modes of person-al presencing in the Life-World, the modes of depth, of growth and of anonymity, I repeatedly used the term 'value'. This term was used in the following senses: (1) in the mode of depth the value-character of the person lies in the person's uniqueness-to-me which merges with my existence in the split moment of silent presence; (2) in the mode of growth, the value-character of the growing person is given to the persons around, in that the becoming person is with me as a special value-being to be cared for in his growing distanciality and, hence, ethical existence; (3) the value of the person may emerge from anonymity to become clearly present to me whereby we maintained that also the anonymous field of persons-around possesses a value-character distinct from things-around.

These three variations of the self-value of the person are by no means exhaustive. But they have in common that the self-value of the person is distinctly experienced in comparison to the experience of thing-values that we 'attach' to things. These value variations have also in common that they reveal at least to a certain degree some psycho-physical independence, whereas a thing-value is nothing but a predicate of the thing. The self-value of the person, however, is not a predicate of a thing. It is an essential datum of *Existenz*. For the body and the mind *of* the person may long have been extinct whereas the respective person is still remembered by us in his value. This leads us, then, to a fourth mode of how personal being presences as a unity: the 'exemplarity of the person.

During our lives the exemplarity of the person is evidenced in many, mostly unnoticed, experiences. Living persons begin to serve as models in early childhood in terms of an exemplary image of parents and/or of the first teachers. Acts of imitation often accompany the awareness of a person the child looks up to and who serves as a model. We know that the awareness of model-persons who have begun to stand out for us from other persons continues throughout adolescence and adulthood and that it is also accompanied by visions we have of ourselves which we strive to fulfil. Leaders and sovereigns of peoples (past or present), a hero of a nation, a genius of art, a particular saint are but a few examples of model persons who may guide a person throughout his lifetime. The function of model persons worshipped by way of so-called person-cults in politics is well known. But our exemplary consciousness is also at work in educational models serving as *Leitbilder* for the young, for instance, the 'gentleman', the '*honnête homme*', the '*cortegiano*', the 'good citizen', etc. The latter instances of exemplary persons already show that there is no demand for only a factual person to 'fill' the sphere of exemplary consciousness which is a constituent factor in man's With-World. For there is no such thing as 'the' gentleman, or 'the' *honnête homme*, 'the' Frenchman, 'the' Italian, etc., rather there can only be more or less close exemplifications of such ideal models of the person. In the foundation oᴸ Max Scheler's ethical personalism such ideal model persons are oᴸ utmost significance in that their five basic types exercise ontologic-ally a 'call-of-oughtness' (*Soll*seins*forderung*) onto us, which call in every historical epoch is felt and experienced in respective variations of emotive acts of pre-ferring. Scheler's detailed analysis of person-al exemplarity does not concern us here directly.[1] But if we take some of his phenomenological bases into consideration, viz., that 'Consciousness of exemplarity is wholly *pre*-logical and *prior* to any comprehension of any possible spheres of choosing', it appears, from a pure phenomenological viewpoint, that the unity of the person must be sought in the noematic nucleus of the *self-value of the person* implicit in all modes of personal presencing.

In summary of these brief remarks on the unity of the person and his value-being, we may say: the 'one-ness' of the person is constituted in at least four dynamic modes of personal presencing in our Life-World, the mode of depth, of growth, of anonymity, and of exem-plarity, and their possible interwovenness. The unity of the person is a dynamic unity of and in *lived* co-experience. This unity must be distinguished from the conception of an objective and static unity as composed of opposites. For the value of the human person, as self-value, is unique.

Undoubtedly, much of Dr Moore's analyses of the person provides for fruitful discussion. But I wish to stress that any discussion about the unity of the person must also consider that the sphere of the person is the locus of *ethical existence* without which there cannot *be* one 'person'.

[1] These will be found in *Der Formalismus in der Ethik und die materiale Wertethik*, in *Gesammelte Werke*, 5th ed., Band 2, Second Part, section vi, в, pp. 568–80, and *Schriften aus dem Nachlass, I*, in *Gesammelte Werke* (Berne, 1957) Band 10, pp. 255–344.

7

THE PERSON:
ISSUES AND QUESTIONS

Ian W. Alexander

DR MOORE is primarily concerned with refuting the Cartesian and neo-Cartesian dualism of the two substances or what he calls the 'two persons' view, present, he believes, in both the Anglo-Saxon and the phenomenological traditions in spite of appearances, Sartre being mentioned specifically in the latter connection.

He argues that this view comes under severe strain in face of a class of phenomena such as dreams, unconscious motives, etc., described as 'unconscious mental phenomena', which form a group of intermediary cases – phenomena to which, although unconscious, mental predicates may justifiably be applied.

He then goes on to provide a reflective criterion for determining the applicability of mental predicates to such phenomena. He instances such statements as 'I realised that I had a headache' or 'I thought that there was another step to go down', spoken by a man who has stumbled. All of these are statements, he argues, which entail 'the claim that some mental predicate was already applicable to the speaker, although he was not conscious of the corresponding mental state or action before'.

He proceeds then to suggest how the concept of unconscious mental phenomena may solve certain specific problems: for example, 'Rousseau's paradox' as to how a language, which is a system of conventions, can be instituted without previous knowledge of language; or Maine de Biran's account of the origin of personality in terms of willed action, which would seem to require both that the act of will be preceded by knowledge of its object and that this knowledge be preceded by the experience of effecting the act. In both cases, it is suggested, there *is* antecedent knowledge, but unconscious knowledge.

Dr Moore also considers a psychological case – the stimulus-response conditioning technique applied in aversive therapy (as in the treatment of homosexuality), which appears to him to involve for its success 'unconscious mental activities of association and interpretation', a particular stimulus being made representative of a whole class of stimuli.

Having presented these arguments he comes up against a form of dualism, as he puts it, which his stated objections appear to leave untouched, namely the distinction between non-psychological propositions and psychological or intentional propositions, his so-called unconscious mental phenomena being normally capable of accommodation under the latter head.

With that, he has, it would seem, come full circle. We are left high and dry with our Cartesian concepts, but aware of their inadequacy in face of facts which, as he says, 'compel us ineluctably to bend our concepts'. His argument, in short, boils down, he avows, simply to a repetition of the anti-Cartesian slogan 'not two persons, but one', and he leaves us with the question 'What then is the one person?'

Professor Frings presents his paper as complementary to Dr Moore's, beginning, he declares, 'where Dr Moore left off'. He proposes to replace the question Dr Moore asked in his conclusion – '*What* is the one person?' – by the question '*How* is "one" person?'

He proposes, in short, a phenomenological approach, undercutting the mind–body distinction and confining himself to the description of the person as he reveals himself or, to use his term, 'presences' as one person at the level of our immediate, everyday experience of him. It is his contention that the person so presented is not subject to any composition of elements (mind, body, etc.) nor indeed to logical definition or analysis, but constitutes a 'dynamic and lived unity'. His unity has therefore to be sought in the 'primordial acted-out experience with and of the person with whom we share our everyday "World".' To understand it we must regress to the ante-predicative experience of the Life-World (Husserl, Heidegger and Scheler are here referred to) where we 'meet the person in immediate, non-theoretical experience' and where we, in relation with others, 'act out' our existence.

Professor Frings then goes on to list four basic modes of 'presencing' of the person in the Life-World. The first is the mode of 'depth'. The person is presented *qua* person as a basic, primary particular, as an individual transcending all objectifying predicates or qualities that we may ascribe to him in our observation of him. In so far as we do make the person the object of such observation and characterisation, he recedes *qua* person into the background. Presencing is therefore said to move between two poles, the immediate, full presence of the person endowed with unique value (as in love experience) and his reduction to anonymity.

Secondly, the mode of 'growth', described by Professor Frings as 'the genetic mode of the presence of a person'. This mode refers to the 'becoming a person' through the person's becoming aware of his self-value and experiencing his existence in the 'distanciality' or distinction from the other member-persons of the Life-World.

Thirdly, the mode of 'anonymity'. The person 'emerges' from the ontological one-ness of the anonymous field of 'persons around' and may recede partially or wholly into it, with corresponding variation in the person's self-value and his awareness of it.

Fourthly, the mode of 'exemplarity'. The exemplary consciousness, the urge towards the ideal model – what Scheler terms the 'call-of-oughtness' – is basic to the personal life and to the establishment of the person's self-value, and is described in Scheler's words, here quoted, as 'pre-logical and prior to any comprehension of any possible spheres of choosing'.

These four modes of personal presencing, that is modes in which the person reveals himself directly and dynamically, as distinct from mere knowledge about or acquaintance with, are, or are among, the principal modes in which the unity of the person is constituted and, Professor Frings urges in his concluding remarks, suffice to indicate the inseparability of personal and ethical existence.

The two papers raise a number of issues difficult to dissociate, all the more because the theme of the person is itself so intertwined with the themes under discussion at other sessions.

Both contributors would probably agree that the concept of the person is primary. In line with Dr Moore's paradox, one might say that we appear to have knowledge of the person prior to personal experience, while at the same time we can gain this knowledge only through this experience (a version no doubt, as Professor Frings points out, of the Platonic argument).

Dr Moore is concerned, however, mainly with demonstrating the inadequacy of the 'two persons', mind–body dualism, although the solution he proposes in terms of unconscious mental phenomena leads to an admitted impasse and to the recognition that the facts, however hard to justify logically, oblige us to 'bend our concepts'. But, if this is so, it may be argued, our concepts are ill contrived. Our concept of the person must be firmly moulded and modelled on

experience. It is therefore reasonable for Professor Frings to suggest
another approach through the description of the person as revealed
in immediate, pre-objective or ante-predicative experience of
personal activity and personal encounter.

This approach seems to be justified by the special nature of the
inquiry. As Gabriel Marcel would say, the sphere of inquiry in this
case belongs to the order of the 'meta-problematical'.[1] The inquiring
subject is involved in his question and his presence qualifies, indeed
modifies, the 'data' on which he is reflecting. He is in the curious
position of being both the questioner and the questioned.

To raise the question of the person demands, therefore, a special
attitude or approach: a fidelity to experience of an unusual kind.
But, as Professor Frings notes, this raises a difficulty. Reflection on the
person, he admits, will always modify the phenomenon under
discussion 'to a certain degree'. How far then can the proposed
description of the person and of what he reveals of himself lay claim
to accuracy or adequacy? This then is a first issue – one of method.
Are we justified in considering the question of the person as unique
and as involving a special, unique attitude or approach, and is the
proposed approach – through a reflective recuperation and description – adequate to the purpose? The whole question of the
phenomenological method is at stake here.[2]

In any case, what Professor Frings and phenomenologists in
general argue is that the concept of the person must be seen acted
out in personal and interpersonal activity in terms of a subject
situated in a Life-World which he shares with other persons. The
unity of the person is described as essentially dynamic: first, in the
sense that the person is constituted by virtue of his other-directed
intentions and projects; and secondly, that he is subject to a mode of
growth, becoming and developing as a person *pari passu* with the
unfolding and realisation of his individual projects and possibilities
and, thereby, with the continual renewal and enrichment of his
self-value which marks him off from other members of the Life-World.

[1] Gabriel Marcel, *Philosophy of Existence* (1948) pp. 8 ff.

[2] The phenomenologist, it may be suggested, might well reject the implied
dichotomy between description and reflection. In reflection on the person and
personal experience the description is part of the reflection just as reflection is built
into the description. The person is not a thing, but an active, sense-giving subject.
The experiences reflected on therefore embody meanings, but while reflection on
them recuperates these meanings by rendering them explicit, it also gives them
new meaning. It is this telescoping, envelopment and extension of meaning that
characterises phenomenological description, which could more properly be
designated dialectico- or reflecto-descriptive. The 'modification' of the phenomena
that takes place is in the direction of extension, deepening and enrichment. (For a
development of this point, see my paper on 'L'Ontologie de Gabriel Marcel', in
Actes du Premier Colloque de la Société Britannique. de Philosophie de Langue Française
(London, 1962) pp. 7–9.)

This then brings forward another issue: the nature of the concept of person, that is of the *one* person, as it is applied in concrete instances. It itself would appear to be 'dynamic' or at least open. It can only be given or acquire meaning step by step with the gradual uncovering and becoming of the person and his possibilities. Knowledge here is tantamount to a process of discovery and one which is not separable from the person's unfolding of himself, that is from his existing. Has the concept of person this distinctive *existential* and heuristic mark and status?

The third issue, I suggest, concerns the notions of the Life-World and of intersubjectivity. These are obviously bound up with the Husserlian 'intentionality', and Professor Frings's exposition of 'presencing' demands acceptance of that thesis. It implies, I think, a direct, non-causal relationship between persons, a type of relation which can be termed neither strictly external nor internal, where the subjects participate and, by the realisation of intertwining projects and intentions, constitute each other reciprocally as persons. With this is linked the question of the *origin* of the concept of person. Should it be sought within this field of interpersonal activity of this non-causal sort? Professor Strawson has observed elsewhere that to see each other as persons is to see each other as connected and related.[1]

Fourthly, there is the mind–body relation which crops up inevitably. Dr Moore is justified in taking it up again under the theme of the person, for it seems difficult to avoid it in connection with the dynamic unity of the person, personal growth or the origin of the concept of person. Professor Frings does not himself consider the 'constitution of the body' in detail, but he would no doubt accept the phenomenological account in terms of the body-subject or 'my body' as a felt presence, itself in direct, non-causal, non-inferential relationship with the Life-World and as a dynamic centre for the realisation of the person's projects.

A fifth issue is the ontological one. Underlying Professor Frings's paper, if not indeed under the whole phenomenological approach, there seems to be an ontological substructure – the thesis according to which the person or personal existence provides access to Being (or conversely, that Being is revealed in and through the person). The notion of transcendence is basic to Professor Frings's modes os 'depth' and 'exemplarity'. The person has to be conceived dynamically, as imbued with what Marcel calls an 'ontological exigency', striving towards an ontological fulfilment not only of his own person but,

[1] 'What I am suggesting is that it is easier to understand how we can see each other, and ourselves, as persons, if we think first of the fact that we act, and act on each other, and act in accordance with a common human nature.' P. F. Strawson, *Individuals: An Essay in Descriptive Metaphysics* (1959) p. 112.

through his interpersonal relationships, of the other member-persons.

Sixthly, and as a consequence, there is posited and assumed a strict connection between the person and ethical existence. Professor Frings speaks of the 'consciousness of exemplarity' and 'the call-of-oughtness' as essential to the person and as one of the factors constitutive of his unity. And he notes that the 'presence' of the person is the revelation of his *value* as transcending all objectivation and language. The full co-presence indeed, he suggests, would be one of 'silence' that 'speaks' of the 'unique one-ness of the value of the person'. There is implicit in such statements an identification of value and being – distinguished from particular values realised in particular projects – as the ethico-ontological ground from which all personal projects spring and to which they tend. Does it make sense, it may be asked, to make the person and the concept of the person the focal point of such ethico-ontological inquiry? And does such an approach provide, as the phenomenologist might claim, a fruitful way of renewing ontology?

Lastly, both papers – the one broadly analytical, the other a phenomenological 'explication' – would, if I am not mistaken, eschew conceptual schemes. Both are concerned with the unity of the person – one in terms of the question 'what', the other of the question 'how'. One could, however, ask another question – *why?* Why *human persons* at all, entities presenting themselves as unities of this dynamic sort? The answer to this might seem to demand the setting up of some sort of conceptual, explanatory scheme. Perhaps some such is implicit in Professor Frings's paper.

Noam Chomsky has pointed out in the field of language that such qualities as power of innovation and freedom from stimulus control could be attributed to animals, since in themselves they do not 'exceed the bounds of mechanical explanation', but that only 'appropriateness to the situation' gives its unique quality to *human* speech and accounts for the 'creative aspect of language use'. Although he uses this in support of a Cartesian thesis – as indicative of 'innate mental structures' which account for 'linguistic competence' or 'knowledge of a language' – the point is well made. And perhaps equally so the claim that it is not sufficient to provide criteria for the recognition of intelligent speech but that *why* there is such must be explained (as he believes it was Descartes's merit to have done).[1]

[1] Noam Chomsky, *Language and Mind* (New York, 1968) pp. 10–11, 62, 75. Cf. *Cartesian Linguistics* (New York and London, 1966) pp. 3–6. Chomsky's views on the creative aspect of language use are of course bound up with his basic distinction between the 'deep' structure, 'purely mental', which 'conveys the semantic content' and 'determines the semantic interpretation' of a sentence and the 'surface' structure, which 'relates to the physical form of the actual utterance' and 'determines the phonetic interpretation' (*Cartesian Linguistics*, pp. 33 and 35).

Does the concept of the human person not also call for some explanatory scheme? Professor Frings provides criteria for recognising persons and activities ascribable to persons, and describes how persons present themselves *qua* persons. Among these criteria he singles out the ability to create and posit values, and he points to a transcendent realm of Being identified with Value, in which particular values participate.

It is this sort of *creative* type of activity that appears to characterise the human person – this *bringing into existence* of Value. The human person stands out in the general scheme of things as the agent for the production and revelation of Value – or the revelation of Being. Is it then possible to dissociate the question of the person from the more general question of establishing a conceptual and frankly ontological scheme?

8

ONE OR TWO:
A SURREJOINDER TO
PROFESSOR FRINGS[1]

F. C. T. Moore

I AM grateful to Professor Frings, as I have often been grateful to writers in the phenomenological tradition, not only for drawing attention to the quality of our immediate experience of people (which is, after all, not only interesting in itself, but also a starting-point for philosophical inquiry), but also for drawing attention to it in so articulate, highly-wrought and thought-provoking a fashion.

When he says, however, that his paper 'is not to be taken as a criticism' of mine, but 'as a juxtaposition and in part a complement' to some of my arguments, he is passing over some substantial and important disagreements. In this surrejoinder, I should like to say what these disagreements seem to me to be, and why I am to a degree unrepentant in my original position.

First, the disagreement. The following passage indicates where Professor Frings finds a serious deficiency in my argument:

> In attempting to explicate the unity of the person as the 'one' person, I suggest that we do not remain within a conceptual framework of past metaphysics. Valuable though this may be, it is also necessary to regress into the a-logical, non-metaphysical plain lived experience of the Life-World, where we truly 'meet' the person in immediate non-theoretical experience.

In this passage, Professor Frings tacitly, and in some ways fairly, claims that I *have* remained within a conceptual framework of past

[1] Circumstances unhappily prevented me from attending the Southampton Conference.

metaphysics, whereas the step into phenomenology might have saved me from bewilderment. But I wish to rejoin here:

(1) that Professor Frings has misrepresented the problem which puzzles me; and

(2) that his own approach actually has the mixed value of sharpening the problem, rather than contributing to its solution.

I hope to substantiate these two claims by presenting a rather condensed argument under four headings.

I. THE LIFE-WORLD

The recognition that the world of immediate experience is not a chaos of raw data waiting for an organising consciousness to give it form is one of the great merits of the phenomenological school over the old empiricists. Instead, it is held that the world of immediate experience is, as we may put it, already organised. And although phenomenologists do not agree upon the nature of this organisation (as Professor Frings notes on page 71), it is nevertheless to the description of experience so organised that phenomenology is primarily devoted.

It may not, however, be assumed that experience so organised and described is coherent. It is always a danger in phenomenology that philosophical problems arising from our experience are short-circuited – that the question is deemed closed by the comment: 'But this is how we *do* experience it.'

The appeal to common sense here, though in a different and subtler idiom, is of the same kind as the appeal to common sense which often appears in the Anglo-Saxon tradition; and it has similar merits and limitations. The important limitation was, of course, seen long ago by Descartes when he wrote with a certain irony that common sense is the most widely shared commodity in the world. For it is precisely the incoherences to which common sense is subject (and hence which are displayed in the fabric of our experience) that give rise to philosophical puzzlement and debate.

Are there any such incoherences in our experience of persons ?

2. 'THE PRESENCING OF THE PERSON'

Professor Frings's condensed and allusive conclusion suggests that there is not any such incoherence. He writes:

> The one-ness of the person is constituted in at least four dynamic modes of personal presencing in our Life-World, the mode of depth, of growth, of anonymity, and of exemplarity, and their

D

possible interwovenness. The unity of the person is a dynamic
unity of and in *lived* co-experience.

The passage is of course a summary of a fairly complex
phenomenological account of the experiencing of other people. It
is not, I think, unfair to detect the following underlying view here:
that certain theoretical problems of 'past metaphysics' do not arise
out of the 'non-theoretical' experience of meeting persons, that they
are merely created by the idling of our concepts out of contact
with experience.

Note the following remark of Professor Frings about the concepts
which cause the trouble:

> In meeting other persons, we do not bring to our consciousness
> that they are endowed with 'will', 'intellect', 'language', etc. Such
> qualities of the person . . . remain initially quite hidden in the
> immediate experience of the *person*.

In an important way, this observation is incontestable. That we
do not characteristically say to ourselves of a person encountered,
'Here is something endowed with intellect', is true. Nevertheless, the
concept of intellect is among those of which some at least must be at
play in any experience of another person. For almost any concept
has a much wider area of employment than in the formulation of
theoretical verbal judgements like the one given above. We may,
like Professor Frings, mark the difference between the overt, verbal,
theoretical use of the concept, say, of intellect, and other kinds of use,
by calling the latter *hidden* in immediate experience. But what is
hidden is thereby present; and what is present, as we have already
argued, may yet be problematic. Indeed, Professor Frings raises and
suggests a line of answer to a certain problem at this point, which he
announces in the following question: '*How* is "one" person?'

3. THE UNITY OF THE PERSON

There are then problems arising out of our immediate experience of
people. I suggest, no doubt over-boldly, that the chief philosophical
problems are the following three:

(1) What is it to be a person?
(2) What is it to be one person rather than another?
(3) What is it to be experienced as a person?

It is the third of these questions to which Professor Frings addresses
himself in his phenomenological analysis of the experiencing of
people. This phenomenological account, however, is not engaged in

by Professor Frings for its own sake alone. For he believes that it is also a means of answering questions about the unity of the person. I quote:

> I wish to propose an explication of the unity of the person in terms of a different question, viz., '*How* is "one" person?'

But what does Professor Frings mean by the unity of the person? It is made clear, I think, in the following passage:

> One reason why Cartesian dualism . . . cannot account for the unity of the person is precisely because of the fact that it cannot account for the particularity of human individuality.

Without further elaboration, I claim that Professor Frings is concerned here with question 2 (What is it to be one person rather than another?). In fact, he is maintaining in his paper that by answering question 3 (What is it to be experienced as a person?), we can find answers to question 2.

Now I have nothing against either of these questions, though I feel that Professor Frings's interesting treatment of question 3 left him little opportunity for showing the bearing of his answers to question 2. But in my paper I was concerned with question 1 (What is it to be a person?); or rather, I was concerned with certain puzzles which still seem to me to make it very difficult to give an answer to that question.

4. ONE OR TWO

Now Professor Frings hints that there is in his view something wrong with this question. He writes, for example, 'asking about the whatness of the "one" person underlies Dr Moore's paper', and goes on to suggest that this is a bad platonising question. I confess that I do not really grasp this objection, and wish I were present to hear Professor Frings's elaboration of it.

As it is, the question is still posed, and posed, I believe, not merely in the debates of professional philosophers, but in the manner of people's experience. For the concepts involved in the experiencing of people, the concepts which we seem to have, do involve, I still wish to argue, a dualism of the kind indicated in my paper, and one which makes of intermediary phenomena such as those attributed to the unconscious mind, a constant conceptual dilemma.

This dualism, of which I hope I may fairly speak in so general terms, is as much and as properly present in Professor Frings's phenomenological descriptions, as it is in the forms of experience of which they are descriptions. Do we not detect it, for instance, through the following Heideggerian remarks:

The They-around must be considered as different in value from the mere equipmentality of things lying around and before us in their matrixes of relations, destinations and serviceabilities. The emergence of the person from its mode of anonymity shows that the one-ness of the person is not a problematic of the individual person with a body 'and' a mind only but also and especially a problematic of the ontological facticity of the anonymous one-ness of persons-around as distinct in value from that of the equipmentality of things.

I shall attempt no further commentary on Professor Frings's paper, although there is much that calls for a more positive discussion than I have engaged in here. Instead, I shall allow the argumentative requirements of the symposium to make me repeat that there is after all a certain dispute between us: Professor Frings holds that the problem I raised can in certain ways be dissolved through phenomenological description; I maintain that the problem comes out of the concepts we have, and therefore is present in the experience we have, and therefore is raised once more – indeed is sharpened – by any adequate phenomenological description of that experience. In fact, the modes of 'presencing' of persons have been interestingly treated by Professor Frings, but do not dissolve the dualistic dilemma. However, so far as I have been inadequately and curiously myself 'presenced' in Southampton, I thank Professor Frings wholeheartedly for his comments and his attention.

DISCUSSION

Nigel J. Grant (Student of Philosophy at the University of Edinburgh):
My main interest in Dr Moore's paper concerns what he calls the
reflective criterion for describing mental phenomena. My line of
argument will be to show that, though substantially correct, Moore's
analysis, Moore's discussion of the reflective criterion has implications that I feel should lead him in quite the opposite direction from
the one he takes. In other words, I wish to question the legitimacy of
Moore's accepting the notion of unconscious mental phenomena. I
clearly do not wish to question the legitimacy or the existence of the
concept itself. Perhaps this will come up in discussion. What worries
me is the use Dr Moore makes of this notion in his particular argument in his first paper.

Moore gives some examples of what he means by the coming to
awareness of previously unconscious sensations, motives, etc. I quote:
'I realised I had a headache. I realised that I was rather amused by
the incident.' It would seem to me that these are fair examples of
what one means when one says that one becomes reflectively aware.
Now Moore wishes to go on to argue that past-tense applications of
mental predicates do entail the corresponding present-tense
application. So I shall sketch out in my own terms Moore's argument
on this point. Let us begin by asking a Kantian-sounding question,
what is the condition for the possibility of being able to make past-
tense application of mental predicates? Or, more crisply, what is the
condition for the possibility of being able to retrospect, to use
Professor Ryle's term for it? Now as you are all very clearly aware,
we have to avoid the Scylla of vicious circularity and the Charybdis
of infinite regression. In other words, unless conscious processes are
in some sense phosphorescent or visible by the light which they
themselves emit, to again take over Professor Ryle's phraseology in
Chapter 6 of *The Concept of Mind*, it would seem that retrospective
avowal is also doomed. For what guarantees when I'm examining
in retrospect my, say, day-dreaming or my feelings, conscious that
I do so, unless it is another retrospection beyond the first retrospection, and so on *ad infinitum*. Unless I am conscious now of my
retrospection without further need of retrospection, how can I ever
become conscious that I was feeling such and such or possibly,

e.g., day-dreaming? And if I can be non-retrospectively aware of
my retrospective view of my day-dreaming, why can I not be non-
retrospectively aware of my day-dreaming itself in the same way?
In other words, why cannot my day-dreaming itself be phosphorescent and visible by the light which it itself emits, to use Ryle's
phrase? Unless it is the case that some act is characterisable in this
way, we cannot escape the infinite regress and neither introspection
as portrayed by Ryle nor retrospection, as also portrayed by Ryle, or
the sort of problem that Dr Moore is concerned with, the application
of mental predicates, will save us: we shall be doomed.

Husserl saw this very clearly. I shall not bore you by quoting
tracts of Husserl with which no doubt you are much more familiar
than I, but it does occur explicitly in Appendix 9 of *The Phenomenology
of Internal Time-Consciousness* (the 1964 Churchill translation). And, of
course, it goes without my having to spell it out for you that the
problem is answered in Husserl, as it is also very well spelled out in
the work of Aron Gurwitsch in terms of the protentional and
retentional nature of consciousness.

Now Ryle also has misgivings about his own view, as he develops
it in Chapter 6 of *The Concept of Mind*, when he writes that there
remains another sense of 'know' in which a person is commonly
said to know what he is at this moment doing, thinking, feeling, etc.,
a sense which is nearer to what the phosphorescent theory of
consciousness tried but failed to describe; also a development of this
where Ryle, I think, tries to see that the problem has a very large –
to use a cumbersome phrase – attentional component (not *in*tentional, but *at*tentional). And I also quote Ryle again: this is from
Chapter 5 on *Dispositions and Occurrences*, where Ryle is discussing
heeding. Ryle says:

> Earlier in this chapter I undertook to explain why it is that though
> applying one's mind to a task does not consist in coupling an
> inspecting or researching operation with the performance of that
> task, yet we expect a person who applies his mind to anything to
> be able to tell without research what he has been engaged in or
> occupied with. Heeding is not a secondary occupation of theoriz-
> ing, yet it seems to entail having at the tip of one's tongue the
> answers to theoretical questions about one's primary occupation.
> How can I have knowledge of what I have been non-absent-
> mindedly doing or feeling, unless doing or feeling something with
> my mind on it at least incorporates some study of what I am doing
> or feeling? Crucially, how could I now describe what I had not
> previously inspected?

Moore also senses this at the bottom of p. 61, where he says that the assertion that 'I thought there was another step to go down', made by a man who has just stumbled on the last step of a set of stairs, does entail that although nothing goes through the man's head at the time, nevertheless, in some sense, he *is* thinking 'There is another step'. This is why he stumbles and he becomes aware of the thought when he stumbles. Now let us take another example. While I was listening to the chairman's remarks, I became focally aware of the fact that I have to make a phone call as soon as possible after the end of this symposium. However, this focal awareness of the urgency of the phone call didn't last very long. My attention was drawn back to the chairman's comments. It wasn't until I began talking about this example some few seconds ago that I became focally aware again of the phone call that I have to make. But it is not quite the same sort of focal awareness as in the first case. In a sense, it is not quite focal. After all, I am now engaged in using this example rather than in concentrating on it for its own sake. But what was going on between the time of the chairman's remarks and now? Had I forgotten my appointment with the telephone? If by that one meant that it was not at the focus of my attention, then one might legitimately say so. But I would only say 'O.K. You can say that, provided that you understand by it some sort of analysis as I shall give now'. I would rather say that the seriousness of my impending phone call slipped from being explicit in my experience to being implicit, in the same way as the pressure of my collar on my neck has been implicit in my experience for the past half an hour or so.

Now the problem that we are left with is what can we learn about Dr Moore's, to my mind, rather cavalier, rather superficial, but nevertheless well-intentioned analysis of what he calls the reflective criterion. For me Moore should have gone further. He should not have been duped into the sort of argument in his paper that leads round in a circle and in fact leads him to ask at the very end the sort of question that I think should have been the first sentence in his paper. I think he too easily accepts that one's mental life, or accepts on the basis of his analysis of the reflective criterion, that one's mental life can be neatly and dichotomously sliced up into something that we call conscious and into something that he calls unconscious.

Phenomenological analysis requires that we adopt the attitude of reflection. It would be thought of as rendering explicit – it could be thought of as disengaging or explicating – what is implicit in our experience. It appears to me that Dr Moore is in danger of continuing the previous discussion 'Mind and Body'. Professor Frings, however, has, I think, set sail in a direction more appropriate to the title of this symposium.

Professor Frings: I should like to make eight points with regard to my paper. The points are intended to clarify my position and I hope that some of the points will answer Dr Moore's surrejoinder. Thematically the eight points group themselves around two concepts: (1) the concept of ontology as I have used it in my paper and in the sense in which Professor Alexander has used it in his introduction, and (2) around the concept of the lived body mentioned in the Mind–Body symposium.

1. Underlying my paper is the thesis that human intersubjectivity cannot be divorced from the experienced form in which it takes place: personal being with its specific self-value character.

2. I have given a brief outline of how interpersonal experience takes place in our natural life-world: the mode of depth, of growth, of anonymity and exemplarity.

3. The experienced unity of the person lies at least in part in the dynamic manifold of such modes. In all of these there appears to be a manifestation of the self-value being or the self-value character of the sphere of the human person, be it that we take the word 'person' as an individual person or as a group person.

4. With reference to Heidegger's *Sein und Zeit*, I tried to make one point, viz., that the givenness of the other (*das Mitdasein*) is radically distinct from the givenness of things around me, of things ready-at-hand (*Zuhandenheit*), in that the other is met in terms of the self-value of his person, whereas things are not. Things have no self-value. Inasmuch as Heidegger conceives the other (*der Andere, das Mitdasein*) always in connection with things, the other's self-value as 'person' is not thematised in *Sein und Zeit*. For Heidegger states that all values are primarily values as attached (*vorhandene Werte*), i.e. Heidegger conceives in *Sein und Zeit* (and in the rest of his work) all values as attached or thing-values. In this he follows, at least in part, Husserl, who conceives values as 'predicates' of things. But I contend in my paper that 'attached values' are incompatible with the person. The person is neither thing nor a predicate. Yet a person possesses manifestly a self-value. Since Heidegger does not take into consideration the specific value-being of the person in the With-World (*das Mitsein*), my world-with-others, *both* the world that I experience in my togetherness with others and the manipulability of things we use, are seen in the light of our being-in-the-world. What I mean to say is this: Heidegger does not make a specific *distinction* between the value character of human togetherness on the one hand, and of things around us in their manipulability on the other.

5. I would like to illustrate the ontological character of the givenness of the other by way of example. You will recall that I used the word 'ontological' (with reference to Heidegger). I tried to show that we find ourselves all the time with others no matter if we are *de facto* with others or consciously in relation to others. For example, each of us this morning experienced others 'anonymously' such that the others were plainly with us. But for Heidegger this is an ontological factor in human experience: we simply cannot 'be' unless we are – to put it pointedly – *through* others around us (*das Man:* the They). Let us focus on this by way of an example. Let us assume a universe consisting only of two opposite eyes looking at each other, and let us take the case that the eye *A* looks at eye *B*. Then we may say that *A* sees *through B* in the sense that without *B*, *A* would not see at all, i.e. it would not have a With-World. If we take away *B* and let the universe consist of only one eye – true, the eye would physiologically 'see', but ontologically it would be blind. For *A* would not see *through B*, i.e. it would be bare of its With-World. That is to say, it would not 'exist'.

6. Max Scheler, in contrast to Heidegger, stressed the value character of our With-World. Going back to our example, Scheler would hold that *A* would not immediately see the eye *B;* it would not see the eye *B*, rather *A* would see the *look* of *B:* a look, so to speak, coming through eye *B* which might, for example, tell *A* that *B* does not want to be seen by *A although B* is seeing *A*, and *A* is seeing *B*. In other words, there is implicit in this argument the distinction between the eye and the 'look' coming through it. And it is precisely this look in *B* that constitutes a *value of difference*, with respect to *A* by which *A* is *distanced* from *B*, *through B*'s existence. It is here, I think, where we may come to see the value differences among persons in their personal self-value-being, which cannot be divorced from its *ethical* character. And I think that both Heidegger and Husserl do not stress the significance of this point enough, whereas Scheler does so in all his work.

7. This leads me to a final remark with regard to the lived body in its relation to the person. This relation is highly complicated, as Scheler showed. I believe that Merleau-Ponty's phenomenology of the lived body fails to take the relation of lived body and the person into account. I think this relation is threefold: (1) the relation between lived body and ego, (2) the relation between the ego and the person, and (3) the relation between the person and the lived body. As far as the relation between lived body and person is concerned, I would maintain that the lived body functions as a lived expression of psychic and interpersonal being in the sense that, in

terms of our example, the eye, taken here as lived body, functions as an expression of a personal look. Yet the eye and its look belong to *one* experience. They are two variations of the *same* phenomenon. Let me explain this by another example. The blushing cheeks of a person deeply ashamed express to me his shame, and the blushing cheeks are experienced by the person ashamed through his shame. By no means is the red colour on his or her cheeks identical with physical red colour coming from a red light that spreads on the surface of his or her cheeks. The redness of the cheeks of the ashamed person is experienced as a physical expression permeating the body of the person ashamed. Whereas he who is not ashamed and looks at the ashamed person can make a 'judgement' and say 'He is ashamed', or 'He shouldn't be ashamed'. But the person's experience of shame and its expression, as seen by the other, are one.

No physical 'body' can shame; only a 'lived' body can, in inter-relation with the sphere of the *person*. The distinction between the lived body and the body object must also, as Dr Spicker stressed in an earlier discussion, be considered and in our context with each of the above three relations.

8. I think the dualism of mind and body and possible inter-mediaries does not suffice. Rather, it is the lived body *itself* that spatialises itself out into right, left, front, back, up, down. It is my lived body that functions as an 'intermediary' between inter-subjective phenomena (such as shame) as well as in my 'seeing' the other in my environment.

Professor Hartmann (Bonn): I would like to take up the issue of the 'lived body'. In a sense, it seems very modern to make statements about the 'lived body', to say, e.g., that 'I am my body', as Sartre would say or as has been urged by Dr Spicker in a previous discussion. We enjoy such a phrase if only because it is a startling thing to say. Furthermore, we might easily be persuaded that with this notion we have found the solution to Cartesian dualism. But what is the basis for such a primacy of the body? Or for the primacy of a totality of mind and 'lived body?' One is led to believe that pheno-menology could, by sheer description, come to such assertions. But can it really? From what Professor Frings has said it appears to me that phenomenology is mere picture-thinking – Hegel would say, mere '*Vorstellung*', others have spoken of '*Bilderbuchphänomenologie*'–pro-ceeding by naïve description. Instead, however, if we go back to classical examples, phenomenology has always found it necessary to set up another primacy, a primacy not of the body, or of the person, but of understanding, and this for methodological reasons: if we may take Heidegger's *Being and Time* as an example, we find that phenomenology has to attach itself to a project of comprehension and thus to a comprehending agent who can give an explication of his implicit comprehension of himself and the world. It is for transcendental reasons that we cannot start with a description of, say, the 'lived body' or of the person but have to operate in a framework of comprehension such that something like the 'lived body' or the person can be made intelligible. Description will not do unless it is guided by intelligibility, unless it is given a genealogy of intelligibility, starting from a stance of comprehension. Accordingly, questions about the unity of the person, or the primacy of the 'lived body' can only be handled in a phenomenology aware of its transcendental framework. Statements of first-hand plausibility about the person, or the 'lived body', will not satisfy as such.

Richard Webster (Rome): I should like to revert to Mr Grant's suggestion that Dr Moore too neatly and dichotomously slices up consciousness and unconsciousness. If it is a question of this Cartesian problem, then it seems to me that it has to be said that Descartes, like logicians in general, was essentially a dichotomiser. This, no doubt, is a common and indeed a necessary tendency, and if we have any philosophical dichotomy – even such a dichotomy as that just suggested by Professor Hartmann of comprehension on the one hand and picture-thinking on the other – the result is a sliced-up condition. But if this is supposed to be based on logical certainty, the dichotomy becomes absolute. Logic, I would say, is a sausage-slicing machine which slices up the universe in that sort of way. On the other hand, if we bring in, or imply, such terms as 'reality', then our dichotomies are not for ultimate philosophical purposes absolute, but become in some sense provisional or heuristic. If this is so, however, we are left with the possibility of intermediaries, and it would appear that while Professor Frings explicitly rejects 'intermediaries', this rejection applies to the logical stance, but implicitly Frings allows the possibility of intermediaries in reality by his application of such expressions as 'mediation' or 'transitional unity'. My contention, at any rate, is that however we distinguish between mental or intentional predicates and physical predicates, it can never be 'absolutely wrong' – even if it may be linguistically odd – to apply, say, intentional predicates to cases not clearly intentional.

Now I should like to back this up by the following considerations. If we take the *body* to be a contingent aggregate, and if at the same time we take the *person* to be the integration of that aggregate, this, I think, solves the problem of the dualism. The personal integration is an integration of an aggregate, and the aggregate thus has two aspects: the aggregated aspect and the integrated aspect. That is the meaning of the 'two aspects'. But then we also have intermediate positions or degrees of integration, as we can see from lower organisms and also from the varying functions of higher organisms or persons. A lower organism is a less integrated being than a person, and there is no hard-and-fast line between them. Thus, for instance, when Miss Ishiguro remarked that it would be incorrect to say that a tree suffers pain, we have surely to add that in some sense, a less strong sense, a tree does suffer: it may suffer from a disease – which is on the analogy of suffering pain in organisms with a central nervous system. The tree, then, is an intermediate case between the person, on the one hand, and the inorganic physical world on the other. The Cartesian dichotomy is provisional or heuristic inasmuch as in reality we always find a continuity of borderline cases, which, in the case of the problem of the person, is a question of degrees of integration.

Dr S. Raschid (London) : I would like to comment on what seems to me to be a rather serious confusion at the very heart of Dr Moore's paper. It seems to me that he is conflating two entirely distinct things. He talks about reflection and the reflective criterion. Now I think that we have to distinguish between directing one's attention, or, to use Mr Grant's term, *focal awareness* and reflection. Take a very simple example in the modality of perceptual consciousness. I am looking at the blackboard, at a particular spot. Now when I do that there is a whole perceptual background, and if I leave the room in five minutes and someone asks, 'What was the colour of the wall?', I can reply, 'Oh well, yellow or brown', or whatever it was. Now a distinction is involved here between reflection and (another term of Mr Grant's which is very helpful) retrospection. In other words, I am directing my attention to the wall to bring it into focal awareness (in retrospection) but there is no question of reflection. Reflection involves an act of a higher level, and if we use that as a criterion for marking off an intermediary class of phenomena, as Dr Moore has done, this leads to all sorts of difficulties. Again, take a simple example. I am conscious of the fact that there are three speakers facing us. I now reflect on this; so I am conscious of the fact that I am aware of the three speakers. I can reflect on that again, and so I can go on *ad infinitum*. Does this mean that there are as many classes of phenomena as there are levels of reflection? Surely not. It seems to me that all these things take place within the one stream of consciousness: it is pre-reflective or reflective, it is in focal or in subsidiary awareness (Michael Polanyi). As I look at the blackboard (focal awareness) I am subsidiarily aware of the wall; I can then direct my attention to the latter (either in perception or retrospection).

Now the other problem is the question of 'unconscious mental phenomena', and here I think Dr Moore's use of the term is very misleading. Mr Grant was probably thinking of psychoanalysis, whereas Dr Moore is using it in an entirely different sense. In psychoanalysis and psychoanalytical thought 'unconscious mental phenomena' are *postulated* as concepts or constructs, i.e. the term is not applied to anything in actual awareness. As against this usage all of Dr Moore's examples, e.g. the motive of jealousy, are of things which are already there in *actual conscious experience* but which have not been brought to focal awareness, or have not been reflected upon. Therefore I don't think there are any grounds for saying that there are any fundamental differences between any of these things. They are all present within the one stream of consciousness. As regards dreaming, there is no special problem here, unless one takes up a very awkward position such as that of Norman Malcolm – a position which, as Professor Lèwis showed in his Hobhouse Lecture, can only be defended by very desperate argumentation.

So I conclude by saying that all these things are united within the one stream of my experience, starting with feelings and going right up to different kinds of awareness: pre-reflective and reflective, etc. There is for me only this unitary flow of my own mental life. The problem about the body, mentioned by Professor Hartmann, can also be resolved in this way. I know my body within the stream of my consciousness. So that there is still only one thing. As to the question of the unity of the person, there can only be two approaches. Very schematically – the unity of myself as a person is given to me from the 'inside', and that of the other from the 'outside'. I experience the unity of myself as a person within the stream of my own consciousness. Perhaps this is akin to the Kantian idea of the transcendental unity of apperception. But I cannot apply this to the other person, because I do not experience his stream of consciousness, and this raises the whole problem of other minds.

Dr Roger Poole (Nottingham) : May I ask Professor Frings to elaborate on that 'mode of depth' which, he says, gives us access to 'the extremely rare presencing of genuine sainthood in history' and of which he gives as examples Buddha, Jesus and Francis? Kierkegaard and Bonhoeffer come to mind as modern 'presencers' of this kind. We 'see' then an *ethical* 'presencing'. But can we ever be aware of the meaning of such personal instantiations of values *cognitively* (this would answer Professor Hartmann's query), or does the 'seen' exemplar of this ethical 'indirect communication' operate at a much deeper, pre-cognitive level? Is there in fact *any* access (phenomen-

ological or other) to *that* depth of experience – the depth upon which
the saint, hero and martyr operate and upon which they make their
deep demand? Can phenomenology link the experience of the 'seen'
and the experience of the 'ethical', or is that a future task for it?

Professor Mikel Dufrenne (Paris): I want to say a word about the
ethical approach to the other. You said very rightly that Heidegger
does not clearly distinguish between the *Zuhandenheit* value of
things, and the specific value of persons. I think this idea has been
underlined by Levinas in his book *Totality and the Infinite* when he
says that the other is always approached as invested with an ethical
value. Of course it is difficult to answer the question where these
ethical values of the other come from. We might rationalise it, as
Kant does, by saying that there is a universal reason which inhabits
him and so he requires respect because he is a rational being.

Let me also try to explain technically the value of the other
through psychoanalysis. I might start by saying that the first
object – Melanie Klein says it is the breast – is desirable and as such
has the value which might be qualified later as ethical when we
become conscious of ethics. But I think there is an immediacy of
these cognitions of the other as giving him value. As Max Scheler
put it, the value is the herald, if you like, through which the other
as a person announces himself to us. But I will insist on that because
I think that it is from the other – not from the other ego, but from
the other who will become ego later – that we learn our own ego.

The person problem might be clearer if we take this approach to
understand what a united person is – not from any kind of introspection, not from any kind of looking at ourselves, but from looking
at the other. I learn what I am from the other. I have no idea of
what my body is or what my mind is, but I have a pretty good idea
of what the other means and thinks. And it is from him and, I think,
through his being of value, that I learn what a person is.

*Professor Stuart Spicker (Fellow, National Endowment for the Humanities,
U.S.A.)*: I should like to comment on a point raised with respect to the
second question and to follow that with a question of my own: If I
have understood Professor Frings correctly, then the second question
suggests that there exists an 'intermediary' between mind and body,
the explication of which will assist in the resolution of the perennial
problem connected with that distinction. That is, Professor Frings
seems to proffer the view that the 'lived' body is such an intermediary; what it mediates is the psychic on the one side and the
world, so to speak, on the other. I do not wish to disagree with
Professor Frings if this is the general meaning of his remarks. I
simply wish to point out that he is here arguing for an 'intermediary'

in a very different sense from, say, the Cartesian appeal to the pineal gland as the physical locus of mediation of consciousness and body. Given this preliminary remark, it seems that we can ask the following question: In what sense would you say that it makes for philosophical clarity to claim that *the body* (and not the mind) remembers, keeping before you that we are here speaking of the 'lived' body? I raise this question because it seems to me that it is perfectly correct – and perhaps even necessary – to predicate of persons that their *bodies remember*. I offer the following case for examination:

Consider the case of a person who has studied a musical instrument for some years during his youth and has come to learn to play a particular piece of music without any longer requiring to read the music as he plays. This case is further elaborated by the condition that this person has not played this instrument for quite a few years and one day attempts to play that piece without the notation before him. It is not uncommon to find that in such a circumstance one can only play the piece through if one can get started correctly at the very beginning of the first measure of the first line. It is invariably the case that one cannot play the piece through if one is asked to begin somewhere after the beginning, and this is so even if our unaccomplished musician is shown the correct finger placement according to the written notation. Such cases as this one suggest the relevance of Husserl's distinction between active (recollective) and passive (retentive) memory. It is of some relevance to note that the person in the case described is not likely to say '*I* remembered the music' but is more prone to say 'My hands remembered the piece'. Surely this is not a case correctly described as recollection (active memory), but is more accurately described as a process of passive memory (retention). What, strictly speaking, *does* the remembering is the 'lived' body; in some very crucial sense our unaccomplished musician might well say '*I* do not remember the piece at all'.

Professor Frings (reply to discussion): I would like to start with Professor Hartmann's remarks. Professor Hartmann asks about the basis for the correctness of a description of the body. I answer: the basis for this is the self-evidence of the experience of my own body. By this I mean the following: We, as human beings, appear to experience our body in terms of variations. There are two poles within which our lived body is given to us. One is the pole which the Germans call '*Sammlung*' and which we translate by 'in-gatheredness'. In the state of in-gatheredness we are detached, as it were, from our body, for example, in moments of a grave decision we have to make and which might involve the life or death of other people. Another case in point is a true act of repentance. Let us take the latter as an illustration. If I repent an evil deed I can repent this deed and I can repent that 'I had *been* so' as to have done this evil deed. The stress is here on my having 'been' (Scheler), not on the repented deed. In such a concentrated personal state of in-gatheredness we are left to ourselves, i.e. to our 'having been so' rather than to body experiences. In sharp contrast to this we can experience our ego such that it is more or less 'dissolved' in our body. We 'live' in our body, for example, when we overstuff ourselves with food. This body-state is well depicted in Breughel's 'Land of Cockaigne', where three people, a clerk, a farmer and a knight, have eaten more than they should and just lie on the round earth of the Land of the Plenty, apparently having no ego-experience of themselves: two of them sleep, one of them staring into the sky. A 'correct' description of the body is possible through the phenomenon of the self-evidential experience of my body which takes place in the two poles briefly described, in-gatheredness and states of living 'in' one's body. In the former case we experience a 'full' ego while the body 'floats' by us. In the latter case it is the ego which is empty of experiences and dissolved in a 'full' body. Many more examples could be given which hold for these poles and states in between them.

Professor Hartmann asks, secondly, about the 'agency of comprehending' with reference to Heidegger's *Sein und Zeit*. I answer that the agency of comprehending is *Dasein* itself as being-already-in-the-world. Both as being thrown into the world and as 'facticity' of its own *Existenz, Dasein* is its 'own' problematic, including that of 'comprehension'.

The next question concerned what was implied in my paper about sainthood. The following I had in mind: with Max Scheler I held that a human person is the locus of five value regions. In other words, human beings are encompassed by a house of values, as Scheler put it, in which we dwell. In phenomenological terms this means that consciousness possesses five value-regions within which persons, things and states of affairs represent themselves in their value-characters. Concerning sainthood Scheler showed that every consciousness possesses the region of the Absolute which, however, can be filled in history with idols, gods, utopias, philosophies (e.g. nihilism) or God. The problem of the dualism of mind and body also pertains to the phenomenology of religion for which Scheler laid the first foundations in his work *On the Eternal in Man* (1921) and in his essay 'Absolutsphäre und Realsetzung der Gottesidee' (1915–16). The dualism of body and mind (if it exists) obtains with regard to an original saint a character very different from that dualism referred to ordinary man. The lived body of a saint, for example, is one of divine incarnation (Jesus). It may well be that the problem of body and mind (dualism) cannot stand the test if examined in terms of the person of an original saint. For the unity of the incarnated saintly person allows of no philosophical splitting between body and mind. When I thus attempt to differentiate between the lived body (and object body) on the one hand and divine incarnation on the other, I have in mind expressions like 'precious Blood' which are used with reference to divine incarnation. This saintly Blood is not precious because we attach a value 'precious' to physical blood, say, by a decree of a church. This Blood is precious, firstly, as *invisible* Blood of divine incarnation. It is 'precious' both to the faithful who saw, for example, Jesus walk through the streets of Nazareth and to the faithful who never saw him. 'Precious' is, therefore, an *indivisible* value in this case of the incarnated person of Jesus in so far as the value of the person itself is *indivisible*, i.e. unique. I also believe that there is a distinction between the lived body and divine incarnation in expressions like 'This Blood has been "shed" '. We do not say that (saintly) Blood 'flowed from' the body. 'To shed' implies here the *personal* value of the Blood whereas 'to flow from' implies the losing of physical blood. Blood shed cannot be 'lost'. I admit that these points require more preparation and elaboration than I can provide today.

Concerning Professor Dufrenne's question, I wish to state that my views about the givenness of the other are based on Scheler's phenomenology of the Alter Ego, and in no way on the writings of Levinas, whom I have not read.

Professor Dufrenne noted that we learn through the other our own ego. I tried to explain this in my model of the two eyes. But a model is always deficient. I meant to say the following concerning the other: A human being is first thrown into a psychic stream of vague experiences of otherness. By otherness I mean to express that we in very early childhood do not yet differentiate between I and thou. The differentiation between I and thou only gradually emerges in terms of gradual awareness of a distance between (my) being in this original psychic stream and a thou to which (my) experiencing is ontologically directed. We live first *with* and among others, before our individuality is experienced *from* them. Scheler calls this being thrown back on to our ego *Zurückgeworfensein*, a term which reminds us of Heidegger's *Geworfenheit*. Hence, in my model of the two eyes the eye *B* is that *with* which eye *A* is (and without which *A* cannot 'be') while eye *A* is cast back upon itself through *B*, i.e. *A* can only learn about its identity through the pregiven difference (distance) *from B.*

And this allows me to answer the second part of Professor Dufrenne's question: the ethical mode of a person's existence emerges from the *distance* I experience from another person. In this distance lies a value-difference between any *A*s or *B*s of any primordial With-World (e.g. family life). And it is on this level that there arises the possibility of an ought. But the ought is grounded in an already laid-out structure of my With-World. Let me explain this with an example. If I am asked a question, I should answer. I can either answer the question or answer that I do not want to answer it. In both cases, however, I answer, i.e. respond to the question. But if I neither answer the question nor respond in any way and ignore the question completely, my action is conspicuous in the sense that it 'strikes' another. A person ignoring another's question in the Life-World stands out with regard to what 'one' does in this situation. The situation of being asked commands as it were by itself a *response* on my part. If this response remains absent I break the normalcy of the With-World which is 'questioning – answering' in character. The fact that I 'ought' to answer is based in the structure of my being with others. The latter is already 'ahead' of what one ought to do. With this, however, something strange is asserted: my 'to be' is asserted to be prior to my what I 'ought to do', or my questioning – answering situation is ahead of what I ought to do in this situation. Whether this can be held in such a radical way I do not know. The kernel of my reply to Professor Dufrenne is, therefore, a question which one can relate to Descartes: Can the *cogito sum* be put side by side with an *I ought, I exist* (with others)?

Then, Professor Spicker, I must confess that you asked a difficult question. Could you repeat it in terms of Scheler's analysis?

Professor Spicker: When you distinguished 'in-gatheredness' from its opposite pole 'total incorporation', it seemed to me that my case of the unaccomplished musician is locatable somewhere between the two extreme poles you described. Thus I was trying to elicit from you a response to the expression 'The body remembers'. For in this sentence we predicate of 'lived' bodies *remembering*. In doing this we would begin to predicate of *bodies* what we have traditionally predicated of *minds*. Such a revision of our conceptualisation could, in time, reveal that the sentence uttered by not too high-minded persons – 'I love her body but I don't love her' – is not only a contradictory set of claims but further evidence of our failing to understand the nature of persons.

Professor Frings: I am not qualified to answer your question with regard to remembering as a criterion, so to speak, of the 'lived' body.

But I think that what you said earlier regarding the dimensionality of the 'lived' body – right – left, front – back, and up – down – will help us to consider criteria for the 'lived' body and, therefore, also to find a solution to the mind – body problem. I hate to talk about mind and body.

Professor Spicker: I too dislike talking of mind *and* body and this is precisely what lies behind my remarks and question. For it seems to me that in spite of your careful presentation of Scheler's thought, his notions of 'in-gatheredness' and 'total incorporation' still contain the residue of Cartesian dualism.

Professor Frings: If I understand you correctly, your question pertains to the concept of 'in-gatheredness' that I used before as opposed to the experience of the body, which, in an extreme case, would imply that my body resists like a weight, as it were, all kinematic activities. One can interpret the face value of this egological polarity (in-gatheredness – body-ego) as a hidden Cartesianism which, I believe, you imply in your question. But nothing would be more from the truth in Scheler's phenomenology. In brief, Scheler neither recognises a so-called 'pure ego', 'absolute ego', nor a 'transcendental ego' nor a consciousness of universal (i.e. not individual) character. Scheler's phenomenology of the ego (which to date has never been sufficiently described in detail) is essentially linked to the fact that (1) the ego is always with and through the 'alter ego', and (2) that any ego is, by essential necessity, connected with a lived body *although* we can, in phenomenological gaze, abstract from this body and focus on the structure of the ego itself. But – and this may serve as my answer to the question – this 'ego itself' shows in what you might call a Schelerian transcendental reduction *no* time-dimensions but only 'threads' which reach simultaneously into *all* of its experiences: therefore, it is the *lived body*, and only it, which breaks the ego into past, present and future experiences. This point would require a lengthy discussion, especially in regard to the basic differences between Scheler and Husserl. But I hope it at least indicates that a Cartesian dualism between in-gatheredness and the body-ego is out of the question. Scheler also went into some detail concerning respective experiences and egological levels between these two extreme poles. If I recall correctly, Mr Webster's question referred to such transitional experiences between ego and body. I think that movements of my body do have, at least occasionally, effects on my mind. If, for instance, I am dancing a waltz the movements of my body conjoined to those of my partner hardly permit me to be in a state of egological in-gatheredness. In contrast to this, a state of in-gatheredness does not lend itself to enjoying a waltz, let alone to my dancing to it. Indeed, in cases when we are, for example, deeply sad we cannot bring ourselves to perform such or similar body movements: we want to be left alone! On the other hand, we may be only relatively sad and force ourselves into dancing to forget our relative sadness. In the latter case kinematic movements are *effective* on states of the mind and we *experience* them as effective. Hence, ego and body are not split but are set off by transitional states that are either closer to the body or to the ego. *Only* body or *only* ego, I believe, cannot be experienced. We are embodied and, therefore, we do not have to 'learn' that we are no 'angels', as Scheler puts it.

On the question asked about intermediaries: I think my notion of transitional unity covers that. I don't want to say that this statement of mine is final. I would just say that this is how this problem about which you were asking regarding intermediaries would pose itself within the framework of my paper.

Mr Webster: I would agree with you really.

Professor Frings: But I would still say that communication between persons is very different from that between bodies. I can communicate with a person without talking to him. With one glance I can say more than words can tell. But on the other hand, I cannot communicate toothache. I can tell someone that I have a toothache, but the other cannot participate or co-feel my toothache. Such body feelings are, as it were, 'dead' because they are not communicable. I can commiserate, I can re-feel someone else's toothache, but one cannot communicate the toothache as one can communicate mental phenomena. Means and ways of communication among persons are very different from those between our bodies. Body-communication is a separate chapter in the problem of 'Two Persons'.

Mr Grant: My position in this symposium has been incredibly ambiguous. In my criticism of Dr Moore's paper I had to steer a tortuous course. On the one hand, I did not want to present a paper of my own on the topic of this symposium, but on the other hand I wanted to try to point out that implicit in Moore's paper were jumping-off points which could have been used to say something more positive than he did: in particular, a further analysis of reflection would have provided more immediate substance. It might have been a tougher paper to write, but, then, none of us pretends that these questions about the person are easy or simple. I think that Professor Frings has demonstrated this.

Professor Alexander: In the brief time available I do not propose to make anything in the nature of a résumé of the issues and of the points raised in the discussion. In general, I think perhaps that the value of the discussion has been more in its clarificatory nature than in anything else.

I doubt, for example, whether we have advanced very far towards a solution, if such a thing is possible, of the mind – body problem. But I believe that both the discussion and Professor Frings's later exposition have clarified the phenomenological position somewhat. I think that one may now have a clearer idea of what the phenomenologist means by the body subject, which has not to be identified purely and simply with the embodied self as known to, and as understood by, the analytical school. The two concepts are not necessarily identifiable.

Again, I would say that the discussion, initiated very pertinently by Professor Dufrenne and carried forward extensively by Professor Frings, of the relationship between personal existence and ethical existence seems a very valuable clarification of the phenomenological concept of person.

I would say that these two clarifications at least have made the discussion a worth-while one. Certainly it has been so in my own case.

May I end by thanking the two speakers, Professor Frings and Mr Grant. We are grateful to the latter for undertaking at such short notice to stand in for Dr Moore.

POSTSCRIPT

Manfred S. Frings

A second look at the constitution of the 'how' of the unity of the
person may bring to light some implications of what we have
said above.

Human intersubjective experience takes place in terms of person-al
being in its self-value character. As previously indicated, the self-
value of the person varies throughout certain modes of the givenness
of the person in daily life. The self-value-being of the person may be
near to me, it may move my moral tenor to care for it, it may
recede into the anonymity of the They, or it may draw me towards
it such that I 'follow' it. These variations of self-value-being
correspond to the above modes of how the unity of the person
'presences' itself in lived experience.

Suppose that it is true that the self-value of the person which must
belong to his unity is always already present in my lived experience
of the person, i.e. prior to my judgements, then it becomes questionable whether logically correct statements correspond, or are
applicable, to the subject under discussion. For example, one can
ask if the above variations of self-value-being are subject to the
criterion of truth used in logic, namely, non-contradiction.

Of course, I do not question the validity of logical statements, let
alone that of a logical formalism, made in any possible area. But
with respect to the lived experience of a person's self-value it seems
clear that 'true' and 'false' statements will not exhaust the determination of the unity of the human person in its ultimacy. For example, it
could be that I am mistaken in stating that, on the one hand, the
person can be 'near' me (mode of depth) and, on the other, that the
person may recede into the sphere of 'anonymity'. One could hold
that respective propositions about the person are meaningless or,
with regard to the unity of the person, are determinable if, and only
if, they are explicable in terms of the criterion of logical truth.
Indeed, if from the beginning this criterion is assumed to be *identical*
with 'truth', then respective propositions in my paper can be shown

to be 'false'. But I do not hold that truth is, except for logic and/or mathematics, identical with 'non-contradiction'. If the person presences himself to me, then this presencing is *neither* true (non-contradictory) *nor* false. This person is first given in factual, pre-reflexive *lived* experience. He is before me in plain evidentiality. And *this* evidence of the other is radically distinct from evidence in the order of logic, the latter being one of cognitive insight, the former that of lived, existential presence.

Should one take propositions of language (i.e. the symbolised language of a formalism) and the above criterion for truth (by which propositions that *say* something can only be *found* to be true or false) as the sole basis for the discussion of the unity of the person, or of the 'two' persons, his position is faced with the serious implication that the unity of the person in the end *consists* in a logico-analytical formalisation. Yet this clearly runs counter to the practical experience of personal being, to say nothing of religious experience of personal being. As a fact of lived experience, the self-value of the person does not at all coincide with true or false 'propositions' about the person.

For example, there is no reason why my being 'good' or 'evil' should (by logical necessity) coincide with 'true' or false' propositions and their functional meanings. Granted that the unity of the person cannot be divorced from its self-value-being and ethical mode of existence – the point which underlies my paper – one must also take into consideration the difference between self-value-being and attached values (e.g. the value attached to a product and advertised on its price tag). No mere thing has a self-value. The value of a thing is attached to this thing by me, as, for example, when in natural everyday experience a thing discloses itself as useful to me. A thing which defies such possible utility to me has no technical value and will disappear into the background of my daily life. Such a value-less thing dissolves, as it were, into a region of pure valueless thingness, unless this thing is value-able to me as a spiritual value such as 'beautiful' (painting). Yet values of things are and are rightfully subject to logical analysis. None the less, the very possibility of things for having value lies within the person who is the *bearer* of precisely delineated value-regions in his conscious being and which the person possesses as *facts of intentionised data* (consciousness-of). Therefore, a thing represents itself within a certain value-region of consciousness in the same fashion as it represents itself in ordered manifolds of colours. Similarly, as such colours are eidetic givens in the structure of my visual perception, values are intuitive facts of my feeling them. As colours, they possess a well-delineated order of ranks. This is not to deny that I can apply laws of logic to already accepted and attached values, whether these be of things, deeds or acts of the person. But this does not at all imply that the value of the person as self-value consists in such logical application, nor that logical application tells me anything about self-value-being. For, whether we refer to the value of the beloved, or the disvalue of the hated who intentionally treats me unjustly, or the value of the sacred person (exemplarity), in each case the value is *indifferent* to logical applicability and language analysis. Hence, I neither question the validity and generality of logical propositions nor their factual significance. But I do question their factual significance with respect to pre-predicative and pre-reflexive *value-experience* which is (following Max Scheler's Value-Ethics) the phenomenological foundation even of moral oughtness itself. While propositions expressed in language (and/or signs) may be 'true' or 'false' in their application to moral experience, it is clear that a proposition or statement made in the order of logic cannot be 'good' or 'evil'. Phenomena such as good and evil occur, first of all, in my With-World and, therefore, belong to my mode of being: *Existenz*. I already ex-ist (= stand out) 'between' good and evil at any moment of my life. I am delivered up to them in my possible life. And it is through this inescapable ontological place of person-al existence that the unity of the person must *be* open to the values and dis-values of moral experience. The unity of the person is the very locus of a *vivo, I ought* whose certainty remains quite unclarified in Descartes's *cogito, sum*.

, Now, a statement may be true or false (correct or incorrect) for ·good *and* evil acts.'But an evil act can *never be morally* extinguished by any 'true' proposition about it. An act of repentance, however, can extinguish moral evil, and, accordingly, I have shown in some detail that we must re-think a 'logic of the heart' (Pascal) that is quite different from the logic of reasoning.

Phenomena such as good and evil are borne only by the self-value-being of the person. If, for example, I blush in shame about an evil committed, the red on my cheeks is not primarily a colour on the surface of my cheeks. Primarily, it is a revealing expression of the psychic fact of 'shame' which is 'understood' by all who see me. And with respect to myself, the shaming person, this red is not simply physical energy (heat) spreading through my cheeks and subject to tactile experience. Shame is, first of all, a *felt self-value difference* between my having *been* so (evil) and my present intuitively felt non-negative value-*being*. I shame within evidential levels of my possible being given *to* myself, and not because I make a non-contradictory judgement on the 'truth' of my evil deed.

It is precisely here where the exemplarity of the person (as one of its modes of being) comes to the fore. The exemplarity of the person, most clearly evidenced in the life of a 'saint', does not depend on his making consistent statements on his moral life, or that of others. His *being* is exemplary in the With-World. His 'following' is one *for the sake of* his self-value-*being*, i.e. his person. Original manifestations of the value-region of sainthood, as recorded in history (Jesus, Buddha), clearly show that the most exemplary persons do not bother to write down moral codes and imperatives. This is done only by a genius of mind, such as Aristotle or Kant. It is the very *person* of the saint that *is* imperative! I can only be for or against *him*, i.e. his supreme value-being. I cannot negotiate his 'ethics'. His very person, as it were, is already above any possible ethics. Indeed, his exemplarity necessitates, on his part, a certain indifference to any possible man-made written code or norms. This is because the mode of exemplarity is a mode 'to be'. Jesus ignored Nicomachean ethics, let alone Aristotle's logic and metaphysics. The completeness of saintly self-value-being, so rare in history, is expressed in similes and pictures of natural language spoken in daily life and understood by common people. The presence of this completeness transcends all 'argument', as does the finite unity of the *value* of the human person.

PART THREE
AESTHETICS

9

THE CRITIC
AND THE LOVER OF ART

R. K. Elliott

IN the last section of the first book of the *Critique of Aesthetic Judgement*
Kant admitted that he was uncertain whether a common aesthetic
sense incorporating a universal aesthetic norm actually exists. It
seems that he recognised that if there is no common aesthetic sense a
universal community of taste could not be achieved simply by everyone's contemplating Nature and Art disinterestedly, for he suggests
that if this common sense does not exist the demand of the judgement
of taste for universal assent will be a requirement of (moral) reason
and that the 'ought' of the judgement of taste will 'only betoken the
possibility of arriving at some sort of unanimity in these matters'.[1]
If I interpret him correctly, he maintains in the later books that
whether or not a common aesthetic sense exists we have a duty of
imperfect obligation to bring a universal community of taste into
being and must therefore presuppose that we are able to do so. If
there is no common aesthetic sense, somehow or other all men will
have to acquire a similar taste even though initially they do not all
respond in the same way to objects which they contemplate from
the aesthetic point of view. In recent times some British and
American philosophers of art have accepted Kant's presupposition
that the judgement of taste claims universal assent and have com-
bined this with a respect for criticism more in accord with Hume's
aesthetic theory than that of Kant. They have tended to identify
aesthetic with critical discourse, stressing its 'objective' character and
assimilating it as far as possible to moral or scientific discourse. If
they have not explicitly asserted, they have not denied that aesthetic

[1] Kant, *Critique of Aesthetic Judgement*, ed. Meredith, p. 85.

judgements are capable of being correct or incorrect. It seems, therefore, that they have either presupposed the existence of a natural aesthetic norm and have at least tacitly accepted the consensus of critical opinion as the criterion of the fulfilment of this norm, or they believe that critical discourse provides an artificial aesthetic norm. If the latter, there has been no suggestion that this artificial norm should be other than in fact it is.

Initially our responses to works in a particular style vary, they change naturally as we grow older, and very often we are able to bring about changes in them because we want or feel we ought to like or dislike some work or type of work. Hume thought that at least there could be no disputing Addison's superiority to Bunyan, and when we try to find a comparison which will better perform the function Hume intended it is significant how immense the contrast needs to be. It is not obviously wrong, on purely aesthetic grounds, to prefer the ballad *Thomas Rhymer* to *A Midsummer Night's Dream*, or any archaic head on a fifth-century Greek coin to a masterpiece of Pheidias or Praxiteles. If there is a natural aesthetic norm its yoke is very easy to bear, so easy that I am not sure that anything which can be seen as beautiful at all could not also be seen as more beautiful than any other thing with which it is comparable, and recent work in various art forms suggests that it would be rash to try to set a limit on the kinds of thing which can be seen as beautiful by persons of perfectly sincere aesthetic judgement. On the other hand it would probably be hard to find a generally admired work whose beauty has not been sincerely denied at some time by someone. Under the circumstances it would be more reasonable for the philosopher of art to presuppose the non-existence of a natural aesthetic norm rather than its existence. But if there is no natural norm, or if although there is a norm it leaves us as much freedom as I suppose, the alliance between philosophy and criticism helps to preserve a situation which is morally undesirable. If critics and laymen alike commonly believe that there is a (strict) aesthetic norm and if philosophers of art either presuppose its existence or believe that the artificial norm provided by criticism is a proper and adequate one, it would be hard to imagine more favourable conditions for the *imposition* of a common standard of taste. Persons whose responses differ from those of the critics would suppose themselves to be lacking in taste and would try to adapt their taste to that of the critics. Yet there would be no reason whatever why they should participate in a community of discourse which seeks to impose a standard of taste. Kant may well have been wrong in thinking that we have a moral obligation to establish a universal community of taste, but even if we agreed with

Kant on this matter we could not want this end to be attained through the existence of a state of delusion and the unwitting surrender of freedom. I cannot rationally demand of another person that he should find beautiful the things that I find beautiful unless I am willing to make the same effort with regard to the things that he finds beautiful, and since tastes can be acquired I must presuppose that my effort to accommodate myself to his taste could be successful. Clive Bell maintained that aesthetic judgement must be disinterested in the sense that the spectator does not offer the work the slightest gesture of welcome,[1] but if there is no natural aesthetic norm a universal community of free taste would be possible only if each person were prepared to receive every work not in the manner recommended by Bell but with patience and favour. Since we should hardly want to establish a community of taste on a basis which would maximise ugliness, we should have to do so on one which would maximise beauty. Everyone would have to become not a critic but a lover of art.

It is possible to distinguish two common types of approach to art. One I attribute to a person I shall call 'the critic', since critics often adopt it, the other to a person whom I shall call 'the lover of art'.[2] Nowadays critics assert not that the work must impose its authority on a totally disinterested spectator but that it must be received sympathetically 'on its own terms'. This is a fair description of the lover's attitude. The difference between them emerges in their respective practice. Ultimately it involves differences in the kind of being attributed to the work and in the part which art plays in the life of the individual, but to begin with it can be said that the critic sets a limit to the patience and favour which is to be granted to the work whereas the lover does not.[3] As a rule, the lover's first recognition of his own nature throws him into a state of crisis, for it comes with the discovery that he is alienated from the critical community of which he believed himself a member. Imagine him to be engaged with the symphonies of Bruckner, as yet unsuspecting of the crisis which lies ahead. When the composer repeats a resounding phrase so many times with little or no variation, at first the lover finds this intolerable, but on subsequent hearings he forces himself to participate in the repetitions, inhibiting his spontaneous unfavourable

[1] See Bell's essays on Criticism in *Since Cézanne*. Since Kant believed that on experiencing natural beauty we necessarily acquire an interest in the existence of beauty in Nature, he could not have believed that an interest in finding an object beautiful invalidates the aesthetic judgement subsequently passed upon it.
[2] I do not wish to suggest that critics do not love art, but that some critics love some works and treat others with disfavour.
[3] The importance of patience in the experience of art was brought home to me by Robert Simpson in *The Essence of Bruckner* (1967) chap. 11.

response in the hope of achieving a new favourable one. Eventually it seems to him that so many repetitions are exactly right, that one more would have introduced monotony and had there been one less the music would not have achieved just this magnificence of emphasis. He may believe that he has at last adapted himself to the time which belongs uniquely to the work and take delight in the composer's success in incorporating an apparent eternity in the duration of a few bars. If to begin with he is dismayed at the composer's habit of bringing a movement to a halt with an orchestral *tutti* and then restarting it after a long pause extremely softly, he makes an effort not to feel the offence. In due course the stopping and starting are experienced with pleasure, and no longer seem destructive of unity. Passages which at first seemed banal are eventually grasped as expressing a profound humility. New aesthetic qualities appear on the basis of those which the lover's patience has discovered – or half discovered, half created – and he may proceed to experiences of a rarer kind. He hears the voice of Nature in the music, and the music seems to be referring him to something which underlies both Nature and himself. The work becomes a part of his life, not in the trivial sense that it has occupied his time but in the sense that it has engaged him in his depth and, it seems, has revealed its own depth to him. The lover believes that he has been doing no more than receive the work with the sympathy to which every work has a right, but when he enters into conversation with persons of critical temperament he discovers that they have not shared his ecstasies, that they consider the work to contain ineradicable faults (the very ones that he has eradicated), and that they regard him as a naive enthusiast fit to be treated with an indulgence more appropriate to a child than to an adult. Somewhere he must have transgressed the limits which the critic sets on favour, but memory does not show him any point at which he lapsed into self-deception. His attitude has been consistent, his judgements always the expressions of felt responses to what were apparently qualities of the work. Now he must either accept the critics' opinion of him and try to learn from them when to be patient and when not to be, or he must accept the status of a freelance. He fears freedom, but he is loth to betray the works (composer?) he has learned to love.

The same problem confronts him in his communion with other forms of art. In many cases an unfavourable response can be replaced by a favourable one if it is possible to find an idea of which the work can be seen as a presentation. A straightforward example is the Laocoon group. If the work is seen simply as a representation of three persons struggling in serpents' coils it may well appear as manifesting a frigid and rhetorical virtuosity. But by the allusion the representation is annexed to the idea of retribution, and the work can be seen as presenting this idea. Then the represented agony may come to life for the spectator and the work seem to possess in itself a character with which in a certain manner he has endowed it. This experience can be brought about if the spectator first grasps it as a possibility, allowing the idea of retribution to be freely present to consciousness although attention is not chiefly directed to it. At the same time he makes himself ready for the imaginative experience of the work as a presentation of this idea, as if he were inviting the work to realise itself in this aspect. When it seems to do this, he is deeply impressed. Once more he finds himself at odds with the critics, who regard the idea of retribution as external to the work or as belonging only to its content. The work is mannered; indeed, the most remarkable thing about it is its perversity. The lover's response is once more put down to enthusiasm and the qualities he finds in the work are taken to be products of his fancy. For his part, he has to admit that the critics' unfavourable judgement does not call into question the aesthetic character of their response. The work can be aesthetically seen as they see it. Nevertheless, it now has an important meaning for him, and since he believes his own experience also to have been an aesthetic one he is unwilling to repudiate it.

The lover of art exercises thought, imagination and will in an effort to find the work as beautiful as possible. In 'The Crucified Christ Appears to St Bernard',[1] a fresco by an artist of the school of Perugino, the cross is placed centrally in the picture. Christ and St Bernard are represented within the lower angle of the cross on the left of the picture. The spaces bounded by the upper angles of the cross are empty and the large lower rectangle on the right of the picture contains only a landscape which occupies about a half of the available area. At first sight the picture, though of fluent style, gives an impression of considerable imbalance. But the represented landscape recedes deeply into the picture-space and the colour and light invite the spectator to realise this distance imaginatively. He may not find this easy to achieve, but if he is successful he becomes conscious of the horizons of the represented world and the vastness of the space represented within their bounds and suggested beyond them. Then it seems as if the beam of the cross were literally a balance extending into the depth of the picture and as if the figure of Christ were a sufficient counterweight for the whole world. This provides the idea which should enable the work to set up a rapid free

---

[1] Cenacolo del Perugino, Florence. Illustrated in *Frescoes from Florence* (Arts Council, 1969) p. 176.

E

play of thought and imagination through which it would appear in its full beauty, but this movement is hindered by the thought that the work is based upon a conceit. If the spectator is a lover of art he will not allow this new unfavourable response to swing him into an adverse attitude to the work but will struggle to free himself from the tendency to find the conceit offensive. Has the suggestion that the idea is a conceit activated prejudice? *Is* the idea a conceit if its force can be experienced imaginatively in the contemplation of the picture as an image? When the lover asks this latter question the onus for the success of the work once more falls upon him. In general, he regards the success of the work as his responsibility as well as the artist's and feels what seems to be the work's or the artist's failure as if it were his own. If he cannot find an idea which will vitalise the work and is unable to discover any other mode of experiencing the work which would enable it to fulfill what he takes to be its promise, he will not be sure whether the artist lacked creative inspiration or whether he himself lacked the inspiration which would have brought the picture triumphantly to life. The critic regards the lover's response as undisciplined and excessive, however.

Many philosophers of art tend to think of aesthetic experience as if it were a form of inquiry. The work is conceived as an object rather like a map, and the spectator as seeking to discern its objective aesthetic qualities, good and bad, in order to arrive at an overall judgement of its merit. Engagement with art is identified with critical contemplation and thought to be worth while in very much the same way as intellectual activities like history and pure science. On the basis of certain conventions of aesthetic relevance those who understand the work closely on the model of a physical thing can say of every property either that it belongs to the work or to the subject, but for the lover the work is not objective in this way. Personal knowledge of the work is an aspect of his engagement with it, but his chief intention – or rather hope – is to enter into a relationship with the work which has the character of friendship. Since on many occasions the lover does not clearly distinguish the work from the artist in so far as he is present in it, and since he does not sharply distinguish this artist from the historical artist, he will claim that shared experience is part of the value of art as it is part of the value of friendship, and that sometimes this sharing occurs at the level of his deepest concern. To achieve at this level a personal relationship which has almost the character of an identity seems to him a miracle, the value of which he cannot properly express. But even when his relationship is not with the artist but with the work as such, it is still like a relationship with a person. There is a reciprocity between the lover and the work. If asked further concerning the value of art, the lover will not think immediately of the actualisation of mental powers or of enjoyment but will talk about the inspiration and perhaps the consolation he derives from art, and may say that some of the works which matter to him constitute or embody a criticism of his own personal mode of life.[1] Since some works reveal themselves to him more completely than others and he feels a closer affinity with some artists, he has no inclination to criticise tastes which differ from his or to declare any work to be unworthy of aesthetic attention.

It is easy to ignore the existence of the lover and to presuppose that the attitude of the critic is the proper manner for a human being to be related to a work of art. It is questionable, however, whether criticism justifies the trust which philosophers have often reposed in it. If the critic assumes the existence of a natural aesthetic norm, then at some point in the contemplation of a work which he eventually judges adversely he must have been convinced that his unfavourable response constituted the failure of the work to satisfy the norm. But he admits that every work must be received sympathetically and that if this is to be done, initial unfavourable responses must be inhibited. How does he know when he has been patient enough? And how does he ensure that he is equally patient with every work? Alternatively, if there is no aesthetic norm, the critic may be thought of as setting a limit to the degree of patience to be granted to the work. If so, how does he specify this limit, and what are his reasons for setting the limit precisely where he does, rather than making it more generous or more severe? If he cannot specify the limit, his claim that he treats all works impartially will be an empty one.

Furthermore, the establishment of any such limit must have a bearing upon the kinds of quality and experience which are acceptable as contributing to the aesthetic value of the work. In the extreme case – that of Bell – there is only one quality (significant form) which is aesthetically relevant. Any limitation set upon aesthetic response devalues some range of experiences which may be greatly cherished by individuals. There is a price to be paid if aesthetic judgements are to be objective in the sense which enables them to be assessed as correct or incorrect. A work may be experienced in a great variety of ways. A representational picture may be seen as a non-representational design, as a represented world having a certain immanent emotional quality, as a representation of *the* world as the artist sees it, or as expressing the artist's mood, emotion or personality. The spectator may identify to a greater or less

[1] See Max Raphael, *The Demands of Art* (1968) chap. 6.

degree with the artist or with some person represented in the picture, or he may not. He may experience the picture from a point outside the world represented, or he may seem to be present within the represented world. Various significances may be granted to the work or denied it, and may or may not be imaginatively realised in the perception of the work. In some cases experiences are reported whose aesthetic status cannot simply be rejected yet which are enjoyed by only a small minority of those who contemplate the works concerned. Many such factors help to determine aesthetic judgement and the degree of praise or blame accorded to the picture. Analogous ranges of factors are relevant for the other arts. If he wishes to set a clear limit to the degree of favour to be granted to the work, the critic or philosopher must indicate which of these various modes of experiencing a work are acceptable and which not, and must state his reasons for the decisions he makes. He must not say that the limit can only be discovered by reference to each particular work, for this would only be a statement of his intention to impose a limit in every case. Nor should it be assumed that clear and consistent limits are in fact adhered to in critical practice and could be specified if it were worth the labour. The philosopher must be explicitly aware of the limits imposed upon patience and favour if he is to be able to estimate whether a form of critical discourse is worth its price.

Though it has long been understood that knowledge of the artist's life and times can lead to a change in our response to his work, the extent of our freedom to change our responses through patience and favour has not been generally recognised. This, together with the great variety of modes in which a work may be experienced, precludes the establishment of a strongly objective form of critical discourse unless extremely severe and quite unjustifiable restrictions are placed on what is to count as aesthetic response. It may appear that a form of discourse of this type is already operating successfully, but this is an illusion if the critics cannot specify the most fundamental conventions which govern their procedure.

The ambivalence of the beautiful and the ugly is a further reason why criticism falls short of the objectivity it claims. In the *Hippias Major* Plato maintains that any object which appears beautiful relative to one thing appears ugly in comparison with something else. The critic makes use of comparisons to support his judgements, but if the comparison is made in a certain way it could be said to create the quality which the critic claims to have discovered. Rouault's pictures do not ordinarily give an impression of delicacy, but a great delicacy enters into them if they are juxta-

posed with certain pictures by Nolde, for example. They do not
ordinarily appear coarse in style but no doubt they would if they
were hung beside pictures by Fragonard. Yet in comparison with
Rouault's, Fragonard's pictures would appear to lack strength. In
making his comparisons the critic also sets a limit on what they are
to reveal: relative to Wordsworth we are to notice not Yeats's
preciosity but his concreteness, for example. Comparison thus
becomes an effective means of injustice, seeming to have the force of
proof when the reader's sensibility dances to the critic's tune. In the
Republic Plato's view is that in so far as beauty is a response quality it
is ambivalent prior to any comparison. It is true that every work
which we commonly regard as beautiful can also be seen as ugly
without our having to compare it explicitly with any other work.
On occasions the paintings of Michelangelo appear to be monu-
mental as well as dynamic, of noble humanity and great spiritual
significance; but on other occasions they seem inflated and turbulent,
as if manifesting an unattractive will to power and pretending to a
cosmic significance which they do not realise. The works of Leonardo
may appear nervously fine in style, subtly expressive and profound
in meaning, or mannered, frigid and enigmatic. St Paul's Cathedral
seems sometimes majestic, sometimes merely grandiose. In each case
the work appears now beautiful, now ugly *as a whole*: it is not a
matter of emphasising first the virtues of the work and then its
faults. Every work, no matter how great, has what may be called
its 'shadow side' which is constantly being seen, but because the
ambivalence of the beautiful and the ugly is not recognised the
qualities which constitute the shadow side of accepted masterpieces
cannot be allowed to be qualities of the works. Their appearances
are attributed to some defect in the subject: the shadow side is
thought to be the correlate of the jaundiced eye. This state of affairs
often leads to sudden major fluctuations in critical opinions. An
authoritative critic sees the shadow side of a commonly admired
artist but, instead of discounting this perception in the conventional
manner, takes it to be a revelation of the true nature of the artist's
work and explores this work from the shadow side with keen
sensitivity. He may provide a background of theory which helps to
remove inhibitions and enables others to see the work as he does. If
he is successful, disfavour becomes the appropriate attitude to adopt
towards this particular artist, and lesser artists in the same style will
be treated with scant sympathy. Yet the critics treat with extreme
favour the works of which they approve, and continue to believe
that they judge with strict impartiality. The majority of readers
distrust their own responses, train themselves to respond as the

critics do, and re-train themselves if the critical consensus fluctuates again. Strictly speaking, if we are to know the limitations which criticism actually sets upon aesthetic response, we should have to know which types of work are to be seen from the outset with positive disfavour, which are to be seen with favour and to what degree, and in which cases, if any, the spectator is allowed to choose his own attitude. It is hard to imagine what reasons would be provided in support of these conventions.

These objections against criticism are applicable only so far as it pretends to a judicial function and is thought to have a type of objectivity which is out of place in the discussion of art. For much of the time the critic writes as a lover of the work he is discussing, but he is also free to receive a work with disfavour or with cool detachment. Objection arises only when he supposes that he has discovered the one true aesthetic nature and value of the work or when he seeks to impose his taste upon others. It would be most beneficial if philosophers of art were to presuppose the non-existence of a natural aesthetic norm and withdraw their support from any group which was, in effect, attempting to establish an artificial norm. If it were allowed that every man has his own taste, discussion of art would continue unabated and would gain in freedom and sincerity. No one would claim that anyone else *ought* to agree with his aesthetic judgements. Kant was wrong in thinking that the judgement of taste involves a claim to universal assent: if every man were allowed his own taste, the expression 'This is beautiful' would not lose its meaning. Its use would indicate that the speaker has responded favourably to the work as a whole and that he was prepared to try to communicate his response by citing qualities or experiences of a kind which others would recognise or be prepared to accept as aesthetic. Factors such as the work's reminding the respondent of some pleasant episode in his life need be taken no more seriously than they are now. There could be a large measure of agreement about what constitutes an aesthetic judgement rather than a judgement of some other kind, and a large measure of agreement in aesthetic judgements, without there being any universal aesthetic norm.

Each person has a capacity for beauty which is developed within some particular tradition of aesthetic response whose concepts he learns, but he may eventually come to recognise that taste is free. This fills him with fear only because he thinks of aesthetic perception as a form of knowledge, whereas it is rather a form of love. It is strange that anyone should be dismayed at the thought that the world has the capacity to respond to his loving regard. No doubt we could get along very well by pursuing a policy of tolerance in matters of taste; but if a universal community of taste were thought to be desirable it could be achieved by everyone's adjusting his responses so that he finds beautiful whatever anyone else does. It would be necessary to adopt a catholic attitude towards the kinds of qualities and experiences for which aesthetic status is claimed, however, for art is important to individuals and some would choose not to enter the community if satisfactory reasons were not given for the exclusion from the aesthetic realm of qualities or experiences which they value highly. Finally, it should be recognised that the attitude adopted by the lover of art is not an irrational or an inappropriate one, and that it deserves the consideration of the philosopher of art as much as that of the critic does. In examining it the philosopher might find that aesthetics has more affinity with the philosophy of religion and the philosophy of personal relationships than has commonly been thought to be the case.

While I cannot attribute the opinions expressed in this paper to Mikel Dufrenne, it must be obvious how much I am endebted to his *Phénoménologie de l'Expérience Esthétique*, surely the most significant work in the philosophy of art since Croce's *Aesthetic*.

10

COMMENTARY ON
MR ELLIOTT'S PAPER

Mikel Dufrenne

(Translated by David Murray)

MR ELLIOTT's very interesting text sets out several problems with reference to receiving a work of art and to judging it. I should say at once that I feel myself in deep agreement with its author; and how could it be otherwise, when Mr Elliott is so kind as to invoke me, and when he has perfectly understood what I have tried to say elsewhere? If I enter this discussion with him, it is in no sense to present a contrary thesis, but to take up and extend his remarks in my own way.

I think that I can discern two presuppositions in Mr Elliott's reflections, presuppositions which are not of his making, but are made manifest by the history of art and the history of criticism. The first is that in our times 'some British and American philosophers of art . . . have tended to identify aesthetic with critical discourse, stressing its "objective" character and assimilating it as far as possible to moral or scientific discourse . . . It seems, therefore, that they have either presupposed the existence of a natural aesthetic norm and have at least tacitly accepted the consensus of critical opinion as a criterion of the fulfilment of this norm, or they believe that critical discourse provides an artificial aesthetic norm.' It is upon this that Mr Elliott erects his contrast between the critic and the lover, the *amateur* who is also an *amoureux*: who tries to do justice to a work by dint of attention, patience and favour, for whom aesthetic experience is a matter of love rather than of knowledge. The second presupposition is that art is manifested to us through works: paintings, monuments, poems. And it is precisely because these works have supremely the objectivity of objects that they invite us to take up before them, as much as the attitude of the lover, the objectivising attitude adopted by the critic, proper to a spectator at once sovereign and disinterested.

Now these two presuppositions may well be put in question by the most recent developments in critical understanding and in art. Let us start with the second. Art seems to me today at the apogee of a course which is taking it away from the notion of the *work*, and which has its origin in Dada and surrealism. The linked concepts of the *work* and of *creation* are contested by non-art, anti-art, and environmental art as well. Curiously, it is the notion of the *object* which is displacing the notion of the *work*, as the notion of creativity that or creation. A painting-object, like those of Pop art and Duchamp's ready-mades before them, resists being a work, that is to say the premeditated, controlled result of a lucid, voluntary operation; and the exercise of creativity which is deployed in gestural painting or automatic writing refuses to be identified with a creative operation. The artist is less concerned to produce a work than to pursue a strange adventure, the quest for the invisible thing which haunts him, and which is the *other* of his work, that which the work, once completed, will be able to show only in filigree, as something which is absent from it. Blanchot reminds us that Orpheus chooses to see what he should not see rather than compose a song; if he sings none the less, before the Maenads rend him, it is to utter the impossibility of song, to open that imaginary space in which the form that obsesses him can be divined, but as inaccessible and never to be shown explicitly, the sense which lies beyond the sense. The work is not an end, then, but a means.

For that reason, it does not demand what the object-end requires: that disinterested, solemn and respectful contemplation which has often been defined as the model of the aesthetic attitude (a model which certainly influenced me in my *Phénoménologie*). It does not call the spectator to witness its perfection; it treats him rather as an accomplice or comrade, it invites him to take a more familiar attitude and also a more active part, it enlists his own creativity instead of his docility. Reading Bachelard, the dreamer of words, co-dreaming with the poem, exemplifies this; or again the sauntering of the tourist in a city, or the visitor to some monument, his attention freely engaged by whatever intrigues; or again the wandering of the eye which grazes the painting, as Klee puts it; but also – why not? – that of the child playing with kinetic gadgets, or who clambers over the iron sculptures in Mont Royal Park in Montreal. The spectator then is really a consumer; but to consume the aesthetic object is not to use it up; the fruit, far from melting formlessly into enjoyment in the mouth, offers its savour without fading, fulfils itself without losing itself, finds its truth in the imaginary: entering the fantastic, the bottle-rack is a real bottle-rack, one which knows no *sommelier* but is known by a happy perception. The consumer too is fulfilled: he rediscovers the innocence and pleasure which daily life too often denies him.

This first comment, as will be seen, merely justifies the concept of the lover of art which Mr Elliott proposes. For what the work, finished or not, asks from us according to this new view is indeed the attitude of the lover: the generous and joyous assent of him who loves the work for itself, who is in a sense involved in its genesis, and who will not let himself judge it. He loves it as it is, for what it makes of him and he of it.

The second presupposition is that at the other pole of aesthetic experience, critic and savant are as one, at least in recognising a natural or artificial norm for grounding a normative judgement. An ambiguity must be noted here. 'Normative' can be understood in two senses, which it is Kant's merit to have distinguished. In one sense a judgement is normative if it refers back to a norm: here, to a definition of the beautiful, set forth in criteria for beauty or in rules for producing it. In another sense, a judgement is normative if it claims universality, if it demands, more or less authoritatively, unanimous assent. Kant has well shown that the judgement of taste can be normative in the second sense while not in the first, since 'there is no concept of beauty'. One can, then, consider the possibility of a community of taste based on universality in judgement, as Mr Elliott proposes doing, without invoking some norm of beauty; and in fact it seems to me that art studies and criticism today no longer seek to define any such norm. The task which draws the aesthetician is rather that of analysing the attitude of one who makes an aesthetic judgement, and it is to this end that Mr Elliott judiciously applies his distinction between the critic and the lover.

But we must introduce a further distinction among those contrasted with the lover: one between the critic and the savant. For it seems to me that the functions of critic and savant are dissociated today. As a matter of fact the status of the critic is now very uncertain; do all those who claim the title, even in the A.I.C.A., practise the same craft? We might well restrict the title of critic to those who 'do the galleries, or dress rehearsals, or the publishing houses' in order to introduce new works to the public. They do indeed make judgements, whose commercial weight is sometimes considerable.

And it is most often they who concern the *amateur*; it is to their judgement that he compares and tries to adjust his own, as Mr Elliott shows very well. These critics are, if you like, experts, and can be men of taste; they may also successfully resist the temptation to follow the latest fashion (or to advance it in order to be surer of following it), or to surrender to the financial interests which attach to certain arts. Where are these more or less institutionalised critics to be located in relation to writers like Borges, Bachelard, Blanchot, Sartre and also the representatives of the American new criticism? The latter have an entirely different relation to works of art, which is in no way that of the judge, but much more that of the lover. They endeavour to embrace the work, to penetrate it, to spread it out by attention and understanding. Their attitude is not, however, precisely that of the *amateur*: their reading of the work is completed in writing; they are themselves creators, they join in the game of writing; they address themselves to their own work as much as to that upon which they comment; and their work is a taking-up of the other, not a discourse upon it in a meta-language; and thus the other appears as calling for this response and being fully realised only in it. Does not every work await its public in the same way? But here the public is truly creative; and the truth of the work is what happens between two creations, in that encounter where each affirms itself only in its relation to the other. If extended, this idea would connect with the theme expounded earlier: that if the work awaits a public, it must exist fully only in the common act of the transmitter and the receiver.

Neither the official critic nor the writer-critic is a savant as historians, psychologists and sociologists of art wish to be, even if he sometimes draws inspiration from the work of these others. But the savants in their turn refrain from judging and referring to norms. One needs only to remember the most recent developments in *Kunstwissenschaft*: I mean the renaissance of formal analysis, also known as immanent analysis, the impetus of structural semiology. These studies bear upon literature above all, but as much upon myths (they have been initiated largely by Lévi-Strauss) or on tales (Propp is a pioneer here) as upon the novel of letters, the *nouveau roman* or the theatre of Racine. But they extend not only to cinematic works, which are always narrative, but to the plastic arts in which the image can further be joined to a text and function as a report. They disclose, in any case, the structures of the object according to the levels of reading which it offers (in which they are extending and specifying the work of Panovsky and the Warburg school). They can even stretch to music, although research here is still very tentative. Now, it is significant that immanent analysis is most often applied to works that might be called manufactured, or standardised, for the good reason that their structures are the most stereotyped and thus the most apparent: except where exotic myths are concerned, their messages are simple, their codes easily discerned. Doubtless this choice is dictated by method; but it also illustrates the lack of interest of the structural approach, for the moment at least, in the value of works; if among its objects of study some are, or have a claim to be, objects of value, it prefers to deal with those which do not aim at beauty, or which tradition has not consecrated as beautiful. In every case, like any scientific enterprise, it abstains from judgements of value; the scientific discourse which is being elaborated under the suspices of structuralism is not critical discourse, in so far as the latter aims to judge the object according to a previously established norm.

Let us note parenthetically, however, that this approach, while non-normative in the first sense of the term, maintains a double relation to norms. On one side, to the extent to which it becomes sociological and refers to the cultural code which presides over the making and use of the object, it evokes the norms as well as the customs which imposed themselves on the artist; but relativising them in the same breath, and thus not taking them on their own terms. On another side, it can – if sometimes almost unwittingly – make apparent two qualities which may give the aesthetic object real value: first its novelty, its singularity, exactly when it transgresses the codes and norms obtaining at the time of its production; in which the work not only attests to the creativity of its author, but itself creates a style, starts a history within the history of a genre. And secondly its depth, measured by the levels of various possible readings, and disclosed by the circularity of the significants in the global shape of the work: depth appears to us as an indeterminateness which is the effect of an overdeterminateness.

The point of these two comments is only to clarify our vocabulary, and, in the present discussion, to place Mr Elliott's contrast a little differently: to make it between the savant and the *amateur*, rather than between the critic and the *amateur*. And the two principal problems raised by Mr Elliott still demand our reflection.

The first is that of the relation between understanding and love in aesthetic experience. The second is that of the normativity of judgements of taste, and of the possibility of an aesthetic community founded on a *sensus communis*. These two problems are linked, and I propose to deal with the second before the first.

One may readily agree that the judgement of taste can be normative, in the second of the senses we distinguished, that of claiming universality, only if its object is amenable to a norm: If there are criteria of beauty which are themselves universally accepted. Historical or sociological studies of art in fact show us that works are produced in accord with the codes and rules which prevail in each culture. But the norm, as we have said, is thereby relativised, and like Marx we may be amazed that Greek statues, which were beautiful for the Greeks, should still be beautiful for us. That is why Kant, anxious to defend none the less the presumption of universality in the aesthetic judgement, bases it on a subjective experience instead of on an objective norm. No norm for the object – no canons which guarantee beauty – for it is always a single object which is beautiful: this tulip, not tulips in general. When I say that some object is beautiful, I seek less to characterise the object than to announce a certain state which I feel in myself: the harmonious free play of my faculties, attested to me by a particular pleasure. My judgement is a reflection, and not a determination. The true criterion of this judgement is the pleasure: the importance of this point cannot be overestimated. And if I stray a moment from the letter of Kant, it is to preserve this point in spirit. For taste is expressed with reference to an object: it is a particular object which provokes our pleasure. Must we not then reintroduce the idea of a norm in the object? Not exactly. One does not say what the object ought to be; one registers what it is. The only norm which can be invoked for it is an immanent norm: it ought to be what it is, to be really itself; which suffices at least to exlude from the domain of beauty those objects which precisely are not themselves: which are false, dubious, insipid or marred. But even if the object is a norm unto itself, it must nevertheless be recognised by us, and perhaps abetted: the whole of transcendental philosophy is there to tell us that the object is constituted only for and by a subject. The appeal made by the judgement of taste, which renders it effectively normative, is this: if you are like me, you can feel the same pleasure that I do – assuming that you, like me, accede to the object which excites the pleasure.

There is no intolerance in this appeal: first, because the imperative is not categorical or unconditioned; here the interests involved are not those of reason. The norm appeals simply to the evidence for an identity of human nature beyond particular tastes or activities and particular products of the imagination and understanding. Nor any dogmatism: no canons for the production of beauty imposed upon the artist, and none for appreciation, upon the audience; there is nothing to hobble the freedom of the genius; and nothing is asked of the spectator but to feel pleasure.

On one condition, however, which we have just mentioned: that
he accedes to the object. And here we come again to the second
problem, that of the aesthetic experience; and again, after a brief
detour, we must side with Mr Elliott in giving a privileged place to
love. That experience (to which, we repeat, we are invited, but which
we may always scamp or decline) joins subject to object, but in a
special way. Whereas cognitive experience is fulfilled in representation, aesthetic experience recalls us to a presence, to a sort of
primitive relation in which subject and object cease to be distinguished and opposed. The initiative, if we may so put it, belongs to
the object. In asserting this, and in suggesting that the object bears
its norm within itself, we seem to contradict both Kant, who on the
contrary insists on the subjectivity of the judgement, and contemporary art, which decries not only docility to rules but the imperial-
ism of the *work* and the cult of perfection. But the disagreement is
only apparent. For where contemporary art is concerned, I think
that it cannot entirely give up the objectivity of the object – I
mean, its imperious presence, its plenitude, even its opacity. Even if
the work is 'impossible', as Mallarmé held of the book, it is still a
work which tells us that; it testifies to the desire which has instigated
it and which informs it, which renders it impossible, but it is there to
testify. And if, strictly speaking, it is unfinished, like the sketch, the
paraph or aleatoric music, and all the current open-ended forms, it is
complete' just through being unfinished. The death of art is the
summit of art; and I doubt that the practice of art can totally
abandon the concept of the work, even if today the work takes on
entirely new guises.

The spectator must, however, participate actively in this epiphany
of the work. It is here that Kant, in underlining the subjective
character of the judgement of taste, supports contemporary aesthetic
practice, were support needed: the appeal to the imagination, to a
free, spontaneous and playful response. The free play of imagination
and understanding in harmony is manifested in the liberation of
desire and fantasy, in the freedom of a perception which is not tied to
concepts, and which meets the inexhaustible depth of sense. A sense
which cannot be spoken or conceptualised, because it is wholly
immanent in the sensible, whose potency and unforeseeability it
merely attests; we can take it up only by playing with the object to
the extent where we lose ourselves in it, and it in us. This communication, which ends in communion, returns us to the origins of
perception, to that unfettered perception of which Merleau-Ponty
spoke, which is also a happy perception because it does not require
us to keep our distance.

This return to the presence, by which the subject overcomes his separateness, is indeed an act of love, and one might reflect, as psychoanalysis suggests, on the relations between aesthetic pleasure and the orgasm. But the problem which Mr Elliott raises is about knowing what part is played in this act by the understanding which the savant elaborates, which is to say representation. Briefly, I think that this relation is really dialectical – reciprocal or circular. On one side, the more important one, the presence emerges through the representation. Certainly the presence is the origin, but it is always lost, and one can rediscover it, always uncertainly and incompletely, only through the representation. To put it another way, feeling requires the mediation of knowledge, the naïve perception requires the educated perception. Notice, besides, that certain works of art urge us more especially to cultivated exegesis: those which offer us an enigmatic pattern from a remote time and place, and which must be deciphered, whether by relating them to the cultural code and the visions of the world which engendered them, in the way illustrated by Panovsky's work, or by analysing them and testing their elements according to the structuralist procedure, as Viollet-le-Duc did earlier with architecture and Vincent d'Indy with music. On another side, everything that the ethnologist can tell us about the fabrication and function of the Negro mask helps us to perceive it better, as does everything we can learn from the regard which Picasso casts upon it when he sees in the nose-segment a solution to the formal problem of a limited space; but we are neither the Negro nor Picasso, we need adopt neither the religious practice of the one nor the pictorial practice of the other; we have only to perceive. But our perception must be illuminated if it is to be clear, and nothing which instructs us is irrelevant. And this is equally true for those aesthetic objects which familiarly surround us, and which do not surprise us: we must learn to grasp their structure and their significations. Beyond these significations, however, at least in the most authentic works, perception discovers a surfeit of sense which cannot be conceptualised, which is tied neither to formal syntax not to the intentions of the content. Of course it can discover it only after these various experiments in readings; but for a moment it must also forget what it has learned, what keeps it within the confines of discourse, in order to surrender itself more profoundly to the object and be possessed by it.

Thus it can happen that, in front of the Negro mask – which ceases to confront us like an object kept at a distance – instead of knowing what the Negro thought or desired, we may really communicate with him, if he too has experienced the mask's beauty without giving it a name; and that we may communicate with Picasso too, if he has drawn his lessons from the mask only because he first felt that same fascination. Thus the presence – rediscovered asymptotically in the aesthetic experience – perhaps realises the condition for a true community: it leads individuals back to that point where they are not yet separated from Nature, nor distinct from one another, but where they will arise from a common matrix: alike at birth, though destined to diverge through individuation and acculturation. The aesthetic community is a communion at a common source, and that is the infinitely precarious work of love rather than of knowledge.

But we said that the relation of love and knowledge was dialectical. This means that the loving understanding of the work, lived as something beyond scientific understanding, is also on this side of it: it inspires that knowledge itself. Were we not sensible already to the expression of the work, we should hardly be able to orient our intellectual reading of it: someone like Freud must respond to the enigmatic beauty of Sophocles or Shakespeare in order to draw his interpretation out of them; it is the live, untamed experience of the work which preserves the formalist or the structuralist from making a reductionist use of their conceptual apparatus. The conceptual project does not validate our fervour; but it opens the way for it and requires it.

I shall end by saying that I subscribe to Mr Elliott's conclusions; and I hope I have not betrayed them in seeking, through a theory of presence which implies a theory of Nature, an ontological foundation whose premises might indeed be found in Kant.

11

CHAIRMAN'S
OPENING REMARKS

Eva Schaper

MR ELLIOTT argues that British (and American) aestheticians are prone to identify aesthetic with critical discourse and that this implies that aesthetic judgements are in principle correct or incorrect. Whether they admit it or not, they are passing verdicts for which reasoned justification could be provided. This view, he maintains, is not merely unduly restrictive, it is essentially mistaken. It presupposes either some kind of natural norm (perhaps a common aesthetic sense), against which we can deploy the usual arguments from the history of taste, or some artificial norm created through consensus, which always involves the danger of becoming something which the critics impose upon a trusting public. Mr Elliott insists, by contrast, that taste is inherently free, and that any alternative view which does justice to this fact and allows for the possibility of a community of free taste, must be preferable. His own view moves the attitude of the lover of art, and not the critic, to the centre of the picture. The lover of art characteristically receives art works 'with patience and favour', in order to maximise beauty and heighten enjoyment.

The case against the critic is made with the enlightened critic in mind, the critic who does not believe in pre-formed standards of assessment against which he measures the work, but who honestly holds that he is letting the work 'speak for itself'. Yet even such a critic, Mr Elliott maintains, will have to set 'limits to his favour', and such limitations cannot in principle be justified, for three sorts of reason. (1) Mr Elliott pictures the critic as first attending to the work and then passing judgement. But, he says, there is no time at which we can say the critic has paid sufficient attention: a little more patience, another look, might reveal aspects until then overlooked, which would have changed the critic's assessment. (2) Moreover, even if the critic has exercised extreme patience with one work, his judgement might well involve comparison with other works about which the same problem arises, and, in any case, simply to compare is to select, i.e. to reject, aspects of the work assessed as irrelevant. (3) A work treated with disfavour by one critic may find favour with another, without this being simply evidence of a jaundiced eye. Works may have their light and shadow side on which it is perfectly legitimate to concentrate separately, although this never warrants the conclusions that a work is constituted by just one or the other of the sides which suggest favourable or unfavourable judgement respectively. For these sorts of reason we have to reject, Mr Elliott insists, the notion of the 'judicial' approach to a work of art, an approach which issues in an assessment of the work's character, quality or value. He thinks that many good critics do not assume this function but in fact adopt the attitude of the lover of art. And it is as lovers of art, in any case, that we should approach art works. The lover of art makes a sustained effort to find beauty in a work, exercising thought, imagination and will; his constant aim is to maximise beauty, first to discern it, and then exhibit it to others, and Mr Elliott has some good and convincing descriptions of how this may be done even in cases which initially evoke no positive response.

There are good grounds for thinking that many of Mr Elliott's points about how we should approach art works are, taken in themselves, unexceptionable, but can they sustain the theoretical distinction between the enlightened critic and the lover of art? For more has to be involved here than the desirability of a sympathetic approach to the appreciation of art, or an admission that there may be more to a work than meets the critical eye – both of which are clearly true. Mr Elliott seems to be arguing that the approach of the lover of art is *incompatible* with any approach which assesses, judges or passes verdicts even when the judgement is thought of as emerging from an unprejudiced gaze. He concentrates here quite properly on cases where the critic's assessment (and usually he is thinking of the *negative* critic) diverges from that of a lover of art. But it is not at all clear that in these cases the two approaches are incompatible. There is a suggestion, for example, that the appreciation of the lover of art for a Bruckner symphony is inexplicable to the critic who has already formed his adverse judgement, when in fact what the lover finds in the work is very well described, and described, moreover, in terms of critical assessment: 'pleasure', 'exactly right', 'magnificence', 'no longer seems destructive of unity', 'expressing profound humility'.

Perhaps the point is that the lover of art will never form too hasty a judgement, but then he might fall into the opposite vice of procrastination. To suspend judgement may be a virtue, to suspend it indefinitely may often be not to say what one thinks. Moreover, there is nothing in the critical approach which says that a critic cannot change his mind. He does not give up his critical function simply by being a lover of art.

This point has to be distinguished from another: on what grounds should we disallow an unfavourable judgement simply because *someone* finds the work beautiful? There is a suggestion in Mr Elliott's argument that we should do so simply because of the existence of the favourable response, and this is connected with Mr Elliott's explicitly maintaining that the success or failure of a work is as much the responsibility of the lover of art as of the artist. It must, of course, be true in one way that *any* positive response contributes to the success of a work, but is this the standard of success we should be using?

One question to which I cannot find a satisfactory answer in Mr Elliott is how he wants it to be understood that we may 'come to love' a work of art. Sometimes it seems as if through patient application we could come to love what we did not love before; at other times the suggestion seems to be that the lover of art comes to understand, and to make explicit in patient contemplation and deeper absorption in the work, *why* he loves it. Perhaps we are to include both. The question remains, however: *what* is it that makes us inclined to 'grant patience and favour'? Is it anything that might be presented to us as art, as it appears in an art gallery, for example, or bears the title of 'novel', or is in some analogous way 'exhibited'? Mr Elliott's claim is that 'every work has the right to the lover's sympathy' (perhaps he should have said 'to *some* lover's sympathy' to be consistent?). Now either we must be prepared on some grounds or other to exclude, in advance, say, pictures on chocolate boxes, and include, say, still lifes by Cézanne or Braque, in the category of art works, or if we are not, we must be able to offer a criterion, however rough, for distinguishing within that category what is and what is not worthy of our attention. In either case the only criterion that I can see offered is just that an art work is that which has a right to our loving sympathy, but this does not square with Mr Elliott's inclination to allow that the art lover's attitude might be directed towards objects nobody would call art, perhaps a natural scene or the local gasworks, and is in any case frankly circular.

A fundamental difficulty I feel about Mr Elliott's description of love and its objects is that he oscillates between treating 'loving art' as analogous to loving a person, and taking literally the demand that our approach to art be that of establishing a relation of love. The former is suggested by his concluding remarks that aesthetics is closer to the philosophy of religion and personal relations than it is to epistemology; the latter, by much of what he says elsewhere in his paper. Treated analogously, the concept is illuminating and even in some ways liberating; treated literally, it raises some tricky problems.

The love that one bears to another, or that God bears to us, we certainly do not think of as requiring justification or explanation. Every person, moreover, though unlovable to many, is capable of finding at least one other who loves, that is, who appreciates, enjoys, trusts, and shares the mystery of another life. We have no doubt here about what can figure as a partner in such a relationship: creatures of God, in the religious context, or persons among persons to whose nature it belongs that they are capable of love and of being loved. We could even say that every person lays claim to love simply as a person. In what sense could art works make such a claim or stand in such a relationship to us? Surely they do not do this simply in virtue of their being works of art? And if they do not do this in a literal sense, in what sense do they?

As soon as we begin to consider these questions, we cannot avoid epistemological analysis. We need to know why we should take an object seriously as claiming our love, and though we do not have to take any critic's word for it either, we surely as critics ourselves are bent on recognising and more or less clearly knowing what it is we are dealing with, and possibly prepared to love. These questions arise simply by pressing the analogy Mr Elliott himself draws. We do after all in the sphere of religious or personal relationships speak of idolatry or fetish or obsession; we do or can dissimulate, and objects sometimes usurp the role of persons or souls. How, if at all, should we deal with these in the context of aesthetics, what analogies should we draw? If we draw them at all, then surely we must say that the critic is right to be circumspect, and to ask whether an object is worthy of love, whether it is congruous or incongruous to love it.

Perhaps Mr Elliott really wishes to say that it is, after all, part of the meaning of 'work of art' that it should be loved. But he does not establish or attempt to establish that this is so. Moreover, he clearly wants to say that it is not our act of love that makes something art, but only that in love the work can be fully realised. Understanding what we love must then be at least a prerequisite of coming to love it at all, and what we understand is as it is, as work of art, whether we all love it or not. Mr Elliott seems to think, finally, that loving something can never be wrong because it realises more and not less beauty in the world. Whether we can in this way 'maximise' beauty depends, it seems to me, on whether we love wisely or foolishly, and the growth of our sensibility in turn depends on this.

Professor Dufrenne endorses, he says, Mr Elliott's conclusions. What he suggests as refinements of Mr Elliott's distinction between the critic and the lover of art, however, results in a view which, it seems to me, is no longer entirely compatible with Mr Elliott's position. Two presuppositions of Mr Elliott's argument receive special treatment: (1) contemporary Anglo-Saxon aestheticians tend to proceed normatively, and to equate aesthetic with critical judgement; (2) art manifests itself in art works. Professor Dufrenne finds the first insufficiently argued for by Mr Elliott and the second, though of great importance, not argued for at all. He therefore investigates the second presupposition first.

Professor Dufrenne points out that the concept of a work of art, that is, of a fully formed, objectified, unique and completed thing, is no longer held to be an indispensable notion in aesthetics. From Dada to Pop, the view that artistic creation results in an artistic object which is fully there for contemplation has come under fire. Where the old work concept has been found too deeply entrenched in art thinking, new forms have deliberately styled themselves anti-art, rather than be burdened with what are considered to be outworn and misleading notions. The use of the *objet trouvé*, collages or the ready-mades of recent days shows a growing tendency to deny that a singular artistically completed structure is a necessary end-product of the creative process. A 'work' in the traditional sense may, at best, appear somewhere en route towards 'art', which is now thought of as a process rather than a final forming. An attitude of disinterested contemplation is no longer demanded, therefore, of the recipient: what is now stressed is participation, manipulation and even consumption of the aesthetic object by the public. What has thus been brought into prominence, Professor Dufrenne insists, is a renewed emphasis on the primacy of pleasure in aesthetic experience, pleasure to be achieved by whatever means, and certainly not only by those appropriate to a remote and finished article.

Professor Dufrenne is here bringing out an extremely important point to which Mr Elliott pays no, or scant, attention: the distinction between 'work of art' and 'aesthetic object'. Much of what Mr Elliott wants to emphasise could be made at once more intelligible and more acceptable if we introduce some such distinction as this, and tie his proposals concerning the lover of art to appreciation of the aesthetic object which emerges from either a work or a process or a thing when we love it. Professor Dufrenne, I believe, wishes to make this point, though he does not do so as explicitly as this. He maintains that the decline of the work concept in recent art does not count against Mr Elliott's conception of the lover's approach to art; on the contrary, it seems to confirm it, since joyous assent is essential to the attitude of love and also to what we are supposed to do with some recent art forms. The new art also demands that we refrain from judging, in the sense of adjudicating a finished thing, and even goes so far as to deny that there is a 'work' to be judged. Though Mr Elliott is silent on this point, his view, suitably refined, could be made to fit both a traditional and a more revolutionary conception of art.

Professor Dufrenne, nevertheless, suggests more than mere refinement of Mr Elliott's first assumption. If, and here Professor Dufrenne agrees entirely with Mr Elliott, a critic were to judge according to either natural or conventional norms, his attitude would have to be rejected as logically inappropriate to art. But Mr Elliott's condemnation is too sweeping to do justice to much good art criticism which does neither of these things, and yet does not belong in Mr Elliott's category of the non-critical lover. Professor Dufrenne here distinguishes two senses of 'normative' in order to show the narrowness of Mr Elliott's category and the consequent *non sequitur* of his conclusions. To judge normatively, he says, may mean (*a*) to judge with reference to a norm, whether natural or conventional, and (*b*) to judge with reference to the universality, even if unrealised or imperfectly realised, of possible consent. He takes (*a*) to be generally rejected by good modern criticism. Though Professor Dufrenne politely refrains from saying so, the implication must be, I think, that Mr Elliott's attack is misplaced. Alternative (*b*) is clearly not open to Mr Elliott's attack, but it also differs significantly from loving patience towards all art works in that it allows for a by no means negligible intellectual and even cognitive component.

What we need here to articulate these distinctions, Professor Dufrenne thinks, is the notion of the savant, who is not the too narrowly normative critic of sense (*a*). (We lack in English an appropriate term corresponding to this notion: perhaps this suggests there is something in Mr Elliott's contention that it is the *critic* who monopolises the Anglo-Saxon scene.) The position of the savant is somewhere in between the critic of sense (*a*) and the lover of art: he is the critic we need. He makes the truth of a work emerge from a fresh and personal encounter which finds formulation in his interpretation of the work. This approach is normative in sense (*b*), not sense (*a*), for the *possibility* of universal assent to the savant's assessment provides both the motive for undertaking it, and the need for putting his cards on the table for inspection and scrutiny.

The two main problems which Mr Elliott's paper raised for Professor Dufrenne can now be reconsidered in the light of these more flexible distinctions. Could not the full aesthetic experience consist, Professor Dufrenne asks, in a rapport between *connaissance* and *amour*? It is right to say that knowledge alone does not do justice to the character of an experience which is close to a personal encounter and involves us deeply; but equally, love alone must be equally unsatisfactory in its blurring of contours and in its ultimate denial of the differences in the character of things. The savant holds the balance.

The savant alone employs the concept of the norm in Dufrenne's second sense, not the fault-finding critic or the fully involved lover, and it is just this concept which is actually central to both our speakers' demands for a community of free taste. Any assent, of course, which takes the form of, say, 'This is beautiful' has a strong subjective element: it is the assent of a person, who loves the work in question. It expresses that the spectator has approved, and one criterion for the right to apply the concept of beauty is the pleasure gained from the free play of all subjective faculties in the individual. Yet one predicates beauty of the object, and not of one's state of mind. Professor Dufrenne proposes that this predicate is granted not to just anything but only to what is 'fully itself'. The norm here appealed to is what he calls an 'immanent norm', and its recognition is not a purely intellectual matter, but neither is it based merely on subjective liking: it is the recognition of what something is with the emphasis on how fully it is, in so being, itself. (Professor Dufrenne is not at all clear on this point, but the general tendency towards a Kantian position is fairly obvious.) Committing oneself to the view that an immanent norm is realised in an art work, one also commits oneself, at least in principle, to demanding that others could gain the same approving pleasure from the same work, and to saying that this is so because the work *is* beautiful. Good criticism does not merely arrive at such conclusions but presents what is relevant to the recognition of beauty in interpretation, stressing and highlighting that which will facilitate assent by others. A piece of criticism, then, has the function of justifying both the critic's own assessment and the appeal to the possibility of assent by others. The condition for recognizing the beauty of something is, therefore, not merely that the individual art lover should feel pleasure, but that he should 'do right by the object'. The privilege of the lover in Mr Elliott's sense is the duty of the savant in Professor Dufrenne's sense.

The tendency of Professor Dufrenne's remarks is then to question the contrast between critic and lover, and, mainly by implication, Mr Elliott's assumption that the identification of aesthetics with purely cognitive judgement holds for all contemporary aesthetics. It is possible of course that Mr Elliott will dig his heels in over the current state of aesthetics in Britain or America, since Professor Dufrenne's examples are drawn almost exclusively from the Continental scene. Of more significance, however, is the question whether Professor Dufrenne's insistence that the relation between critic and lover in the savant is a *dialectical* one is much help. 'Dialectic' is too useful a word. It is apparently intended to mean more than the reciprocal shift of emphasis from one to the other, and the mutual enrichment and reinforcement of both attitudes in one person. What more remains obscure.

In Professor Dufrenne's notion of the aesthetic object, i.e. the work seen or experienced as being fully itself, we are given some tentative ground for that object analysis which is lacking in Mr Elliott's view. It enables us to say that, however much we may try to love them, some things are not beautiful: 'we exclude from the realm of beauty objects which are not fully themselves'. Mr Elliott cannot do this, but how Professor Dufrenne would do it in detail is another matter. The important point seems to me that he is prepared to do so, and that his standpoint in principle allows it.

How, finally, must we see our speakers' relationship to Kant? Mr Elliott refuses to accept that the Kantian community of taste is free. Professor Dufrenne is equally unwilling to sacrifice to Mr Elliott's persuasive attack on the critic who 'limits patience and favour' the normative aspect which he believes to be contained in the loving assent to what a work is. Kant, he says, was not trying to impose any standards, but to bring out that the judgement of taste 'let the work be what it is'. Professor Dufrenne's savant reveals a work's presence not just for private but for public enjoyment: the freedom of the Kantian judgement of taste is not in question. Mr Elliott, of course, does not question that we are free to assent, but rather that there are cognitive-epistemological issues involved here. On this point the two speakers are irreconcilable.

DISCUSSION

Mr Elliott: I regret that in the rather limited time at my disposal I was unable to provide the kind of paper that M. Dufrenne's work on aesthetics deserves. Possibly an explicit treatment of his idea of the work as a quasi-person, or of his concept of the world of the work, for example; both these exceedingly important concepts are ones which it would be very useful for us to have close and careful discussion of. Unfortunately this was beyond my power to do at the time. What emerged was a meditation on a Dufrennian theme that the spectator is the accomplice of the work as much as its judge. In my paper in effect I try to press this idea to its limit, and also to express certain other ideas which began to seem to me disturbing as well as exciting.

First, concerning the aesthetic norm, M. Dufrenne is right in reminding me that aesthetic pleasure–if we take this to include a variety of pleasant experiences, which are recognised as involving a harmonious interplay of sense, imagination and reason–is the ground of my calling an object beautiful. Indeed this is so, and of course this experience involves seeing the object as having a certain character. But does this experience involve any claim to universality? It seems to me that there is no more than a supposition of communicability. This may amount to no more than that others can imagine, perhaps only very vaguely, how I experience the work. In aesthetic discussions, as soon as the other person can imagine how I experience the work and grasp how I attach value to the experience, this seems to me to be enough, even if he cannot actually see it in that way. I heard a talk on the radio, a man talking about looking at an archaic Greek statue. He said he experienced the statue as if it were alive and spoke of a sense of infinite benediction coming from the statue. It was quite clear that the man experienced the statue like this. I cannot myself experience archaic Greek sculpture in this fashion but I can imagine how he experienced it. I have had other experiences of a somewhat similar sort which enable me to do this, and I can acknowledge his aesthetic experience, so there is a bond between us even if it does not amount to actual shared experience.

If there were a moral obligation to bring about a universal community of taste, no doubt we could go some way, a long way perhaps, towards fulfilling it by doing everything we can to put ourselves in the other person's place, and so on. As we train ourselves to respond in the way that some fashionable critic does, so no doubt we could train ourselves to respond as our neighbour does. But if there is no such obligation, then how can the judgement of taste make appeal to a universal voice? Is it not just that I attribute beauty to an object on the basis of a certain kind of experience and suppose, usually correctly, that others will at least be able to understand the sort of experience I have had and why I value it? But if in a particular case they cannot imagine it, I may decide to go it alone.

M. Dufrenne mentions also an immanent objective norm, as if the work sets its own standard and in experiencing the work we judge whether it reaches the standard or falls short. But it seems that different people discover different immanent norms for the same work. Persons of the type I have called 'the critic' may declare the work to have failed to fulfill its own norm when the person I have called 'the lover' declares it to have succeeded. But the norms are not the same in each case, and the work as the correlate of aesthetic perception is not exactly the same in each case, not even if the critic and the lover both regard the work as successful. Nevertheless, both of them believe that they have done justice to the work. Both of them believe that they have let the object be itself. Here of course the relation of the aesthetic object to the work of art is once more in question. M. Dufrenne mentioned that when the audience cried '*plus fort*' that also was in the work. But how much is in the work? For the lover the work contains more than it does for the critic. Isn't he judging it by a different immanent norm?

The idea of the objective norm amounts to this: that the work must actually appear beautiful to me if I am to judge it to be beautiful. It is not so much that if I take the work to be a presentation of some idea it must be an idea which is appropriate to the work, but rather that I must *actually see* the work as the presentation of that idea. For the lover of art, as I have described him, self-deception is a real danger, since in his willingness to find a beauty in the work he may imagine it to be there when it is not. But the success of his effort depends on how the work actually appears to him, not on how he imagines it as appearing. So the ideal objective norm reduces to something like freedom from self-deception, just as the ideal subjective norm reduces to something like a supposition that other people will be able at least to imagine how—and how pleasurably—one experiences it.

It is salutary, I think, to be reminded how we ordinarily use the word 'critic'. Ordinarily when we talk about 'the critics' we mean journalists who give their opinions about new works, productions and performances. This is quite true. But perhaps the position in England is not quite the same as in France. As regards literature, at any rate, there is a very influential body of academic critics–two critical establishments, one old and one new. Both, I think, are judicial in the way that I described in my paper. Both, I believe, influence taste in the way I have suggested. These critics combine the functions of savant and critic, but their primary concern is with the aesthetic value of the works they deal with. A similar influence has been exerted by types of criticism based on aesthetic theory. It is possible to see a work of art as ugly because it does not look appropriate to its function, or because it is not a pure example of its genre– sculpture which is pictorial or pictures which are psychological. It isn't that these critics judge a work to be ugly for doctrinaire reasons, even though it actually *appears* beautiful to them. The work really does seem ugly to them, because it doesn't look appropriate to its function or is not a pure example of its genre. Such works actually seem ugly to them and they make them seem ugly to others.

As regards loving and knowing, M. Dufrenne is right in distinguishing the role of the savant from that of the critic, and in saying that knowledge is a prerequisite for aesthetic response. And he is right in saying that love and knowledge are reciprocally related in our communion with art. Knowledge gives rise to love and love to knowledge. However, in speaking of the critic as seeking knowledge, I had in mind rather knowledge of the work's aesthetic qualities and defects, and I was thinking not so much of actual critical practice as of how philosophers have at times construed aesthetic experience as nothing but the recognition, discernment or perception of aesthetic qualities or features, usually within a very limited range. This is a sort of *knowledge* rather than a sort of love. An analogy could be made with Spinoza's idea of personal knowledge, something which is knowledge of the individual, of the individual's most subtle qualities perhaps, but still only personal knowledge and not personal relationship. I think the wide use of the term 'aesthetic perception'–people who used to talk about 'aesthetic experience' now talk about 'aesthetic perception'–is symptomatic of this understanding of the experience of art as if it were essentially a sort of inquiry. I think this is wrong.

I did not say in my paper, did not dare to say, that the lover's attitude is *the* aesthetic attitude, the *right* aesthetic attitude, though it is the attitude with which I have most sympathy. All the attitudes I have discussed are aesthetic attitudes. I cannot deny the aesthetic character of any of them, and I have to recognise that some persons who adopt more restricted attitudes than that adopted by the lover are nevertheless persons of the keenest sensibility. If there is no moral obligation to create a community of taste, I cannot deny anyone the right to respond only to formal values, for example, if this is what he wants to do. How can I say that it is not an aesthetic attitude?

One point about a matter which has disturbed me considerably. It seems possible that if one whole-heartedly adopts the attitude which I have ascribed to the lover of art, then any work whatsoever, and, what is more, any natural object, could be seen as beautiful. It also seems possible that any object could be seen as ugly or displeasing. I know that for certain individuals there is a limit. I once tried to see a warehouse as having a beauty in the manner of Romanesque architecture, but felt a nausea and was unable to complete the perception. There may be a naturalistic limit for the species, but I do not think there is. I don't suppose there was anything at all that might not have appeared beautiful to St Francis.

Reflection on the attitudes of the lover and the critic suggests that Plato was right in his contention that sense reports the beautiful always together with its opposite, not mixed with it, but in such a way that whatever can be seen as beautiful as a whole can also be seen as ugly as a whole. I think this phenomenon lies at the basis of many of those fluctuations of taste which we sometimes call 'revaluations'.

Professor Dufrenne: I would like to add some remarks about the background to my reply to Mr Elliott's paper. My two main points were, firstly, that there is a problem about the relationship between the savant or scientist and the lover and, secondly, relating to the question about the universality of aesthetic judgement as, for instance, it was raised by Kant.

I will come directly to the displacement I proposed of a distinction drawn by Mr Elliott. I substituted for the distinction between *critic* and *lover* the distinction between scientist (savant) and lover. This distinction has been in my mind since I have become preoccupied by the debate which is now taking place on the Continent – mostly in France and Italy, where aesthetics is now flourishing – between two approaches to art: semiology and phenomenology.

Two weeks ago I attended a congress in Urbino the general topic of which was 'narrative structures'. This congress was organised by the Association for Semiology. Semiology is a way of approaching the work of art by trying to analyse its structure. As a matter of fact, structurising has exerted a great influence on semiology since Saussure. Usually semiologists do not pay any attention to the value of the work of art. They do not evaluate it at all. They prefer working on stereotyped works like detective novels, folk-lore tales like myths, or ordinary music like popular songs. What they are looking for is the cluster of properties and of structures which underlie a genre. What they try to do is to determine what a genre is and what its evolution is – for instance, how the novel has a proper history from the *Roman de la Rose* to the *nouveau roman*, and so on. Another example would be of how the sonata has a history from the Church sonata to those of Debussy or Roussel. So you can see that there is absolutely no value judgement in such research. The problem is to define a genre, the rules of composition, the cultural codes which prevail, which are adopted by a certain culture or a certain class at a certain level of civilisation.

This approach opposes itself to a phenomenological one. But what I have tried to show in some of my papers is that there is no such conflict between the two approaches. Phenomenology can approve of, even reinforce, the semiological approach if the main object of phenomenology is what Husserl called 'intentional analysis'. This analysis has two ways – the *noematic* and the *noetic*. We have to understand and analyse these intentional links which put into relation the object and the subject. And so we have to dictate what kind of intentions are acted on by the subject, for example, the way he looks at a work of art and what kinds of structure in the work of art answer to those intentions. This intentional analysis, as Husserl puts it, is 'noetical – noematic'. This is exactly what semiology does. It tries to disclose the properties of the structures of the object and, at the same time, it also examines and analyses what kind of attention the subject gives to the object. But what is peculiar to phenomenology is that its approach results in a closer communication between subject and object than the semiologists allowed for. And this is where the word 'love' might legitimately be used.

The levels of meaning (semiology being a kind of semantics) of a work of art are not completely grasped when it is analysed only according to positive or cultural codes. For instance, I look at a painting of the Nativity and I see a young woman who has a baby in her arms. First I must recognise a woman who is a mother, and this might not be done, for example, by some people from a primitive tribe who do not recognise their picture from a photograph. You need certain codes, certain habits of perceiving in order to recognise a young woman with a baby in her arms in a painting.

Conversely, as a matter of fact we do not perceive a Negro statue very well because we have not the same way of looking. We are not culturally informed in such a way that we would have the same way of looking at the statue as the people the statue was made for. So first we have to look at a young woman carrying a baby, but then we have to know that this is the Virgin, and for that we need a certain cultural background, and we have to get acquainted with the New Testament, and so on, and this means acquiring a cultural code. Now Panofsky observes that in paintings before the thirteenth or fourteenth century the Virgin was depicted kneeling in front of the child and it is only afterwards that she is shown carrying the child in her arms. This means that there is another conception of the Virgin as a mother and not merely as a mother of God who adores God but also as a mother who loves her baby, so it implies a new conception of this dogma, and so on.

Those are the things we should know in order to have a reading of the meanings of a work of art. But if it is a genuine work of art there is something else which precisely distinguishes it from the stereotyped work, something which makes the genuine work of art transgress the rule of the genre, or transgress a tradition, and say something for itself. And this is what phenomenology ends up trying to decipher and to explicate, the feeling which we have in front of such and such a particular work of art. This is a result that semiology cannot reach by itself for it requires feeling; more precisely it requires what Mr Elliott calls 'love'. We might give it another name. But what needs to be recognised is that we have to participate in the work of art, and that is where contemporary art teaches us something. It requires us to have another connection with the work of art and the relationship to be more intimate, even in funny ways. I quoted in my paper something I had seen which seemed to me very characteristic. In a beautiful garden in Montreal there are some modern sculptures in iron. The children climb those iron structures and it is great fun. That is a genuine way of using a work of art. Another example: sometime ago there was a performance of Cage in Brussels. You know how the music of Cage is. The Belgian people were not much used to it and there were some movements when the music was very loud, and some people in the audience yelled '*plus fort*'. Those expressions belong to the music and have to be produced within it and they were in it. This is participation, this is love, a way of living the music, nor merely receiving it passively in a solemn way as in a cemetery or a funeral but reacting to it, living it. This of course is a limiting case!

I come now to the second problem, that concerning the conception of a loving relationship with the work of art. I am grateful to Mr Elliott for having stressed this. Such a relationship involves finally a philosophy of nature. What I call a philosophy of nature would show or undertake to describe a primitive state of man or consciousness where man just emerges from nature, with the presupposition that man is part of nature. What I would call nature is reality itself as experienced in *presence* – and I would oppose *presence* to *representation* – but reality 'before man', i.e. before this organisation of nature into a world as worked out by perception or into a universe as worked out by science. Nature is something I cannot tell because, since I am here to tell something, I am always 'after man'. So nature is a limit of thought. But we *may* go close to the idea of nature precisely when we describe, as Merleau-Ponty did, a certain *'perception sauvage'* where, at the limit, we would be one with the object, where the object is not put at a distance; where we are not looking at it as from in front of it; where we are not that disinterested spectator Husserl spoke about; where we are not only in agreement with the object but are living it within ourselves; where we *are it*, in some ways; and that is precisely what I would call 'aesthetic perception'. The aesthetic object drives us back to this kind of perception when we participate in it; when we take an active part in its genesis; when we are both creators of this object and are also created by it. In this reciprocal relationship, in this very close involvement, we are driven back to the origin.

We cannot have a separation of ourselves, we cannot be completely absent, or have an experience of nature as before man. We cannot get rid of our ego, of our transcendentality, of our constitution and powers as Husserl would say. But at least we are very close to such an experience. And this would be the root for this idea of a universal community of taste, as Kant would say, and as Mr Elliott was interested in, because in such an experience I am no longer myself as a distinct individual. Not only do I deeply communicate with the object but also I may communicate with the others who are all similar because we are no longer ourselves as separate personalities. We are back to the mother, mother nature, to Gea, to the Earth, as the Greeks said and as all the primitive religions (which are the true ones) have said. We are coming back to brotherhood because we are coming back to Mother. This kind of community is without any normativity, any rules, any law. It is just a kind of limited experiment, nothing more, but it may be that this is what would justify Kant when he says that my aesthetic judgement is normative – 'normative' in the sense that everyone should assent to it. That means everybody should have the same experience if anybody is to do justice to the object in the same way that I do, so there might be some inkling towards a philosophy of nature in this experience of our judging the object not from our point of view as a separate subjectivity but as being united with it.

Those were the two points I wanted to make as a complement to my paper.

Professor C. A. van Peursen (Leiden): I should like to make some remarks about the similarity that struck me between this discussion and the previous one on 'Freedom and Determinism', as to the methodology of both problems. Both problems concern notions which it is difficult, even impossible, to fit into rules: for instance, freedom into the rule of causality, art into the rule of criteria.

I have four points to make. Firstly, I should like to call these notions 'metaphysical' in a specific sense. In a positive sense of 'metaphysical' these notions may be said to be very *stimulating*. They are not emotional, as is often said, but are stimulating more in the sense that they can provoke further reflection and study. Outside the field of study, however, they are more 'regulative', as Kant would have said. In a negative sense of 'metaphysical' it may be said that they are not verifiable, i.e. it is not possible to apply criteria of truth or falsity or of correct or incorrect judgement with regard to them.

Secondly, there is, nevertheless, a possibility of a progressive translation of these more metaphysical notions to more logical and schematic ones. To give a historical example of a third notion which was also metaphysical – the notion of life, which has been dealt with by Kant in his *Critique of Judgement*. Now in modern sciences of life we have created a means of approaching this phenomenon of life, giving the criteria, like quantity of information, organisation, structure, etc. It might be possible to effect such a translation in aesthetics by the use, for instance, of information theory, structuralistic analysis, etc.

My third remark is that, if this progressive translation is possible, there are two necessities here. One is that you need to have a kind of universality, i.e. inter-subjective categories, prescriptions, etc. The other is that you have to maintain, so to speak, the metaphysical residue which is left or, in other words, the distance which remains between your scheme or rules and the thing itself. This means that you must participate in the thing itself apart from your schematisation. Thus knowledge and love come together here, so to speak.

Finally, I have the impression that in these two discussions there is a special task for phenomenology. I see phenomenology as an intentional analysis where the self-givenness of the thing in itself – perhaps requiring an endless process of analysis – is at one pole, yet is related to the various modes and intentions of the subject – the noetical – noematic method referred to by Professor Dufrenne. Thus there may be a bridge between these more metaphysical notions which it is so difficult to discuss and the translations one tries to get into all sorts of schematisations, theories of information, etc. As to these translations, the specific task of phenomenology would always be to keep a wider horizon to prevent these methodological approaches from becoming too narrow-minded, from identifying the thing itself with the criteria, modes and provisional rules.

Professor J. N. Findlay (Yale): I was fascinated by a remark in Mr Elliott's paper in which he suggests that every work of art has two sides, a sort of daylight side and a night side. This is a point I have not seen especially noted in aesthetic literature. But it does seem to me so profoundly true to one's own aesthetic experience that it is very worth while underlining it.

This capacity for looking at things in two ways can itself, however, be looked at in two ways. Proust has an example when he talks about how people in the Second Empire in France used to paint their walls with decorations which they regarded as Pompeian. We, however, do not, when we look at a Second Empire decoration, see it as Pompeian. *We* see it as Second Empire. We like it because we think it a beautiful example, having all the redolence of the Second Empire, and so on.

This is just one example of this kind of shift from one meaning to another. And what is suggested in Mr Elliott's paper is that this abolishes the notion of the aesthetic norm, something that everyone can share. There are, as it were, two norms, the norm of the person who likes and the norm of the person who does not like a given work. Now I am quite willing to think that the language should be approached in this way. But, after all, it is equally correct for one to say that, when an object is seen as expressing something quite different, it is in a sense a different 'aesthetic object' – the kind of aesthetic object I have when I look at a Second Empire wall paper and say, 'This is *real* Second Empire and no mistake', and enjoy it as such. This is something which a Second Empire person could not possibly have done. The Second Empire experience was not *that*. Similarly, I doubt whether anybody could have an experience of Greek sculpture as it was to the Greeks. Graves, and things of this sort, are totally different to us from what they were to them.

Now the question is, whether the normativist cannot say that, if you really have the same experience of the object, i.e. if you learn to look at the object in the same way, then you will agree with other people about it. And this does seem to be true.

I want to propose that people should consider seriously the view that aesthetic surface is not really very important, or at any rate not so important as people have thought. People have always thought that aesthetic enjoyment is, for philosophers at least – not ordinary people – of the expression of some sort of pattern in some sort of sensuous material. I suggest that Plato was quite right in suggesting that sensuous material was entirely dispensable. It is not in virtue of any equivocation that certain mathematical concepts may be said to be beautiful, certain stories a beautiful structure (even though they may be ill-written), and so on. There is such a thing as good form. The normative person is the person who recognises and enjoys good form. The fact that somebody else, who sees the object quite differently, does *not* enjoy it – this fact does not contradict normativism.

There is one final objection which Mr Elliott has raised. And the question is, does this mean that everything is beautiful, if you are not able to define the concept under which the particular can be ranged? Well, I think this consequence must be faced. Everything *is* beautiful. But is it worth while making the effort to *regard* everything as beautiful? A St Francis or a St Teresa in ecstasy might see incredible beauty in a warehouse. But I do not think there is any reason why we should bother.

Mr Elliott: I would like to make two points in reply to what Professor Findlay has said. Firstly, he has raised the question whether, *when one person enjoys a particular work and another sees only its shadow side*, we do not have *two* different aesthetic objects. There is a constant problem about the identity of the object. But I think I would say that there was *only one* object, since there is, still, the content in common. A person also has aspects, is seen now in one way now in another. One constantly sees oneself in opposed aspects, antithetical ones, yet it is the same thing that is being experienced.

Secondly, I think Professor Findlay is right in saying that, even if everything is beautiful, it is not worth the effort to see it as such. Since life is short, let us see those things as beautiful which are easier to see as such, give us more return for our effort. The answer I would give to this is that, *for the individual*, the effort may be abundantly worth while. For instance, it requires more effort to see the beauty of Traherne's poetry than, say, that of Donne. But, for a person with an affinity with Traherne, it is well worth the effort. There are occasions on which such effort has been much rewarded, I suppose, because of something between oneself and the work. But in general, of course, I can only agree with Professor Findlay on this point.

Mr P. Pettit: I am surprised that the distinction has not been made between the 'aesthetic object' and the 'artistic object'. If one regards the 'aesthetic object' as something having natural beauty, the 'artistic object' will obviously be the work of art. If you take a landscape – an 'aesthetic object' about whose beauty there is not normally much question – somebody may say, 'I find that very beautiful'. One may be inclined to reply, 'Do you really?' or 'I agree; I do too' or perhaps 'I do not'. We may search for a common aspect under which we can agree to see the landscape as beautiful. But this is a matter of taste. Taking the 'aesthetic object' in that way, it is *what* is seen as beautiful.

Now I think there may be two reactions to an aesthetic object. Firstly, there is the reaction of the non-artist, who may say 'I see that as beautiful' and try to present in words or in some other way the aspect under which he sees it as beautiful. He tries, in other words, to give reasons why it appears beautiful to him. Then there is the reaction of the artist who, instead of simply giving reasons or trying to elicit the aspect under which he sees the object as beautiful, will create a work of art – an 'artistic object'. Now if the 'aesthetic object' is *what* is seen as beautiful, could we not call the 'artistic object' *how* what is seen as beautiful is in fact seen?

I know that I am taking as my model the case of the landscape artist – perhaps a rather trite case of the artist, in a way – but it may be useful as a paradigm. If, then, the artistic object is *how* what is seen as beautiful is in fact seen, is it not quite reasonable to expect that an artistic object should be the subject of evaluation? Perhaps the procedure of evaluation would be something as follows: when one finds an artistic object – it might be a work of music, where the corresponding aesthetic object is something not defined in any terms except in terms of that music itself – one is expected to be able in some way to share in this artistic object and to see what is 'seen' in the way in which the composer saw it. Is one not expected to test the piece of music in one's own experience by finding out whether one can interiorise this 'how', whether one can share in this way of seeing the aesthetic object, however undefined, as enjoyed by the artist? The artistic object is in fact a giving of reasons of a type, it is how the artist sees the aesthetic correlate. When we evaluate an artistic object, we try to share in this way of seeing. If we know the terms of the artistic object – if, in other words, we are competent critics – we are in a position to say, 'No, this artistic object fails for me and I think it would fail for anybody who knew the terms of the artistic object'; we can then go on to give reasons.

If one makes this distinction between the 'aesthetic object' and the 'artistic object', and if one regards the process of artistic criticism as a matter first of all of experiential sharing in the artistic object and then judgement on the success or failure of that object, one has a scheme which is more differentiated and which may perhaps offer a more fruitful approach to the problem of the norm in artistic criticism.

Mr D. M. Murray (London): I like very much what Mr Elliott has been saying about the shadow side of the work of art. But I am not so happy about the way this has so far been unpacked. Specifically, I am worried about the claim that there are different aspects of the work of art which can be separated out – a 'light' aspect and a 'shadowy' aspect. There was an interesting example relevant to this on the radio recently when a Neanderthal Edwardian critic was discussing Mahler. He was trying to explain why he thought Mahler a bad composer and took, as a case, the last movement of the Third Symphony. What was interesting about his comments is that he had, in the most ordinary sense, no technical criticism to make whatever. He agreed that what was being expressed was expressed with extreme clarity, with complete technical control, without waste of time, and so forth. But, he said, it was 'indecent'. He could recognise its emotional basis, but thought it an improper one, one which should not be shown in public. I do not think it makes any sense to say he was recognising an 'aspect' of the work which was different from the aspect recognised by those of us who are particularly fond of this movement. I think it is precisely what I love about Mahler that this critic finds deeply offensive and even obscene. If there are aspects to be distinguished, they may be aspects of the appreciation of the work or aspects of one's responses to it. But I do not think there will be any way of making precise a claim to the effect that the last movement of Mahler's Third has that aspect which this critic dislikes and an independent one which I like.

Dr Schaper: Let me try to sum up the discussion and impose a certain pattern upon it. 'Only connect' is always the chairman's business. In this conference we have been trying to see whether we can bridge what has seemed to many an unbridgeable gap between what might be called 'analysis' and phenomenology. My impression is that, in this session, largely the same language has been talked, but I think it is a language already loaded to one side. Both the speakers have been very much in agreement. They have put forward a view which is a plea for an approach in aesthetics that gets away from what we in Britain and on the other side of the Atlantic have been used to.

Some speakers have tried to raise issues which either bridge or divide. The challenge of the first question (by Mr Spicker) was, I regretfully noticed, not taken up. The question, directed to phenomenologists, was whether phenomenology can actually do, either in a *more* satisfactory way or in *as* satisfactory a way, what

British analysts are trying to do when they consider the problem of other minds – whether analysis of the aesthetic experience (so persuasively presented to us by both speakers here) could help towards a solution. This is something we could discuss from both sides of the Channel, perhaps meet, perhaps reluctantly decide that we do not meet. So here is one issue which was touched upon but which did not quite come through.

Professor van Peursen, very interestingly, brought out some methodological trends in the papers, and suggested that a bridge between, let us say, the more metaphysical and the more analytic talk could be found in intentional analysis. This probably is a way (if there *is* a way) to meet, if we could make use of the somewhat underplayed results of Anglo-American studies of the language of critisicm and the valuable attempts on the Continent to analyse, or at least to describe phenomenologically, the kind of experience which we have put in words in critical discourse.

The next point made concerned the difficulty of 'participation' whilst allowing for the value judgement which one wants to make at certain points. This was brought out, I think, in the question whether structural analysis could embody any value judgements. 'Structuralism' (in the French sense), we are often told, avoids value judgements. Professor Dufrenne assures us that it does not. Now here perhaps there is another point where we have to ask more specific questions of the structuralist – after all, we do not fully understand in Britain what structuralism is about. We only have an assurance that structural analysis can show us the way to embody the historical value judgements and the value judgement that transcends historical singularity.

It surprised me that the last point made, about the aesthetic and artistic object, was not brought up earlier. It was raised very clearly and precisely by Mr Pettit. There may be a way in which we could overcome the talking at cross-purposes which has been going on at some stages in our argument. Very often when we speak of the 'aesthetic object' someone means the work of art, someone else that which he sees, someone else that which he sees someone else as seeing, and so on. Here many more distinctions would be necessary before we could agree that part of what we, and the speakers, have been saying applies to what I would call the 'aesthetic object'. We could find ways, I suppose, to use some of the analyses which have been made in recent years on exactly these points: should we say that the aesthetic object was the same as the 'artistic object'? Is the artistic object only available as an aesthetic object? And so on.

I shall close with a reference to Professor Findlay's contribution.

Is everything beautiful? Professor Findlay suggests that it is, but asks if the *effort to see* everything as beautiful was worth while. He says that it might be or it might not. I suggest that we might want to go further and say: all right, everything is beautiful, but we are not talking now about aesthetics, at least not about philosophical aesthetics. Nobody can be stopped in his ecstasy for warehouses or worms. St Francis, who was mentioned several times, may have found everything beautiful, and if we want to follow him we may. But St Francis was not making aesthetic judgements.

POSTSCRIPT

R. K. Elliott

ALTHOUGH my explicit intention in my paper was to stress the favour with which the lover of art receives the work and to indicate especially the part played by the will, no doubt in my illustrations I described instances of that participation which M. Dufrenne rightly regards as a valuable element in aesthetic experience. The love of art has this 'erotic' element, as well as the 'agapeistic' element with which I was more particularly concerned. Both are neglected by the philosophical approach which seeks to understand aesthetic experience so far as possible on the model of ordinary perception. It is not absolutely clear what the request for a bridge between analytical and phenomenological aesthetics amounts to. I find it hard to believe that M. Dufrenne's phenomenological method will prove a serious obstacle to Anglo-Saxon philosophers of art who read his admirably lucid paper. But if communication has already been effected, or waits on no more than the exercise of ordinary philosophical goodwill, there is no need for us to seek some magic formula which will enable us to break through to each other.

Part of what I tried to say in my paper was that the aesthetic form of life allows us to be related to its objects according to a great variety of modes, and easily tolerates very extensive disagreement and fluctuation in opinions. That theme was a Wittgensteinian one, even if the language in which it was expressed was phenomenologic-ally loaded. There did not seem to be any need for a special bridge by which alone communication would become possible.

It is not the case that only the 'untranslatable' parts of each philosophy can be of any real value to the other, or that if our existing understanding of phenomenology is only partial then it is of no real consequence. If in our philosophising about art we have imposed too simple forms on the phenomena of aesthetic experience so that despite our precision we have let much that is important about art slip through our fingers, reflection on the respective methods and achievements of the two philosophies could make us aware of it. This enlightenment would not depend on our first having attained a perfect understanding of the fundamental concepts of phenomenology, and we could at once make use of informal methods of phenomenological description in order to bring our philosophising into closer contact with its subject-matter.

In their remarks during the discussion Professors Dufrenne and van Peursen stated the importance of phenomenology for aesthetics succinctly and with insight.

PART FOUR
BODY AND MIND

12

A PERSON'S FUTURE AND THE MIND–BODY PROBLEM

Hide Ishiguro

IN this paper I shall attempt to throw light on the role of the concept of future in our understanding of the notion of personal identity, which I hope will help to do something to solve some difficulties in the mind–body problem.

There are two areas in the mind–body problem which have been the focus of recent discussion in the Anglo-Saxon philosophical world. The first problem concerns the primacy of the concept of person, i.e. the concept of beings to which are ascribed both physical features (such as location, shape and colouring) and mental features (e.g. forming intentions, having thoughts and feelings, perceiving). This view is not in itself new in the history of philosophy. What *is* new about recent views on the primacy of the concept of a person derives from the assertion that it is necessary to admit this primacy not merely in order to solve the other minds problem, but even in order to state the problem.[1] The second problem concerns the identity or non-identity of physical events and mental events. The question is how one could set up criteria of identity of events. Many of the recent arguments defending or attacking physicalism have been centred around this problem.

This paper is only concerned with the first problem, the solution of which is presupposed in any answer to the second problem. Several interesting arguments relating to the second problem have been formulated in terms of the identity or non-identity of a physical-property universal with a mental-property universal which

[1] Wittengenstein, *Philosophical Investigations* (1969); Strawson, *Individuals* (1964).

applies to the *same logical subject*.[1] Other arguments have been put in terms of the identity or non-identity of the events of certain bodies or certain parts of the body being in a specific physical state with the event of a *person's having certain sensations or thoughts*.[2] I think it is well worth noticing that the specification of the second term in the supposed identity presumes a prior understanding of the criteria of personal identity. It presupposes the principle of collection for the mental experiences of one and the same person. (If not, one would have to specify the mental events as those causally related to the individual brain or body in question, in which case the identity thesis is in danger of becoming self-refuting.) So, before one raises the question of the identity of mental and physical events, one has in any case to try and clarify what exactly is involved in the concept of a person – the kind of being to which both physical and mental features can be ascribed.

Many sceptical opinions have been raised against the *primacy* of the concept of a person. And it is first of all important to make clear what it is to claim of a concept that it has primacy. Granted that human beings are very different from any other kind of animal, and granted that there are many predicates that are only true of human beings and of nothing else, why should this lead to the view that human beings belong to a special and totally unique category called persons? Why should there be a more fundamental difference between human beings and apes than, say, between apes and amoebae, between apes and worms, or even apes and cats? Certainly this does not seem to be the case if one is just concerned with the ownership of experiences by organisms. Why single out human beings and create a greater ontological gap between them and everything else, whether we call them persons and the rest material things, or call them *pour-soi* and the rest *en-soi*? Isn't this as absurdly anthropocentric a view as that of Descartes with his free-thinking substance, or Kant's view of the noumenal self? Professor Bernard Williams has convincingly pointed out the difficulties involved in holding that the primacy of the concept of person means that we can ascribe to a person not merely those predicates which we can apply to material bodies, but certain predicates which it would make *no sense* to ascribe to material bodies. (To claim that a dog decided to overcome his desires may be simply *false* rather than senseless, just as it may be to claim that a tree feels pain.)

[1] See, for instance, W. Sellars, in 'The Identity Approach to the Problem', in *Review of Metaphysics* (March 1965), who is sceptical about the value of formulating the problem in this way.

[2] Thomas Nagel, 'Physicalism', in *Philosophical Review* (July 1965), who is sympathetic to this way of stating the claim.

I believe, however, that the primacy of the concept of person is worth a stronger defence, and that the thesis can be defended independently of the question whether the non-application of certain mental predicates to things which are not human beings derives from the question of sense or of truth-value, and independently of the question whether there may not be greater ontological distinctions between different kinds of beings which are not humans than there are between humans and non-human animals. For there may be many other beings than men who are persons, and yet the set of persons may not be a subset of animals. It is not a logical absurdity to suppose that one could encounter man-made machines which need to be treated as persons. The concept of person might be primary in the sense that there was a whole huge cluster of predicates none of which we would understand unless we already had somehow grasped what a person is.

And in trying to understand the cluster of predicates, I want to take seriously the view implicit in the thought of Heidegger and Sartre that a man's relationship with his future states is essential to our understanding of what a person is.[1] In general, in the Anglo-Saxon philosophical world, discussions about mental criteria of personal identity from Locke to Shoemaker have been too much concerned with either the mere ownership of consciousness or with experiential and factual memory. It is logically possible to think of a person who at some given moment has total amnesia – a person who at a particular time has no factual memory of what he himself did previously. It is even possible to ascribe to him various character traits and psychological dispositions and habits which he acquired in the past and still retains, though not through experiential or factual memory. It might be difficult to see how someone who *always* suffered from total amnesia, i.e. someone who never recalled any of his past, could count as a person.[2]

Memory or apparent memory is scarcely, however, a sufficient condition of personal identity. It does not seem impossible for there to be human beings who inherit their parents' experiential and factual memory. What their parents remember doing, the children 'remember' doing in the first person; but they learn to distinguish their parents' and other ancestors' experience from their own by learning the biography of each person. But what is important is that they would still find it important to distinguish each as a different person because each would have adopted different moral attitudes,

---

[1] 'The primary meaning of existentiality is the future.' (Heidegger, *Being and Time* (1962) II 3, p. 376.)

[2] Cf. D. Wiggins, *Identity and Spatio-Temporal Continuity* (1967) p. 49.

or have chosen to realise different desires. In other words, the ownership of a certain amount of memory is necessary in order for a being to identify objects around him, and to count as a person, but the possession of thoughts about his future, and the possession of intentions which he executes, and which in various degrees are effective, seem to be what makes us take a special attitude towards him. And this attitude is presumably what one means when one talks of interpersonal relationships. I want to argue that a being who fails to think of any state of affairs in the future which he sets out to bring about, and has no awareness at any time of what he is doing which carries some reference to the future, cannot properly be described as a person. I believe that even when memory is important in the question of personal identity it is partly because we have memory of ourselves doing things to bring about things in the then future and memory of our failing or succeeding to bring them about. Memory provides us with past futures, and it is this which gives content to our understanding of ourselves as agents.

The claim that the concept of future is essential in the concept of a person might raise immediate suspicion and objections in many minds. A person who has a concept of himself as a person may die in the next instant and may even know that he will die in the next instant. Since this would not affect the knowledge he has of his identity, perhaps it might be thought that whatever else it depends on, our concept of ourselves as persons cannot depend on any understanding about our future. A person, it might be said, necessarily has a past since, without at least remembering some of his past, he would not come to grasp the kind of continuous existence he has; but it is entirely contingent whether he has a future. I reply that it is indeed obvious that a person may die at any given moment; but this does not make the possession of a future something as contingent as our possession of, say, a particular colour of hair. And my aim now is to show why it is not, and why this has relevance to the mind–body problem.

Why do I think I am the same person as the person whose existence began with the birth of my body? I probably can establish that my body is the same living organism, the same animal, as the one which was born on a particular date at a particular time. But can this exhaust the interest of the question?

Professor van Peursen has written that 'A good many thinkers equate the soul with the "I" – which in point of fact is exactly what we do in everyday speech.'[1] I am not sure whether some difficulties

[1] C. A. van Peursen, *Body, Soul, Spirit,* English ed., trans. H. H. Hoskins (1966) p.128.

have arisen because of discrepancies in Dutch and English usage, but this is a claim I do not quite follow. When I say 'I was born in Timbuktoo', 'I am ill', or 'I have lost weight', I am certainly not talking about the soul. It is not even certain that in claims about activities which might be most easily performed by a Cartesian disembodied soul, such as those reported by 'I am thinking about the mind – body problem', the word 'I' has to be taken to refer to a soul which would be the case if the soul and the 'I' are identical.

Ordinary language may in any case be misleading on this question. In 'I was born in Timbuktoo', or 'I am ill', or 'I have lost weight', for example, it would be odd in ordinary language if I were to replace 'I' with 'my body'. Yet it seems that the truth condition o¹ the above statements would be similar to the truth conditions of statements about, say, the birth, the unhealthy state or the loss of weight of a worm. And one may well argue that the worm is nothing more than the physical organism which *is* the live body. This is problematical, but at least if *A* and *B* are expressions which are used to refer to objects, and if replacing *A* in a sentence by *B* results in an odd sentence, then it cannot follow that the oddity in itself proves the non-identity of the referents of *A* and *B*. The oddity might come from certain contingent features of a particular language. In Japanese, for example, I cannot say that I – using the first-person pronoun – have pain, but only that my body has pain, although in Japanese I would say that I am standing and not that my body is standing.

So rather than investigate the assumptions behind the use of the word 'I', I will try to investigate what lies at the centre of our concept of person when we do so much as *raise* the question whether a person is or is not identical with or independent of the body. Can one retain, without religion, and with hard-headedness, the concept of a person? It does not, for example, seem to me that our having perceptions, sensations or memory, by itself, justifies our retaining an unambiguous concept of person.

We would certainly want to ascribe awareness of external things to most animals, and there seems to be no difficulty in *agreeing* to make the identity of a particular animal body both a necessary and sufficient condition for determining the identity of a stream of consciousness. But although the identification of a state of consciousness at any moment presupposes the identification of an animal which has it, the stream of consciousness need not be individuated in exactly the same way as the animal. Just as one could make many different films by cutting up a continuous reel, one can individuate a stream of consciousness in phases, even though the whole stream of consciousness was causally related in a special manner to *one* animal body. The long reel was causally related in a special kind of a way to one camera, but it was not necessary to individuate the film by the identity of the camera to which it has a special causal relation. (In this analogy I mean the cine-camera which is continuously filming from the moment it comes into being until the moment it breaks down, and the films made by the camera to stand to one another in the same relation as the human body stands to the stream of consciousness which is causally related to that human body.) It is therefore not of great help either to say that a person is a set of bodies which successively own the same stream of consciousness. For without memory having a privileged position, which I have denied it has, it seems impossible to individuate the stream of consciousness without reference to any body.

It seems that when we have any reason for *worrying* whether the criterion of personal identity coincides with that of bodily identity, we are thinking above all about the notion of agent. That is why recent investigations in the so-called 'split-brain' human (and animal) behaviour have led some philosophers to examine anew the concept of personal identity. Patients whose *corpus callosum* has been sectioned as treatment for epilepsy could – *under special experimental conditions* – be trained to learn different things in different halves of the body controlled by different hemispheres of the brain, for the normal process of transference of the learning acquired by one hemisphere to the other via the *corpus callosum* is no longer possible. The left hand can carry out acts which the patient learnt through instructions flashed in the right half of the visual field, and the right hand can carry out acts that cancel it based on instructions flashed in the left half of the visual field. Pucetti concludes, for example, 'Thus all the evidence is for two independent spheres of consciousness created by separation of the cerebral hemispheres with two centres of learning, emotional response and so on'.[1] But, as I will come back to later, the problem seems much more complicated than Pucetti indicates. An awareness of an agent is not the same as a mind's awareness of the world around it, or even of its own states at any given moment. We do not always know why (or following what information) we are acting. We also sometimes carry out self-destructive acts or a set of mutually contradictory acts. So the existence of such facts does not of itself make us conclude that there is another agent embodied in our body. But are we right?

We assume that the criterion of identity of an agent is that which gives us the principle of collection of acts the responsibility for which

[1] *Analysis* (Jan. 1969).

is ascribable to that agent. We do not think that this identity is a matter of convention. We must see however whether our assumption has any basis.

How does a man know himself as an agent? Professor Stuart Hampshire writes, in *Thought and Action*:

> There is one continuing object about the existence and identifying features of which he (a person) is never in doubt and which he can always use as a fixed point of reference: himself. However uncertain he may be in referring to things in his environment, he can always identify himself as the man who is doing, or trying to do, so-and-so. He is aware of himself as the centre from which all his perceptions radiate, and he is aware that, as he moves or is moved, his perspective changes.[1]

But does the peculiarity of a person's self-knowledge lie in the fact that he can always identify himself as the man who is doing, or trying to do, so-and-so? It is possible to identify another person as the man who is doing or trying to do a particular act – as when I am told that Pierre Boulez is the man who is conducting the symphony on the stage. So obviously it isn't the case that I am the only person whom I myself can identify by picking out the person who is doing a particular act. Nor is it the case that I stand in a privileged position to myself and that I can always pick myself out as a person who is uniquely doing a particular act at a particular moment, whereas I can only do so on certain occasions with other people. It is therefore misleading to say that I can identify myself *as* the man who is doing so-and-so (although, as I will argue later, Hampshire points towards an important truth). It is rather that there is no question of my identifying myself among many people who are doing various acts now. Strictly speaking, there is no question of my identifying my present self, as Kant has correctly realised. It is because of this that I know what I am doing, not vice versa. When I am writing this sentence I do not identify myself *as* the person writing this sentence. On the contrary I know directly that *I* am writing this sentence because for *me* there is no question of how to identify *myself*. Thus although it might be true (with certain qualifications to be discussed later) that I know what I am doing or am trying to do, I do not identify myself *as* the person who is doing or trying to do a particular act. My knowledge of the identity of myself cannot come *after* my knowledge of what I am doing. I want to suggest that my knowledge of what I am doing or trying to do presupposes a view about my

[1] *Thought and Action* (1959) pp. 68-9.

personal identity which is inseparable from a notion about my bodily continuity in the future.

I am aware, for example, that I am writing a paper on the mind – body problem. And, as Sartre says, I know this not only when I think about myself, but when I am simply thinking about what I am doing, i.e. about the words and sentences that I am writing. I know this because I know the connection of the particular sets of acts I am carrying out and a state of affairs in the future which I intend to bring about by my acts. I grasp and direct my present acts in terms of these states of affairs in the future. I do not know what I am doing on the basis of the observation of what happened in the immediate past. And if I were suddenly to die now, or if some catastrophe arose which stopped me from continuing my activity, it would not become false that I had been writing a paper on the mind–body problem – for a correct description of my action carries a reference to my intention.

In brief, if I am aware of myself as an agent by being aware of what I am doing, and if the correct description of what I am doing carries a reference to a future state of affairs which I am trying to bring about, then my understanding of myself as an agent seems to involve a reference to the future. A future which might not exist for the agent, but which has to be assumed by him to exist. Hence the concept of an agent necessarily carries a reference to the possible future – where the agent subsists and continues to carry out the action in time.

I want now to examine two assumptions which I have just made in formulating these arguments, which require clarification and justification. The first assumption is also made by many philosophers who have argued about intentions: viz., that we have a direct non-observational knowledge of our actions such that in doing something we necessarily know what we are doing under *some* description. The second assumption I shall examine concerns the bodily continuation in the future which lies at the basis of the notion of myself as an agent who will carry out some action in time, and which is indispensable to my intention to bring about any state of affairs in the future.

The first assumption requires various qualifications. In the chapter 'Avoir, Faire et Être', in *L'Être et le Néant*, Sartre argues that knowledge of what we do is dependent on the knowledge of our conscious projects which we know directly. For Sartre a piece of behaviour is an action only if it was done by a person 'intentionally to realise a project of which he was aware'.[1] People might object that

---

[1] Sartre, *L'Être et le Néant* (1943) p. 508.

by Sartre's criterion actions would be only a tiny fraction of what we would want to say that men do. We do not usually have any conscious project when we tap the table with our fingers, or chew our food. I will not take up this objection because, although what it claims is true, it is not very important. I think that it is precisely because of the existence of the small class of actions captured by Sartre's definition that people are led to discuss the question of personal identity in a way which makes it not the same question as the identity of animals. And Sartre writes quite correctly that when a man knows what he does, he knows not in the sense of knowing all the things which might be achieved or be happening as a consequence of his behaviour, but in the sense of being aware of a project or aim which gives sense to what the man is doing. According to Sartre, when a man knows his project, he knows it directly.

But in what way is this awareness different from the awareness we have of things we observe around us and in us? From the awareness a person may have of phenomena he perceives or of his sensations? Even if intentions are not the kind of thing one observes, can't it still be the case that a man knows his own intention by inference from something given to him in the present? For I can observe a leak in the pool and describe what is happening as the pool draining itself by *inferring* the ensuing state of affairs, but this does not mean that I have a direct knowledge of the future state of affairs which is the 'goal' of the changes taking place in the pool. So what is special about the agent's knowledge of his action? As we know, Sartre is insistent that people do not know their aims and projects in the way they know psychological facts by observing data, nor by inductive inference from data. But in what sense aren't they known as psychological facts? In the sense, presumably, in which when I am crossing the road I do not come to know that I am crossing the road by some inner observation of psychological facts which tell me what my purpose is.

It might be objected that even if projects are not data, motives are psychological data; and these can be empirically discussed. Sartre does say that if an act is done for a purpose, then the person has a motive. So wouldn't it follow that I can know what I am doing by observing and discovering my motives and inferring what my purpose is? For example, if motives are like desires, can't I focus my attention on them, as I might on a toothache, attempt a correct description of them, and then make a hypothesis about the aim of my present action? (If this is so, the whole point about the irreducible relation between the concept of future and the awareness of an agent disappears.) Sartre claims I cannot, because he believes that the way a person identifies his motive for doing a certain act presupposes his knowledge of his intentions and not vice versa. For example, I discover I am motivated by revenge by becoming aware that I intend to hurt the person who injured me. 'A motive has to be experienced *as* a motive.'[1] Of course a person can be mistaken about his motives, and come to find out what his true motives were. But this is because he realises that he was misdescribing his actions to himself. By finding out a more correct description of what he was intentionally doing, by finding out the aim or point of his acts, he identifies his motives. And so we are back at the knowledge an agent has of his intention, i.e. the thought with which he does what he does. An agent is aware from within, as it were, of its aims and projects – a knowledge inseparable from the awareness he has of what he is doing as a physical being.

This is not too far from Kant's way of singling out the uniqueness of human beings. In contrast with everything else in nature which is simply rule-governed, men alone have the ability to follow or not follow laws, and act according to the principles which they choose. It must be noticed that this is somewhat different from the Wittgensteinian claim that one knows what he does intentionally without observation in the sense that he directly knows a description under which he does it.[1] Even when a person knows a description under which he carried out an act, it does not follow, as I have already pointed out, that the description always carries a reference to any projected future state. (Professor Melden even suggests that the reason why the concept of rule-following is important in understanding action is because talk about choices and ends has led philosophers to ignore actions which are not done out of deliberate choices, not with any specific end in view.)

Why then have I reverted to the Sartrian talk about our projects and the future rather than adopt the concept of rule-following? The reason is the following. When I do something with an aim, I know my aim without observation but I do not always know what I do. The awareness I have of following a rule is, as Melden says, not an observational one; I am not always *aware* of following a rule when I act. Thus the concept of rule-following does not by itself guarantee that when I act I know what I am doing under some description without observation. I might not even know what would count as following the relevant rules. If I were doing mathematics, or if I were speaking a language, or playing chess, then even if I could not

1 Ibid., p. 512.
2 For example, A. I. Melden, G. E. Anscombe, A. Kenny, Charles Taylor and also perhaps Richard Taylor.

explicitly state the rules of mathematics, grammar or chess, at least someone could formulate the rules, and my action could be said to consist in behaving in accordance with the rules or failing to obey the rules. But since I hardly ever speak just in order to utter a bit of language, my knowledge of grammar would not give the awareness I have of what I am saying, and what I am doing in saying it. And when I paint or set out to annoy someone, although what I do can be understood (even for myself) only in the context of certain practices, as Wittgenstein would have it, it is not clear what the rules are which I am or am not following. The introduction of the concept of rules does not make it more easy for me to have a direct knowledge of what I do.

As has been pointed out by some philosophers, I can often fail to know what I am doing.[1] Suppose I take a pen to write a particular pun, but my ink has run out and nothing is written on the paper. What do I know without observation in this case? It cannot be that I know that I was writing that pun, since I cannot have known what was not the case. Perhaps I know that I was trying to write the pun. But this should not be taken in the sense of my deliberating on what I should write. I was carrying out a physical act. I moved my hand with which I held my pen. But the way I moved my hand depended on my thought of the pun which I wanted to write, and my knowledge of how to write. What I did, or rather the movement I carried out, was, in a sense, exactly the same as what I should have done had I succeeded in writing the pun on paper. Our language of 'doing' usually involves the specification of what was done in terms of the consequences achieved, and we do not always have appropriate verbs to express what I did do when by some unexpected causal lapse the normal consequences were not achieved. So what I do know without observation when I do something is that I am engaged in carrying out the kind of act that I would carry out in normal circumstances when I succeed in carrying out the action. In the cases mentioned above, I carry out the physical act which I believe brings about a certain state of affairs. To assess whether I have succeeded or not in doing it I must observe. Which is to say that when I do something, what I know without observation is the intended result of my action. But I do not necessarily know without observation *what I actually do* under any description. I know I am writing a paper on the mind–body problem partly because I know without observation my *intention* in doing what I am doing, but partly also because I know by observation that I am not failing to do so. Sartre seems to be right, then, to claim that what I know *directly*

[1] Cf. e.g. Keith Donnellan, 'Knowing What I am Doing', *Journal of Philosophy* (1963).

is my conscious intention in doing something, rather than *what* I am doing. (Professor Melden has written that when someone asks me 'Do you know what you have done?' the affirmative answer I give is in no way predicated upon any observation I may have made. But as I have said, the affirmative answer I give is also based on knowing by observation that I am succeeding in doing what I intend to do. If my answer is in error, it could be that I had not observed what I had done and did not realise that I did not do what I intended to do.)

What seems to distinguish a person is that he is often aware of his intention in doing something – not only in terms of results that can be obtained simultaneously with his execution of the act (as in eating, scratching, which might well be shared by primitive animals which we would not often see the importance of calling persons) but also in terms of states of affairs in the future which he attempts to bring about and which he knows from experience that he will succeed in various degrees. He not merely predicts his future, he contributes towards bringing it about. That is why he can 'take' a moral attitude.

I must now examine the second assumption which I mentioned and which relates to my bodily continuation in the future. It might be said that even granting that I am often aware of myself as an agent doing something which I believe has reference to the future, I need only assume that I am a *mental* agent who will continue to exist in the future, and achieve or fail to achieve the various things that I am now doing by causing my body to do various things. But can I? When I carry out an act with an intention, the intention is not a kind of mental effort which I can identify or specify independently of the action. My knowledge of my intention does not depend on any awareness of such effort. Of course I can deliberate whether I should carry out a particular act before I do it, and be aware of a desire to do a certain act before I do anything – but, as it has been often said, such deliberations, and such prior awareness of one's desires are not necessary in order for me to act intentionally. Nor is the existence in me of an intention to do φ followed by my φing sufficient to make what I did an act done with the intention to φ. I may intend to injure a man and then fall down the steps injuring the man by accident. Thus my awareness as an agent does not consist in my awareness of the situation plus an awareness of a mental effort which is distinct in quality whenever it accompanies a different act, and something whose existence would provide a necessary and sufficient condition for the occurrence of the act. Thus I cannot reproduce the purely mental state of intending to do a particular act φ and hope that somebody or other will carry out the act φ following my intentions. Acting with an intention is not like wishing. When I intentionally write a pun, and when I tear a piece of paper, the difference in the intentions I had in doing these acts does not consist in different mental states detachable from the physical acts. I can only know what it is to do φ intentionally by learning to do the kind of act φ is. I have often intended to do things in the past and observed what I could bring about or failed to bring about. I noticed what was happening around me as I did these things. Even for extremely simple acts like moving one's fingers, which one normally knows without observation, I learnt what it was to manipulate them by observing the success of my action – by seeing them move as I moved them, or, if I was blind, by the sense of touch.

I am not merely saying that a person does not succeed in doing what he intends unless he has observed the results of his attempts to do similar things in the past. I am saying that I cannot know what I am doing in the sense of acting with the intention of φing, as distinct from ψing, without having observed myself in action in the causal world. The way in which I envisage and set out to bring things about forces me to treat myself as an individual physical object causally related to other objects in this world. It is not merely that in order to assign temporal existence to myself I have to pre-suppose something permanent in the world I perceive and from which I distinguish myself, as Kant has said. If I think of myself not as one distinct perceiving mind but as an agent, then not only must I distinguish myself from the objects in the world, I must also treat myself as one such enduring thing which causally interacts with those objects in the world. Even the split-brain patient behaves as one person in normal circumstances, and does not seem to have special problems about his personal identity. This is not merely because, being creatures who turn around, the environment of our left perceptive organs and right perceptive organs are very similar, and there is very little different information stored in the left hemisphere and the right hemisphere even when the *corpus callosum* is cut. It is rather, it would seem, because, in carrying out most acts, whether it be crossing the road, leading a student revolt or obsessively collecting Egyptian pots, it is the whole body of the person which is involved in carrying out the act, and very seldom just a left or right limb. Thus, for most acts, it is the whole body of the person, which also takes a stand in the world and meets obstacles – and of course both hemispheres of the brain store these experiences. Thus, two centres of consciousness would not seem to develop as easily as it has been claimed. The unity of body has a much deeper relevance to agency.

It might be objected here that although it is true that in order to be aware of myself as a physical agent I must have the same body for some time, I need not think of myself as having the same persisting body in the future, in order for me to be aware of acting with the intention of bringing about something in the future.[1] I have already argued earlier that one does not identify oneself or one's body in order to know that one is doing something. It would then seem that the awareness one has of continuing and finishing a task in the future does not depend on being aware of the subsistence of oneself as the same physical body which carries on the act. Could I not intend to carry out an action without committing myself to any belief about whether the physical body which will carry out the act is identical with the physical being which I know myself to have now?

I think that a careful examination will show unexpected difficulties in such suppositions. Let us first take a very simple example. Suppose I am standing on a pavement and take a step intending to cross the road. Could I make sense of what I am doing if I did not suppose that the same bodily agent was to begin crossing the road and end crossing the road? What would it be to begin crossing the road as one physical agent, suddenly discover that one has a *numerically* different body (not simply a drastically altered body as in Kafka's *Metamorphosis*, but, for example, notice that a body which looks exactly like my own recent body is following just behind me, as I walk on), and finish crossing the road? It seems that one cannot coherently think of such examples without reverting to a theory of Cartesian disembodied souls which operate on bodies, and which as a corollary allows mindless live bodies to come into being at times.

It might be objected that this difficulty only arises because the action of crossing a road is a simple one which does not involve different sub-actions. If, for example, I were setting out to rob a bank on the other side, I could break down my act into, e.g. crossing the road, opening the door of the bank, thrusting a gun at the accountant, grabbing the money and fleeing, and, it might be said, when I begin crossing the road to rob the bank I am not committed to any belief that *I* who will carry out all these steps have the same body. I do not claim to have worked out fully the defence of my position. But it seems that our awareness of ourselves as continuously existing agents depends on the awareness we have as continuous causally interacting items in the world. Of course I can imagine myself undergoing radical physical changes – e.g. becoming physically handicapped and not being able to carry out the kinds of

[1] A point raised to me by Mr D. Parfit.

projects I had – and yet be quite clear that I am the same agent. But in all those imaginary cases of brain transplants, one cannot just transpose intact the awareness we have of our identity as one bodily agent. I would have to give sense to what I mean by grasping myself as an *identical* agent through time without assuming that I have the same body. That some bodily agent continued to carry out a plan originally intended by another does not by itself prove that they are the same agent, even if he appears to have 'memories' of the other's experiences.

I will thus not interest myself in the notion of 'person' which would still hold in an imaginary world radically different from our own. It is in this world where we must justify and make clear what we mean by persons, these beings to which we ascribe moral attitudes and with which we assume we can enter in interpersonal relationships.

A person is someone who can often be aware of himself as an agent, and knows that he is acting with the intention of bringing about a certain state of affairs. I have tried to show that this entails that a person is a physical agent, one who is giving direction and shape to the act he carries out in terms of a state of affairs he intends to bring about in the future, and assumes his bodily continuity in the future. He knows what such intentions are because he observes that he can, in many cases, do things with his body which he wants to do. What I am is not only related in a special way to what happened to me, but more to what I brought about and what I am bringing about – i.e. to all these multiple actions and projects of various duration which overlap in time in the past, present and future. My stream of consciousness cannot be divided up into arbitrary time chunks (as a reel of film can be) to make up different persons, because I cannot arbitrarily divide up the continuous overlapping effects of what I brought about and what I am bringing about in the same body. It is not strange, then, that the criteria of personal identity more or less coincide with those of bodily identity, although the concept of a person is different from that of a body, or of a live body, or of a conscious body.

Thus even Sartre, with his excessively dualistic vocabulary, writes that '*l'âme est le corps en tant que le pour-soi est sa propre individuation*'.[1] Like Kant, Sartre distinguished the empirical self – the self that I know through observation about my bodily features or psychological data – the self which I can describe retrospectively in an autobiography, and the *pour-soi*, the self which I grasp without observation as a free agent; but at least Sartre did not relegate

[1] Sartre, *L'Être et le Néant*, p. 372.

choice to a non-empirical world. Kant had left no way of identifying the two, but as a matter of fact any understanding of what it is to be an agent, and any grasp of what it is to have a project, is given to us in the causal and physical (Kant's phenomenal) world. It is the subsisting body which gives sense to my having knowledge of my action, i.e. of the intention with which I do anything and of myself as an agent. And although concepts such as 'projects' and 'reference to the future' can only be grasped in the causal physical world in which we discover ourselves as agents, they give a new dimension to the knowledge or description of actions as distinct from those of bodily movements. This does not, of course, lead to the view that only human beings *could* be persons, or that they are the only persons.

13

A REPLY TO
'A PERSON'S FUTURE AND
THE MIND–BODY PROBLEM'

C. A. van Peursen

1. The paper presented by Miss Ishiguro offers a reasonable approach to – even a way out from – the mind – body problem. It combines certain methods of British philosophy (e.g. the analysis of the logical priority of the concept of 'person') with those of Continental philosophy (e.g. the more phenomenological analysis of the future-dimension of human existence).

1.1. The first group of theses starts from the necessity to presuppose 'identity' of the human person (the sameness of person – identity) in order to discuss the eventual identity, of physical (φ) and mental (ψ) events (the mind – body problem as identity). The paper concentrates on identity, and defends the primacy of the concept of 'person' by defining the human person through his relation to the future.

1.2. A second group of theses results from the previous ones. The concept of the person, as an agent intentionally directed towards states of affairs in the future, implies that a non-observational knowledge of what we do is possible. (Sartre's position is mentioned with approval.) This means that one need not base the identity of the person on the awareness criterion. Neither is the other criterion, that of bodily continuity, a presupposition required for the identity of a person, as in this case it is implied in it. I can only know what intention is by learning to do things as a physical agent. So, in a very elegant way, Miss Ishiguro's paper leads from the identity of the person to the identity of ψ events and φ events. (For instance, to specify the intention of writing a pun is to refer to physical phenomena.)

2. These theses find further specification by the rejection of some other ways of approaching the mind – body problem.

2.1. The concept of rule-following as criterion in understanding action (Wittgenstein and others) is not sufficient. It is often not clear to the person as agent what type of rule he is following in bringing about new states of affairs.

2.2. It is not very useful either, to investigate the assumptions behind the use of the word 'I'. Here a passing critical reference should be made to the example Miss Ishiguro gives in this connection, as this example relates to my book *Body, Soul, Spirit*. I think she is correct in stating that, in saying 'I', one is not, generally, referring to one's soul. The thesis defended in *Body, Soul, Spirit*, however, was quite different: (*a*) with many philosophers, and often in daily language, the word 'soul' refers to the I; (*b*) the book itself defended, against theses (*a*), the claim that both the mental and the physical are one-sided objectifications. They have, I maintained, both their presupposition and their possible integration in the human 'I' as the total acting and orientating human existence. But this critical remark on the exemplification of thesis 2.2. does not, as such, touch the thesis itself.

3. The two main theses meet with difficulties that need more extended elaboration. The aim of this paper will not be a kind of refutation of Miss Ishiguro's paper, which contains, as has been said, many valuable suggestions. By stressing some of the difficulties in this paper, I shall only try to offer some amendments or to suggest a slightly different approach.

3.1. The Cartesian view of man gives the criterion of self-consciousness, of introspection, for the identity of man. This fails in two respects. It brings about a sharp distinction between the mental and the physical without the further possibility of convincing arguments for the unity of man. The link between soul and body is not established until afterwards. Secondly, it implies the logical and factual isolation of human self-awareness which makes its relationship to other minds as well as to the world of daily activities disputable. A more voluntaristic approach is to overcome these difficulties by defining man as an intentional being, related to future states of affairs. In this way one renounces criteria like memory, self-consciousness, etc., which might lead to isolation of the mental. This means, in many respects, a fruitful restriction to the correct description of what somebody is doing with reference to a future state of affairs.

3.1. The difficulty here, however, is the opposite of the Cartesian one: will a mere external criterion, like this one, be sufficient? Does it imply that an extreme behaviouristic description of acts related to the future indicates the identity of a living being? Animal behaviour expecially that of instinct, can often only correctly be described by a reference to future states of affairs to be brought about. Any mention of extra factors risks the reintroduction of Cartesian introspective notions (unless the concept of a rule is used as a distinctive factor, as will be explained in 4.1.).

3.2. The notion of intentional behaviour might overcome the difficulties connected with a purely external criterion that could lead to a physicalist type of description (as perhaps is possible – although even this is disputed among biologists – with respect to animal instinctive behaviour). 'Intentional' has to be taken here in the sense of phenomenology: consciousness in itself does not exist, since consciousness is always consciousness *of* something (Husserl). This implies that the structure of the intended object (e.g. a perceived house, a remembered event, a mathematical proposition) manifests always specific acts of consciousness. Or, in G. Ryle's description of Husserl's intentionality: 'to every piece of mental functioning there is intrinsically correlative something which is the "accusative" (*Gegenstand*) of that functioning'. The same conception, but within an existentialist framework, can be found in the earlier work of J.-P. Sartre: it is not by isolated description nor by Cartesian introspective knowledge that human consciousness comes about.

The problem now is, whether one can defend the thesis of a non-observational knowledge of oneself as agent (1.2.) along Sartrian lines without assuming the more metaphysical theses that Sartre himself presupposes. The difference between a more 'objectivist' (e.g. behaviourist or physicalist) analysis of intended projects and a more 'subjectivist' (e.g. phenomenological, existentialist or neo-Marxist) analysis of projects as the intentional 'accusative' of human acts is that the former is concerned with facts, the latter with 'meaning', i.e. the ways in which things are taken as this or that (e.g. as desirable or not desirable, according to the perspectives of intended projects). This 'meaning' is, as it were, constituted or projected by the subject. And this is only possible if the human subject (*existence*) accomplishes a kind of negativity (*néant*) in the objectively given world. 'Action implies necessarily . . . an objective deficiency (*manqué*) or even a negativity (*négativité*).[1]

It is, I think, an advantage in Miss Ishiguro's paper that she does not endorse either this thesis or the correlated ones of Sartre: pure freedom of choice giving meaning to meaningless reality and pure subjectivity of consciousness as non-being (*néant*) over and against

[1] *L'Être et le Néant*, p. 508.

opaque reality (*être*). For this results in a new kind of Cartesian dualism, this time between *pour-soi* and *en-soi*. However, the question remains whether, if one rejects the too metaphysical consequences of Sartre's analysis of 'consciousness' and 'meaning', it is possible to avoid reducing 'intentions' and 'states of affairs in the future' to mere facts (empirical data, *données*).

4. An effort will be made to escape the difficulties mentioned (3.1. and 3.2.). The principal theses of Miss Ishiguro's paper will be maintained. But this will be done by making use, in a positive way, of approaches she rejects (2.1: 'rules'; 2.2: the 'I'). In this line the numbers 1.1., 2.1., 3.1. and 4.1. correspond to each other, as also do the numbers 1.2., 2.2. and so on.

4.1. The notion of following a rule can be used as a good, although perhaps provisional, model for the identity of man, as well as for the identity of mental and physical approaches to human behaviour. A first advantage is the distinction between following a rule where the understanding of meaning is implied, and the reference to past and future states of affairs along lines of mere causal influence. Two quotations will exemplify well-known explanations of 'rules'. *Wittgenstein:* 'The prophecy does not run, that a man will get this result when he follows this rule in making a transformation – but that he will get this result, when we say that he is following the rule.[1] *P. Winch:* 'It is only because human actions exemplify rules that we can speak of past experience as relevant to our current behaviour. If it were merely a question of habits, then our current behaviour might certainly be *influenced* by the way in which we had acted in the past: but that would be just a causal influence.'[2]

Rules can serve as patterns for analysing human intentional behaviour, even in cases where the acting subject does not know himself exactly what rules are involved. M. Polanyi states that 'the aim of a skilful performance is achieved by the observance of a set of rules which are not known as such to the person following them'.[3] It is clear that following a rule is a provisional model in the sense that, after further elaboration, it can only become a good discrimating criterion when the invariance of the rule is 'pragmatically' related to the identity of the human person. The distinction between syntactic, semantic and pragmatic rules, following Charles Morris, can be of much help in the analysis of the meaning of human intentional behaviour. For this behaviour is interrelated with the total cultural horizon, which is not instinctively given but historically

---

[1] *Remarks on the Foundations of Mathematics* (1956) p. 94.
[2] *The Idea of a Social Science* (1958) p. 62.
[3] *Personal Knowledge* (1962) p. 49.

intended and pragmatically brought about. (Cf. Wittgenstein's 'forms of life', Husserl's 'Life-World'.) H. Feigl, writing on the mental and the physical, says 'that the very link of the intersubjective language with the experience of the "knowing subjects" who use that language is given by the pragmatic context of their utterances'. Various authors of differing philosophical orientation try to analyse rule-following as a tool for gaining wider control over the surrounding world together with establishing the identity of the human person (e.g. J. Piaget).

4.2. Rules relate an acting person to the group or culture to which he belongs. He identifies himself within those rules as someone who can follow or not follow rules. He situates himself as a subject to whom the word 'I' refers. This is never either a body describable in purely physical terms or a pure individual consciousness. It is the presupposition of any objectification of mental or physical aspects.

Idealism tends to reduce objectivity to the subject, positivism to reduce subjectivity to the object. It has hitherto seemed impossible to produce a complete translation of terms of subjectivity into those of objectivity. Therefore it seems wise, at any rate on behalf of a comprehensive theory about the identity of man, to safeguard this correlation between subject and object. (It need not be repeated that the subject cannot be identified with the soul or the mental; the mental and the physical are both objective, secondary categories for description.) This correlation is a methodological one and must not result in a kind of metaphysical description (like *pour-soi* and *en-soi*). But this implies that the human 'I', indicating the identity of the person, must find its translation within the structures of the various sciences. It is no use having a philosophy of mind and body that does not act as a possible integration of scientific information and theories.

5. Philosophical discussion about body and mind has often been too remote from scientific research. New developments in the fields of the formal sciences, natural sciences, sciences of life, behavioural and social sciences present us with a flood of new information. In addition they present us with new theoretical approaches to their fields of research in such a way that new possibilities for the application and readjustment of a more philosophical conceptual analysis become manifest. A few instances of this will be mentioned here; they represent tasks to be performed rather than results already achieved. The purpose of this list is a restricted one: to show the possibilities for further philosophical investigation of the mind – body problem, as well as the way in which both themes dealt with (no. 1 and no. 2) in the previous paragraphs are interrelated and even shade off into one another.

5.1. In the field of the formal sciences one of the most interesting – and most difficult – discussions is about the theorem of K. Gödel concerning the impossibility of proving, within a formal system, the consistency of that system (i.e. to prove it without the help of a meta-system). The relationship of this problem ('rules') with that of the self-identification (the 'I') of man has been indicated by various authors, such as W. Bridgman, G. Freyx and J. Ladrière. The last-named mathematician refers to these limits of formalisation as the impossibility of self-referential systems. The question has been posed, by these authors and others, whether the human 'I' – perhaps at the same time also the human brain – cannot be defined as a system possessing this possibility.

5.2. In the field of the natural sciences the relationship between the field of research and the observer, methodologically between object and subject, has been stressed now for many years. This has been done particularly by the Copenhagen School (Bohr, Weizsächer, Heisenberg): natural sciences are not concerned with an independent nature, but with the various relations between the human observer and the phenomena.

5.3. In the field of the sciences of life, information theory has offered new methods of formulating rules for the measurement of genetic information. The increase of information in the course of evolution goes hand in hand with an increase in organisation. The category of 'uniqueness'. could thus be applied, in a scientifically justified way, to the increase of evolution-capacity (Medawar). Other biologists, such as Thorpe, distinguish in higher animals between the more centralised rules of behaviour and the central nervous system in animals.

5.4. In the field of the behavioural sciences one finds an extensio·. of this type of analysis. Human experience (the mental) and human behaviour (the physical) can be translated into a hierarchy of rules: processes of learning. Many authors, of divergent schools, are of the opinion that human learning, in distinction from animal learning, shows an increasing variety of 'strategies', by which man as subject gains a wider control over the surrounding world (similar concepts, e.g. in neurophysiological research, game theory, etc.).

5.5. In the social sciences, linguistics and history, concepts come to the fore that also point in the direction of a possible relationship between rules and the identification of an acting subject, and this as a kind of grammar for both mental and physical descriptions. C. Lévi-Strauss writes, for instance, that the human mind can be analysed under objective structures constituted by the reciprocal operations of the mind of the investigator and that of the group to be studied (respectively: the subject and the object of the research).

5.6. In presenting these cases, I do not at all pretend to have given a survey of new developments in various disciplines. They only give some possible clues for further investigation into the subjects referred to in the main paragraphs (1-4). They can, therefore, only serve as illustrations for the necessary interrelationship between scientific information and philosophical method, on the one hand, and, on the other, the main themes concerning 'body and mind' which have come to the fore in contemporary philosophy (no. 1 and no. 2).

14

CHAIRMAN'S
OPENING REMARKS

P. F. Strawson

MISS ISHIGURO raises or alludes to a number of issues in her paper, and Professor van Peursen raises or alludes to a great many more. I could not hope to review them all adequately in these opening remarks, even if I were competent to do so. So instead, since Professor van Peursen seems to be in general sympathy with Miss Ishiguro's central line of argument, I shall confine myself to some comments on that central line of argument. I am in sympathy with it myself, so my function will be expository rather than critical. If I am guilty of misrepresentation or misinterpretation, I hope Miss Ishiguro will correct me.

Miss Ishiguro undertakes to argue in favour of the primacy of the concept of a person from the nature of intentional action. That is to say, she seeks to establish that the concept of intentional action has a certain character, and that from the fact that the concept of intentional action has this character it follows that the concept of a person has the primacy which is sometimes attributed to it.

Now of course it will be important, in considering her argument, to be clear what Miss Ishiguro has in mind when she speaks of the primacy of the concept of a person. I think it is clear that by a *person* she means, *inter alia*, something that is, not just contingently, but essentially, embodied; something that, not just contingently, but essentially, has corporeal characteristics and is in various physical states at various times. And I think it is also clear that one of the things she has in mind in speaking of the *primacy* of the concept of a person is what might be called an anti-Cartesian point about the *relation* between the concept of an individual person on the one hand

and the concept of an individual (personal) mind or soul or consciousness on the other. I think she holds that the former concept (that of a person) has primacy *over* the latter concept (that of a mind or consciousness) or is logically *prior to* it; or, if you like, that the latter concept is logically *secondary to*, or *derivative from*, the former. And I call this point an anti-Cartesian point because of course accepting it involves *rejecting* the Cartesian view that the concept of a person (say, a human being) is a certain sort of logical compound of the two simpler concepts of an individual soul and an individual body. On this Cartesian view you indeed normally have one item of each sort standing in a peculiarly intimate relationship in the case of each person; but the *concepts* of each sort of item are capable of logical exposition independently *both* of each other *and* of the notion of the sort of union of one item of each sort which you normally get in the case of a human being. Evidently, you must reject this view altogether if you hold that the concept of an individual (personal) mind or consciousness is logically secondary to that of an individual person.

But though I think Miss Ishiguro would probably agree that this anti-Cartesian point is what she has mainly in mind in speaking of the primacy of the concept of a person, I think she has certain reservations about the effectiveness, or the exact bearing, of some of the arguments that are often used in support of the anti-Cartesian point. These arguments often turn on problems about the identity, and the identification, of particular things, especially, of course, of particular subjects of experiences or states of consciousness. They tend to show that the criteria of *distinctness* and *identity* for a particular individual consciousness must have the secondary or derivative character that the anti-Cartesian point requires them to have. But I think Miss Ishiguro feels that it is not clear that such arguments in general have a particular relevance to *persons* or to *personal* consciousness rather than to the wider class of, say, sentient beings, which, unlike Descartes, we are inclined to think of as including non-human animals. And I think it is possible that she might want to go further than this and say that once we see such general arguments as applying to conscious beings at large, including non-human animals, then we can no longer see them as doing for us quite what we wanted done in the case of persons. For we wanted to be able to exhibit the way in which the criteria of identity and numerability for personal minds or souls were logically secondary to, or derivative from, those for persons by means of the simple rule of derivation: *one* person, *one* personal soul or consciousness; *same* person, *same* personal soul or consciousness. But it is not clear that we should want to adopt the same rule in the case, say, of cats and crickets: to say *same* cat, *same* feline consciousness; or *same* cricket, *same* cricket-soul.

I have some doubts of my own about these further doubts that I have attributed to Miss Ishiguro: doubts about whether I am correct in attributing them to her and doubts about whether they are correct or – if correct – whether they are of any real importance. But even if these further doubts of hers don't really matter much, we are left with the point that, as it seems, some of the standard arguments for the anti-Cartesian point are not really or specifically arguments in favour of the primacy of the concept of a *person* over that of an individual personal consciousness, but, rather, more general arguments in favour of the primacy of the concept of an essentially embodied subject of consciousness of any kind over that of a pure individual consciousness of that kind.

In the face of this point, or these points, Miss Ishiguro, I think, adopts the following strategy. There is, she holds, a certain class of predicates which are *essentially* applicable, and *peculiarly* applicable, to persons. If the anti-Cartesian point can be shown to follow from the notion of *predicates* of this *class*, then we shall indeed have an argument which can properly be described as an argument for the primacy of the concept of a *person*. For to anything which could count as a person, some predicates of this class must truly apply, and anything to which any predicates of this class truly apply must count as a person. So the argument will both be sufficient for its purpose and will apply to nothing but persons. The general form the argument must take is also, I think, clear. If the Cartesian view were correct, then it should in principle be possible to effect a Cartesian reduction of all predicates which are applicable to persons: *either* such a predicate could be immediately classified as purely mental or as purely corporeal *or* it could be analysed into two components, one purely mental component and one purely corporeal component with, perhaps, some account of a causal relation between the components. If such a reduction can be shown to be impossible in the case of the class of predicates in question, then the anti-Cartesian point is established and established specifically for persons.

The predicates in question, of course, are those used in ascribing intentional actions to human beings – intentional actions of the kind which essentially involve an externally observable change or movement of the body of the agent and which may, of course, involve much else as well by way of physical or social outcomes. By means of such actions we enter into interpersonal relations and qualify as moral beings. And the possession and the realisation of the capacity for such relations and such a status are necessary and sufficient conditions for being a person.

How, then, does the argument go? Of course the fact that actions of the kind in question essentially involve the body is not sufficient in itself to establish the anti-Cartesian point. For this fact by itself does not rule out the possibility of a Cartesian reduction of the concept of such action or of the predicates ascribing such actions. How, then, would the Cartesian reduction go, and what account would the reductionist give of the agent's knowledge of what he was doing in performing an intentional action? Well, the Cartesian reductionist, it seems, would have to say that the action-ascribing predicate or the action-concept in question was analysable into two components, one mentalistic, specifying the intention, and the other physicalistic, specifying (at least) some appropriate range of observable bodily movements or changes – though the specification here might be very open and couched in terms of effects (e.g. some movement causally capable of producing such and such effects). Further, the analysis would have to say something about the relation between the two components, i.e. at the very least that the mental element was co-present with or preceded the bodily movement. As regards the agent's knowledge of what he was doing, the reductionist would have to say that the agent was aware of the mental element without benefit of observation or sense-perception of any kind, where as he knew that the appropriate physical movements were taking place by means of observation or sense-perception including the proprioceptive sense.

Now, even as thus incompletely told, there are, no doubt, all sorts of things wrong with this story. But Miss Ishiguro rightly dismisses one too short way with it, which consists in the well-intentioned but careless doctrine that we know what we are doing without observation. For the really rather obvious fact is that we can't know that our intended action is actually coming off – can't even know that we are performing bodily movements – without dependence on sense-perception of *some* kind; though the accurate description of the facts in this area is a complicated and tricky business, which has been illuminatingly handled by a number of writers, including Mr Vesey and Mr D. G. Brown. What we can be said to know without sense-perception – which is not to say that we can never deceive ourselves on the point – is what our *intention* is. But of course this remark by itself is perfectly acceptable to the Cartesian reductionist.

This anti-Cartesian line, then, must be abandoned. A more promising line is opened up by inquiring, as Miss Ishiguro does, how we are supposed to acquire the concept of intention or intentional action and how we are supposed to learn to do things, to perform intentional actions of various kinds. It is when we consider how the

Cartesian reductionist must react to these questions that we see the difficulties of his position. Not, of course, that there is any difficulty in explaining how we learn to do lots of things, like driving a car or buying a house. We learn the appropriate techniques. We learn to do these things *by means of* doing other and simpler things. But these answers refer us from intentional action to intentional action and do not touch the problem of general analysis of the concepts of action and intention. When this problem is pressed in connection with the questions I mentioned, it seems that the Cartesian reductionist has two options open to him of which the second admits of variations.

The first and less attractive is to say that there is no logically necessary connection between the occurrence of intentions in the mental life of a being and the actual performance of actions by that being; that it would be perfectly logically possible for intentions to *occur* in the mental life of a being who was and had always been quite incapable of action; though, of course (the reductionist adds), what happens in fact is that intention-having human beings discover that very often when certain intentions occur or are formed or are formed in the right sort of way, there also occur appropriate movements of the appropriate body; and this is what constitutes intentional action.

The second and rather more attractive course is to begin by conceding that a condition for the *occurrence* of intentions in the mental life of a being, or indeed for the possession *by* a being of the *concept* of intention, is that *that* being should be capable of actions and should actually perform actions; and then proceed to claim that this point can be explained in a way consistent with the Cartesian reduction. The explanation might be that there are certain mental states of a kind *akin* to desire or favour which are often associated in fact with appropriate movements of the body, where 'appropriate' refers to the content or object of these desire-like or favour-like states of mind; and where such states occur in the case of a being for which this association does often or sometimes hold, they are properly called 'intentions'. For the concept of intention is the resultant of:

(1) the internal nature of these states, and

(2) their occurrence in a being for which this association holds.

It may indeed be the case *in fact* that these states occur *only* in the mental life of beings for whom such an association holds. But this, if true, as it very well may be, is a *contingent* truth. And because it is a contingent truth, a Cartesian reduction of the concept of action, and of predicates ascribing actions, is indeed possible. As for the question how we learn to do things, well, in the case of basic bodily movements we don't learn *how* to perform them, in the sense of mastering *methods* of performing them, at all. They perhaps occur at first in a fairly random way and may become objects of these favouring mental states; and when they occur *in association with* these favouring mental states, this *counts* as our performing them, as our intentionally doing things.

Of course any such story would have to be, and could be, considerably improved and elaborated. And perhaps, if elaborated with sufficient care, it could not quite so easily be shown to be incoherent as is sometimes thought. Nevertheless it is clear that Miss Ishiguro would reject any such story; and so would I – if not as quite certainly vulnerable to incoherence-demonstrating argument, at least as forced and contrived to an unacceptable degree. It seems more plausible to hold that the concept of intentional action, though not of course a simple concept, is a *primitive* or, in a certain sense, *unanalysable* concept: it resists any sort of dismantling analysis, such as a Cartesian reductionist is bound to offer. It is perhaps worth running over once more the source of the illusion that it is a dismantleable concept. It consists quite simply in the fact that when you have intentional action, you incidentally have a physical movement; and since you can clearly have just the same physical movement *without* intentional action, it looks as if what makes such a movement a case of intentional action, when it is one, is simply the *addition* of something – say a mental component – somehow related to the physical movement. But when we come to try to describe or characterise this additional thing, we find we can't do it in any acceptably plausible way except in terms which involve the concept of intentional action itself. Thus suppose we try to characterise the kind of knowledge of our current˘intention that we have when we do something, knowledge that is indeed independent of observation or sense-perception. The most plausible kind of characterisation of this kind of knowing goes something like this: it is knowing what we are doing provided nothing is going wrong in the physical world. And here, of course, is a reference to doing, i.e. to intentional action. So this characterisation is no kind of contribution to a dismantling style of analysis of the concept of intentional action. And if this dismantling style of analysis is indeed impossible, then there is indeed a valid argument from the nature of the concept of intentional action to the anti-Cartesian conclusion.

Now I think it might conceivably be objected to Miss Ishiguro's general thesis that it really isn't entirely clear that the anti-Cartesian argument from the nature of the concept of intentional action has a peculiar application to *persons*. For, after all, we attribute intentional action to non-human animals. And I think it might reasonably be

replied to this that we do so only in an analogical or at least a highly
attenuated sense: that we don't really think of animals as *knowing
what they are doing* in at all the way in which we think of ourselves as
knowing what we are doing. And this is in contrast, for example, with
the spirit in which we ascribe to them the experience of suffering
pain.

But I think Miss Ishiguro would also have something else to say,
about the justice of which I am not so sure. It is quite clear and
indisputable that persons have projects and intentions and undertake
courses of actions of kinds which could not be correctly ascribed to
non-human animals – including those which bear on their status as
responsible moral beings. And I think Miss Ishiguro holds that the
entertaining of such projects (or some of them) and the undertaking
of such courses of action (or some of them) is inseparably bound up
with the notion of oneself, not just as continuing as one person
throughout the period of their execution, but as continuing as one
and the same *physical* agent or bodily being throughout the period of
their execution; and, given the overlapping and interdependence of
our projects, this virtually means that the thought of oneself as a
moral agent is bound up with the thought of oneself as continuing as
one and the same physical agent or bodily being throughout one's
life. For, she seems to suggest, we could entertain the thought of any
alternative possibility only by reverting to the position of the
Cartesian reductionist which has already been discredited by
reference to the concept of intentional action in general. So we have
an argument, in this case uniquely applicable to persons, to explain
why the criteria of personal identity do, and must, yield more or
less the same results as those of bodily identity.

Now here I do think Miss Ishiguro is a bit overplaying her hand;
and, if I may make the suggestion, even consciously a bit overplaying
her hand. But as to where the lines should be drawn here – as to
what is conceivable and what isn't – I shall make no suggestions;
partly, though not only, because I have talked enough already.

DISCUSSION

Miss Ishiguro: I should like first of all to say something about the doubt Professor Strawson has raised as to whether I move too quickly from the awareness one has as a moral agent to the criteria I have as a *physically continuous* moral agent. I quite agree that my *positive* arguments are probably not quite adequate. But at the moment I am not able to give any sense to speaking of a continuous agent of any kind which does not somehow involve all the kinds of knowledge we have as continuous *bodily* agents. The grounds normally given for speaking of an agent's identity as a continuous agent which is separable from that of a bodily identity is in terms of memory. It seems to me, however, that if loss of memory by itself does not force us to regard ourselves as different agents, and if the awareness we have of the intentions with which we do things is, as I argued, inseparable from the knowledge we have of ourselves as items in the causal empirical world, then we cannot show how the continuous identity of moral agents can be specified independently of their being bodily agents. It is from this kind of *negative* consideration that I made my suggestion.

Next, a point of clarification about what I have said, since I do not quite follow Professor van Peursen's distinction of 'internal' and 'external'. Many arguments have been put forward[1] to show that the fact that intentions and actions are *logically* connected does not disprove that they cannot also be *causally* connected. And I agree with this. We should, however, make a distinction between (1) the relationship of our desires to the intentions with which we carry out our actions when we do act, and (2) the relationship between the intentions with which we act and the actions themselves. I think that, when people want to talk about intentions as the causes of actions, they are often slipping from this first relation to the second one. I am quite willing to accept that causal relations might be established between certain kinds of desires and the intentions with which people sometimes do certain things. But this is a different question from that about the relation between the intention with which one acts and the action itself. It is this latter question which cannot be properly understood without reference to the concept of

[1] For instance, by Goldberg, Davidson and Pears.

future, *which the agent himself has*. In this sense this is something 'internal'. But I wanted to show how this in turn is dependent on causal concepts about ourselves in the 'external' world.

At the end of his paper, Professor van Peursen is concerned with what might distinguish human beings from other beings. He makes several suggestions, one of which has to do with the fact that human beings are able to follow Gödel's proof. But the whole of Gödel's method is to construct a function which maps meta-mathematical statements into mathematical formulae, and to show that the formula corresponding to a certain meta-mathematical statement cannot be proved. Nor can the formula corresponding to its denial. This is demonstrated algorithmically. Therefore the proof itself[1] could perfectly well be proved by any machine that could follow all those steps. I am not sure that I see the difficulty said by Professor van Peursen to have been raised by Ladrière. I do not therefore see that human beings could be marked off from other kinds of being in *this* way.

Professor van Peursen: I would like to make three points in further clarification. Firstly, as to the difference between the two papers, I think that Miss Ishiguro puts forward, more or less, a phenomen-ological thesis in a more analytic language; whereas in my paper, at any rate at one point, I put forward a more analytic thesis (about rules) in a more phenomenological language. Miss Ishiguro remains, perhaps, more true to a positivist train of thought in giving objective criteria – relationship to the future. I, on the other hand, stressed the role of the ego – and this, not from an analytical, but from an epistemological point of view.

Secondly, relating to the discussion between Professor Strawson and Miss Ishiguro about bodily continuity, I should like to say something about the role of phenomenology. I will do this by drawing attention to three aspects of Husserlian phenomenology, stressing only that Husserl's descriptions are always very dynamic, are not descriptions of the essences of things but of their constitution. It is perhaps even justified to say that such a constitution is nothing else than the way by which a meaning is being elucidated: f.i. 'The purpose is . . . to make ourself clear about what it, strictly speaking, means: "thing" . . .'/'. . . what is, so to say, being profiled, covered, conceptually meant by a word.'[1]

(*a*) In Husserl's writing the word 'rule' (*Regel*) is used again and again. A classic example from Husserl is when you see a house from

---

[1] Namely, that there is an undecidable but true sentence in a consistent axio-matic system that is rich enough to include arithmetic.

[2] Husserl, *Ideen*, II 34, 35.

the front and know that it has also a back side. In seeing the front
you are already anticipating the hidden side of it which you will go
and see in a moment. Husserl often stresses the fact that you can
have an endless series of perceptions from different perspectives of
one given object. His point here is twofold. Firstly, he is analysing
not the object itself but the *how* of the object, the way a given
phenomenon is getting its meaning in language. Secondly, he is
saying that the thing as such becomes a series of rules in which the
expression 'etcetera' plays a role.

(*b*) In Husserl's descriptions of time-consciousness, the difference
between perception and memory is, *inter alia*, that when I perceive,
for instance, a play being performed before me there is a direct
relation of the play to the present moment in which I am to be found.
If I recall the play I saw a few months ago. I recall a direct relationship between the play performed then and the 'now' I was then in at
that moment. So here is a derived form of direct relationship – being
related to a certain structure of time. Here Husserl always stresses
that time has a relationship (past or future) to the present, taking up
certain lines of thought that can be found already in St Augustine.

(*c*) The rules of seeing a thing in a series of perspectives are related
to a certain point of perceiving, and this point is an embodied subject.
Future states have to be recognised and this means they have to be
related to the 'now', where the subject of awareness is. As in modern
physics a given description shows methodologically a relation to the
place in space-time of the observer, so any description in human
thought and language is, according to Husserl, related to the
epistemological subject.

I give these three examples not merely to stress the dynamic
character of Husserl but also to put some critical questions: Is this
description of the ego subjectivist, idealist, unverifiable? This reminds
me of an old story in which the positive role of the ego in the analysis
of situations is brought out. It is the story of the visitor to New York
who was unable to find a hotel with a room free. In the end he went
to one in the poorer quarters, and there he found a hotel with some
rooms free, but this turned out to be for 'blacks' only. In desperation
he went out and blackened his face and hands with some shoe-cream.
He returned to the same hotel and, on this occasion was told: 'Yes,
sir, room 25 is free for you.' He asked the porter to rouse him at
6 a.m. and retired to bed. In the morning the man was wakened by
the porter. He went to wash his hands and face but found they would
not turn white again. Why not? Because the porter had made a
mistake. He did not rouse the man in Room 25 but the one in
Room 26. The humour of this story turns on the place of the ego –

the story changes the transcendental standpoint, and this is what makes it rather stretched.

Finally, what is the relevance of this for our discussion in this symposium and at this conference? We are discussing the identity of the person and this identity is different from that of objects or phenomena. For instance, you can have an interesting discussion of how to identify the Gulf Stream. But whereas that is a system which is identifiable according to certain rules, in the case of a person there is something more. A person involves a kind of self-identification – it is a self-referential system. This is a difficulty to which Husserl's analysis draws attention. And phenomenological methods may help to trace the methodological problems here. Husserl gives a good deal of attention in his work to what he calls 'reiterations' (that means you can come back on yourself again and again). It might be asked whether this is perhaps even relevant to methodological problems in various disciplines.

In the last part of my paper I gave certain clues relating to this question, though it is not within my competence to discuss them. But it seems that various competent authors regard Gödel's proof as an essential limitation of any formalisation. The mathematician Ladrière, author of various studies on Gödel's theorem, writes: 'It is just to the extent to which formal systems are able to construct self-referential expressions that they are liable to limitations. . . . This self-referential operation has its limitations: when we render something logically thematic, we make the infinite finite. . . . Formal thinking . . . forces itself to represent just those operations by which . . . the essential mobility of consciousness, the transcendence, manifests itself.'[1] And P. W. Bridgman writes in *The Way Things Are* about Gödel's theorem: 'To prove freedom from potential contradictions, it is necessary to use theorems which can be proved only by going outside the system', and he thinks this similar to 'the insight that we can never get away from ourselves' and he concludes, 'The brain that tries to understand is itself part of the world that it is trying to understand'. All this stresses the problem of how to formulate a self-referential system logically. Man, at any rate, can be considered such a system. And every system created by man on paper or simulated by computers has its presupposition in man himself.

Dr S. Raschid (London): Nothing has been said about the very profound problem of consciousness which must, surely, be central in a discussion of the mind–body problem. Here I would like to address myself, firstly, to Professor van Peursen. You seem to be taking some sort of quasi-Husserlian position and yet you have said nothing about

[1] Ladrière, *Les Limites de la Formalisation.*

consciousness in the sketches you gave of Husserlian 'constitution'. For Husserl, however, consciousness is the only and universal medium of access to the world – it is the foundation of the world. His critical analyses are carefully worked out within the framework of a whole theory of consciousness, i.e. under the phenomenological reduction. I should be glad if you would say something about this. Then, would Miss Ishiguro like to give a definition of 'consciousness'?

Professor van Peursen: I find it most difficult to explain what Husserl meant by 'consciousness'. Within phenomenological reduction it is not *empirical* consciousness. Rather it is sometimes the same for Husserl as time-structure – at any rate it is the possibility of the constitution of objective phenomena in relation to a centre – what he calls 'the transcendental ego'. In other words, when he describes consciousness within the phenomenological reduction he describes it more as a logical, dynamic structure. This implies that consciousness is the intentional starting-point for analysis of objects. So one can go further and say that in any empirical consciousness this logical structure of transcendental ego must be found.

I did not discuss 'consciousness' because, as soon as one starts to discuss it, one risks the language of a purely mentalistic approach. I think that, when Husserl speaks of 'consciousness', this does not imply a mentalistic approach necessarily, since this consciousness is given empirically as an embodied consciousness. Even the structure of bodily presence in the world is the same structure as this conscious intention towards the world. This is true of Husserl and, even more so, of the later phenomenologists.

Miss Ishiguro: I did not, of course, give any definition of 'consciousness'. Nor would I attempt to. The only question I had which was connected with this topic was whether the kind of awareness one has of the outside world is categorially different from the kind of awareness one has as an agent, and as such, the consciousness I am talking about is a personal one. And, I take it, we all know what is meant by speaking of 'being aware' of the outside world.

Professor H. D. Lewis (London): Miss Ishiguro admits that we are aware of our intentions without observing them. What is wrong, in such a case, with saying that we are aware of something distinctively mental? Is *this* the difficulty she and Professor Strawson confront us with – that I cannot *form* the intention to do something without assuming that I am going to persist as a physical entity?

I quite agree that, in the case of most intentions, we cannot form them except on the assumption that we will have the same body to go on doing whatever it is we intend. Do you, then, conclude from this that I must therefore *be* the physical body or, at least, that I cannot be conceived except as being embodied in another way than that of the Cartesian union of two distinct kinds of thing? If you do conclude this, it does not really seem to follow. All that *is* established in this way is that I cannot in fact form the kind of intentions which I form in this world without having a persistent body. And all that follows from *this* is that, in life as I know it now, I do function through my body. It does not follow that I am actually *identified* with my body in any way. It does not rule out the possibility of my functioning at a future date with quite another body. I might, for instance, start on some enterprise, such as digging a very large garden, and complete it with a body which I have acquired later on.

Miss Ishiguro: I have explained already why I think it is misleading to say that when I know the intention with which I do something, I am aware of something distinctly mental. But concerning my awareness as a bodily agent, there are two issues: firstly, whether I have to assume that I am the same bodily agent in forming and carrying out an intention. Professor Strawson doubts whether I have made my case quite strong enough at this point. But to doubt this is not necessarily to revert to a Cartesian position about pure souls. For one might think that persons go through different bodies and yet – and this is the second issue – think that at any given stage a person has to be embodied. Your last point might, therefore, be an attack on my position but it cannot be directed against Professor Strawson, since he himself has cast doubt on what I said on this first issue.

Professor Lewis: Yet what your argument proves – it seems to me – is that we are not able to do *bodily* things without bodies. But this is quite obvious.

Miss Ishiguro: It did not seem obvious to Cartesians who thought one could have mental volitions which you could cause some body or other to act out for you. If you are a strict Cartesian, you can perfectly well have a notion of a mental soul which causes all sorts of bodily movements.

Professor Strawson: It is, of course, common ground between the Cartesian and the anti-Cartesian that one cannot perform bodily actions without a body. The question over which they would presumably differ is as to whether you can effect a Cartesian reductive analysis of the description given of performing an intentional action in the body.

Professor Lewis: I am not quite clear, however, what argument has been produced to show that this cannot be done.

Professor Strawson: For my part, I sketched how a Cartesian reduction might in general look and said that it was not so easy as is sometimes thought to reduce such an account to incoherence. But this does not mean that one has to accept it. It might be found that it was just too forced and contrived and that a more natural and plausible account would be one which would show that the reduction cannot be carried out. It is not enough to say 'Why cannot the reduction be carried out?' It is a task which has to be done. And, in fact, it has not been done.

Mr Stuart Spicker (Fellow, National Endowment for the Humanities, U.S.A.): At the beginning of this discussion Dr Raschid remarked that consciousness is our medium of access to the world. It seems to me that what has been shown – at least in the existentialist literature and, though not so well, in Husserl – is that the 'lived body' is the mode of access to the world.

One problem which arises here concerns the employment of the concept 'physical object' or 'physical being' when Miss Ishiguro says she treats herself 'as an individual physical object causally related to other objects in this world' (p. 175). She also speaks of a person 'as a physical being' (p. 176) and a 'physical agent' (p. 176). These phrases, and others, indicate that no clear distinction is drawn between the concept of 'physical object' as employed in the ordinary sense and the concept of 'lived body' as descriptive of persons. The German language fortunately reflects this distinction in the terms *Körper* and *Leib*, respectively. Miss Ishiguro wants to retain the notion of 'physical body' as an appropriate predicate of persons while at the same time she wishes to maintain that the bodies of persons are spatio-temporally continuous. And this seems perfectly consistent so long as the bodies of persons are conceived as nothing other than 'physical things' as ordinarily employed to describe the things around us. But if Miss Ishiguro is truly sympathetic with the existentialists in this matter, then an analysis of persons as lived bodies must not contain a description in terms of predicates ascribable to physical beings as is indicated when Miss Ishiguro stresses that bodies of persons are physical things and spatio-temporally continuous. As long as the lived body is described in the language of physical body predicates, there will be no way of avoiding a regress to Cartesianism.

We might well ask what the predicates are which are applicable to lived bodies or persons. Human bodies, lived bodies, can of course be described *as if* they were merely physical bodies, and in that case the language of physics and chemistry would seem perfectly appropriate. But then we must ask ourselves whether we are in fact describing persons. One philosopher has made some progress by speaking of lived bodies as 'upright', 'asymmetrical in the lateral mode of left and right', and so forth. Merleau-Ponty, Marcel, Scheler and, in places, even Husserl have given serious thought to this problem. It is no minor point that Marcel argues for the thesis that 'I *am* my body' as opposed to the thesis that 'I *have* a body'. To be sure, Miss Ishiguro warns us of the danger of conceptual confusion when we think that we can simply substitute 'my body' for 'I' *salva veritate*. But my point is that if one wishes to maintain the thesis that bodily continuity is a necessary condition for personal identity, especially bodily continuity in the future, then one will have to re-examine the way we have been describing lived bodies in terms of predicates more appropriately applied to the things around us.

In these few minutes allowed me I merely wish to point out that the concept 'physical body' contains the sediment of the history of the mathematisation of nature as far back as the school of Pythagoras and this has led to the unfortunate situation in which we casually apply the same set of predicates to living bodies or persons without serious reflection. This is partially evidenced when Miss Ishiguro in describing her previous act of writing a pun says that 'I was carrying out a physical act. I moved my hand with which I held my pen' (p. 173). In my view Miss Ishiguro is correct when she says that the concept of a person is different from that of a body, where I assume she means physical body or thing; but I am not convinced that the concept of a person is different from a lived body or what she calls a 'conscious body'. Part of the difficulty here is that for Miss Ishiguro the human body stands to the stream of consciousness as *causally* related to that human body (p. 168); if the term 'causally' were replaced by 'intentionally' in the phenomenological sense, the shift might prove revolutionary. But in all fairness it should be said that the phenomenologists and existentialists are not fully clear on this matter either; this is indicated by their frequent use of the terms 'incarnated consciousness' or 'conscious incarnateness', terminology only partially divested of the invidious side of Cartesianism.

Dr Raschid: It is assumed in this last remark and in others that have been made in this discussion that there is only *one* phenomenological position. This is not so. As far as the body is concerned, the concept of the 'lived body' was introduced by Marcel and was further developed by Merleau-Ponty; but it is not a Husserlian concept. The existential position *is* that my *lived body* is my mode of access to the world. But the Husserlian question is: How do I have access to the *lived body*? And the answer is, through transcendental consciousness.

Professor J. N. Findlay (Yale): Professor Lewis raised the question: Why have we got to have bodies? There is, I think, a much simpler answer than that given by Professor Strawson to this question. It is the kind of answer Kant gave in his *Refutation of Idealism*. Our awareness of ourselves depends on the antithesis of acting and suffering and it can only be real if we have something the Germans call *Anschauung*, i.e. it must involve an awareness which is not merely emptily cogitative. There must be the possibility of an *intuitive* presentation rather than a merely *cogitative* one. For a cogitative presentation would be unmeaning if there were not also the fulfilled presentation.

There must, therefore, be some sort of place where one stands – a point of view from which one acts in relation to the world. There is, that is to say, an *a priori* body. Such an *a priori* body differs in many respects from the bodies I actually see. You would have quite a sufficient body if you were just a kind of poltergeist having some kind of locus in which you can act. Provided you retain your life-style you might transfer it in hundreds of different ways. It is a great mistake to pass from talk about this kind of *a priori* body to talk about the kind of body which we contingently have.

Mr J. Sullivan (*Leeds*) : It is not very helpful, perhaps, to attempt a definition of the body in terms of the physical. To do so would be to miss the *meaning* of the term 'body' as it is used in the context of a discussion about the *person*.

In the *Parts of Animals* (640 b30–641 a34) Aristotle criticises Democritus for identifying *form* with shape and colour. A corpse, he says, may have the shape and colour of a body, yet it is not a body. That alone would be a body which could *perform the functions of a body*. Going beyond Aristotle, whose point of view here remains zoological, we may add that the functions in question are not accessible to a merely behavioural description. Such a description would fail to distinguish between a zombie (a behavioural object manipulated by an alien intelligence) and a living human person. We are concerned here not so much with empirical description as with deciding what would count as a body, with arriving, by means of what Husserl called 'imaginative variation', at a phenomenological essence. That would count as a body, it seems to me, which assured the active, and social, participation of a person in a world. Thus, the body would be seen, in Aristotle's terms, as the manifestation of an energeia actuating, and limited by, the peculiar potentiality of any given world. Thus too is safeguarded the *meaning* of the body as neither identical with, *nor instrument of*, the person, but rather *the organ of a person's action*.

Professor van Peursen: I think there have been two main problems in our discussion. Firstly, the question of intentional action. What is the criterion for an intentional action? Is there intentional action, for instance, in animal behaviour? Is instinctual behaviour intentional? Or do animals not have that type of awareness which we have? This last question is a difficult one, since that kind of awareness is not public and is not open to inspection. Could we therefore translate the kind of awareness we ascribe to persons into rules of some kind? Secondly, the question about the body. One issue which was raised again and again was about Husserl and consciousness. This is a difficult issue, depending as it does on the interpretation of certain texts of Husserl. My own impression is that Husserl, when he described consciousness within his phenomenological reduction – not taking it as empirical consciousness but as a system of rules – he used 'consciousness' in a sense in which it does not exclude consciousness as the structure of human bodily presence in the world.

I come now to some questions which were put to me, for instance, about the solution of words like *Leib*, *Körper*. I did not use these words since I was speaking English and I find them rather difficult to translate. The difficulty when you say 'I am my body – the subjective lived body' (*Leib*), or 'I am not my body since it can also be an object' (*Körper*), is that, whereas it may form a good starting-point for further philosophical investigation, it does not touch directly the objection of a more positivistic approach or perhaps those coming from various scientific disciplines. That is the reason I made use of the expression 'self-referential system' instead of 'lived body'. I think that, as Husserl describes the body, it is not a physical body but a bodily point of reference. It is a bodily self-referential system which is not merely physical (is not merely an *aggregate* of elements) but has a certain structure (is an *integrate* of those elements). Husserl writes:

> All these series of sensations . . . belong directly to the human body as to his body, which is a subjective datum, distinguishing itself from a pure material thing-body by this whole layer of localised sensations . . . however, the intentional experiences themselves are not directly and properly speaking localised, they do not constitute a layer in the body. The perception, as the feeling apperception of a form, is not to be found in the feeling finger, . . . thinking is not really localised in the head like experiences of nerve-tensions, etc.[1]

And in one of his manuscripts (published by M. Farber) he offers an analysis of movement as understandable only by its reference to a

[1] *Ideen*, II 153.

centre affording its description. He identifies this methodological (Husserl would say: transcendental) point of reference with the earth on which the bodily ego exists.

This last point may be more easily grasped if I offer an analogy from biology. Chemical analysis is less important for biology than is informational analysis of the genetic code. Structure poses various problems concerning this self-referential system of the embodied person. For instance, some of the questions put forward by Professor Lewis are interesting, because they point to the fact that we are, nevertheless, inclined to speak about intentions and to ask whether they need bodily continuity. If this is done, intention and bodily continuity are already divorced. But there is, I suggest, no intention without this *a priori* body (as Professor Findlay has called it). Intentions are always directed towards concrete events, passing through bodily perceptions.

Miss Ishiguro : I would like to answer some of the questions directed to me in the discussion. Firstly, of course, it would be very difficult to have a criterion of identity of acts if one did not have the language in which to speak of unfulfilled intentions, i.e. of intentions which did not express themselves in behaviour. But I think this indicates not that there is a realm of intentions which is independent of the physical world in which we act, but on the contrary that we would not have a concept of action and hence of intention if we did not know in most cases whether we had failed or succeeded in doing what we set out to do. It seems important to our concept of action that we should normally do what we intended to do. The contingent empirical facts about ourselves in the world should not be disdained, as they are what give the logical or *a priori* basis to the concept of action we have.

This point seems to connect with what Professor van Peursen was saying about 'self-referential' systems. I think we shall have to be careful in what we take 'self-referential' to mean. For if the point is that a machine cannot register the state in which it is in, as he suggested with reference to Gödel's proof, then it seems to me to be wrong. For, as Hilary Putnam has pointed out, a machine might be able to do just this. Many machines which we would not be tempted to regard as persons can in this sense be 'self-referential' systems. But that a human being can know what he is doing in terms of the understanding he has of what he believes he is setting out to do as a thing *in* the empirical world, as well as the choice he has in the future state he envisages, is probably very basic to beings we call persons. This is a very special kind of self-referential system. And I think one has to take some kind of understanding of action as primitive *so long as* we cannot reduce it to or analyse it away by the *particular* causal models which have been hitherto offered.

Regarding the question about the body raised by Dr Spicker, I think that, even from a physiological point of view, there are all sorts of non-arbitrary unities of a complex kind. I do not think that even Locke thought that the unity of an organism, which, in the case of human beings, he called the identity of 'man', coincided with cell identity or molecular identity anyway. Probably, what Bergson or Dilthey or anyone interested in life-stream was talking about was something different from bodily unity and closer to what Locke called 'personal identity' based on unity of awareness. But it cannot be said that people who talk about bodies rather than persons are merely interested in molecular identity or that bodily unity is completely arbitrary. Nevertheless one of the points I was trying to make was about the inadequacy of this Lockean personal awareness – this unity which was, for Locke, *different* from bodily unity. I wanted to say that something more than awareness is involved when we are interested in *personal* identity. For personal identity has much more to do with our capacities for action rather than just awareness of things that happen.

In many causal analyses of reasons and actions in terms of desires and beliefs,[1] it is difficult to distinguish our awareness as agents from the kind of awareness we might have in the following circumstance. I have a desire to draw *X*'s attention, as well as the belief that my blushing would draw people's attention including *X*'s. My desire makes me blush with discomfort, and I draw *X*'s attention as a consequence. Our knowledge of our actions is obviously not of *this* kind. The blush was caused by my desire and belief, both of which I was aware of. Nevertheless it was not an action. That is why I wanted to take our understanding of action and our self-awareness as agents as something primitive.

[1] e.g. Donald Davidson, 'Actions, Reasons and Causes', *Journal of Philosophy*, 1963.

POSTSCRIPT

C. A. van Peursen

IT seems to me that the following conclusion comes to the fore in the various contributions to the discussion with regard to the problems of the identity of the person and the mind–body relationship.

1. Personal identity is not substantially given (*a*), nor does it imply a private, ethereal consciousness (*b*), as man is always acquiring his own identity (*a*), through the various relations (biological, psychic and social interactions) he is involved in (*b*). Human consciousness of his own identity implies, in this sense, his bodily presence in the world.

2. This first point would be insufficient if man's identity would be merely related to his awareness of these interactions. There is more than simple awareness or consciousness: man is always directed towards actions with regard to the future. Human relations are never to be defined solely by his presence in the world, but also by their dimensions of intentionality towards the future.

3. Animal instinctive behaviour is also directed towards future states of affairs, but lacks biologically such a highly centralised system of cortical behaviour, and psychologically such possibilities of self-reference as to enable the personal identity. Philosophically speaking, with a formulation of Husserl: 'The concept of "person" has to be demarcated from the empirical subject. . . . As to my own centripetal, ego-related acts I have the consciousness of "I can".' As it has been said in the discussion: for Husserl one has only access to the òwned body through transcendental consciousness (Raschid). Or again, in other words: there is an *a priori* body, a point of view from which one acts in relation to the world (Findlay).

It could be a further task to analyse how methodologically all anticipations in logic and in scientific disciplines on processes directed towards the future, and on self-referential systems, have their presupposition in human identity.

PART FIVE
GOOD AND EVIL

15

DOING GOOD AND SUFFERING EVIL

James Daly

Is it a moral outrage that a man should suffer as a result of, or in spite of, acting justly? Or is it improper to expect that 'the way things go' (to use D. Z. Phillips's phrase) should satisfy moral demands? The thesis of the pointlessness of morality, that virtue is its own reward, may answer the question in his own case for the mature moral agent. But can the just man – even if his own sufferings are disregarded in the light of the importance of acting morally – regard with equanimity the sufferings of the innocent and the morally undeveloped: children, mental defectives?

That morality has no point is a position of D. Z. Phillips's which has shown an interesting development from its first statement as a grammatical point about 'morality' to his recent statement that what is at stake is not the point of view of ordinary, but of a religious morality. The thesis of 'Does it Pay to be Good?'[1] is that there is no non-moral justification for moral beliefs, that the relevance of morality does not depend on whether it pays or not. A corollary is that, in Peter Winch's terms, the good man cannot be harmed (except in the case of an affliction sufficient to rob him of his goodness). Phillips follows Kierkegaard in holding that to be moral is to will one thing, the Good, and though the man who chooses justice may not profit, and may even have to die for his choice, in his regard for decency 'in the only sense relevant to morality, he has accomplished all'.

But in his later article 'From World to God?'[2] Phillips says that

---

[1] *Proceedings of the Aristotelian Society* (1964–5) p. 45.
[2] *Proceedings of the Aristotelian Society*, supp. vol. XLI (1967).

Plato's 'way of talking goes beyond ethics in its usual sense. In
short, Plato is expounding a religious morality'. The difference
from the earlier position is crucial from the point of view of the
demand for cosmic justice. Phillips's account of ordinary morality
leads logically to a demand for cosmic justice, but a religious
morality does not:

> The man who pays attention to moral considerations will not
> worry if he does not attain the worldly advance which immoral
> action would have brought him. Still, he does have certain
> moral expectations. He has certain rights which may or may not
> be satisfied. . . . [Sometimes] his rights are wrongfully neglected.
> At times such as these, he will feel harmed, and expect some kind
> of restitution . . . and in so doing, see things from the world's
> point of view. Much of what is meant by seeing things from the
> point of view of the eternal (from God's point of view) can be
> grasped by understanding what it means to die to the expectations
> created by desire or moral rights. . . .

The Book of Job illustrates this distinction well. At first, Job
wants an explanation of the misfortunes which have befallen him.
What he comes to recognise, however, is the necessity for renouncing
the desire for explanations and consolations. By coming to see that
the contingencies which had befallen him had no explanation, Job
is delivered from dependence upon them. The indiscriminate nature
of fortune and misfortune is used by him to teach himself that he is
nothing: he ceases to be the centre of his world. Simone Weil
expresses this point well: 'If I thought that God sent me suffering by
an act of his will and for my good, I should think that I was something, and I should miss the chief use of suffering which is to teach
me that I am nothing. . . .'[1]
  Unlike C. K. Grant, who in his reply to Phillips's article in the
same volume claimed that the man whose standpoint is a moral one
is not particularly concerned with how the world treats him,[2] I
agree with Phillips that the (ordinary) moral agent is as justly concerned with his rights as with those of any other rational being.
The question is, can he adopt a religious point of view which means
giving up those rights and regarding himself as 'nothing'? To see
things from God's point of view rather than from the world's is
presumably what is sometimes referred to as overcoming the
demands of the ego; but the only criteria we have that the result

---

[1] *Gravity and Grace*, p. 101, quoted in op. cit., p. 147.
[2] 'From World to God? II', op. cit., p. 160.

will not be demonic rather than saintly are moral ones. Simone Weil seems to make an impersonality which transcends moral criteria the absolute norm for man:

> Every time that a man rises to a degree of excellence which by participation makes of him a divine being, we are aware of something impersonal and anonymous about him. . . . It is then true in a sense that we must conceive of God as impersonal, in the sense that he is the divine model of a person who passes beyond the self by renunciation . . . that is why we have to adore the perfection of the heavenly Father in his even diffusion of the light of the sun . . . the renunciation of personality makes man a reflection of God. . . .[1]

This seems to advocate a going not beyond but below good and evil. Christian love may be called impersonal in the sense that it transcends the particular interests and desires of individuals, but it is impersonal only in the way that the Kantian imperative is impersonal: to treat all rational beings, ourselves, included, as ends in themselves. This means that we too have rights. Simone Weil, says Phillips,[2] has a pentrating analysis of the moral claims which we think the past gives us over the future:

> First there is the right to a certain permanence. When we have enjoyed something for a long time, we think that it is ours, and that we are entitled to expect fate to let us go on enjoying it. Then there is the right to a compensation for every effort whatever its nature, be it work, suffering, or desire. Every time that we put forth some effort and the equivalent of this effort does not come back to us in the form of some visible fruit, we have a sense of false balance and emptiness which makes us think that we have been cheated. The effort of suffering from some offence causes us to expect the punishment or apologies of the offender . . . Every time we give anything out we have an absolute need that at least the equivalent should come into us, and because we need this we think we have a right to it. Our debtors comprise all beings and all things; they are the entire universe. We think we have claims everywhere. In every claim which we think we possess there is always the idea of an imaginary claim of the past on the future. That is the claim which we have to renounce.[3]

In this passage Simone Weil tries to reduce rights to deluded and greedy demands, psychologically conditioned, and having no validity as principles. The expectation of respect for our rights and just

---

[1] *Waiting on God*, p. 114.   [2] *The Concept of Prayer*, p. 69.
[3] *Waiting on God*, pp. 150 f.

treatment from the impersonal world of nature may be deluded and greedy, but Simone Weil seems to relinquish such an expectation even from other moral agents, which would make morality unintelligible.

The demand of justice, that every agent should be rewarded commensurately with the good he has done, is one which is not met by 'the way things go'. 'Is it for nothing that people have wondered for so long why the wicked prosper?'[1] But for Phillips as for Weil, such wondering, while a religious attitude, is a mistaken one. It involves thinking of God 'naturalistically' as the creator of the design of the world, in which case 'one attributes moral responsibility to him as well, one makes him an agent among agents'.[2] I fail to see how one can attribute personality to God, as Phillips does, and not attribute moral responsibility to him. And the assertion that it is mistaken to regard God as an agent is incompatible with the representative quotation of Simone Weil, 'God sends affliction without distinction to the wicked and to the good, just as he sends the rain and the sunlight'[3] – or with her statement:

> Matter is entirely passive and in consequence entirely obedient to God's will. It is a perfect model for us. There cannot be any being other than God and that which obeys God. . . . What is more beautiful than the action of weight on the fugitive waves of the sea as they fall in ever-moving folds? . . . The sea is not less beautiful in our eyes because we know that sometimes ships are wrecked. On the contrary, this adds to its beauty. If it altered the movement of its waves to spare a boat, it would be a creaure gifted with discernment and choice and not this fluid, perfectly obedient to every external pressure. It is this perfect obedience which constitutes the sea's beauty. All the horrors which come about in this world are like the folds imposed upon the waves by gravity.[4]

This is surely a clear statement that the laws of nature are the will of God. Compare Phillips's:

> A religious person, such as Job, would see his wife's death as an offering to God. She had been given to him by God. (Why should they have met? Why should things have gone well for them?) and now God has taken her back to Himself.

---

[1] D. Z. Phillips, *Proceedings of the Aristotelian Society* (1964–5) p. 47.
[2] *The Concept of Prayer*, p. 86.
[3] *Gravity and Grace*, p. 101; quoted in *The Concept of Prayer*, p. 102.
[4] *Waiting on God*, p. 72.

There seems here to be an ambiguity; it is not clear whether natural events are part of a system of nature for which God would be an unnecessary hypothesis, or whether there is a divine agency of some sort in the world. In the latter case, surely Phillips is wrong in saying 'Once one judges God, as Camus has said, one dethrones Him: "When man submits God to moral judgement, he kills Him in his own heart".'[1] On the contrary, not to judge God would surely be to kill one's own moral being. Acceptance and obedience to God's will in nature are justified in Stoicism where the will of God in the design of the universe is conceived of as rational and good, but an unjust order, whether directly God's will or not, surely deserves a Camus's response.

The influence of Simone Weil is also found in Iris Murdoch's Leslie Stephen Lecture for 1967, which had the Platonic title 'The Sovereignty of the Good over Other Concepts'. It is a measure of the cultural adaptability of Idealism that the closest virtue to the pointless Good is said to be humility, 'selfless respect for reality'. Humility is seen in its extreme Weilian form: 'The humble man, because he sees himself as nothing, can see other things as they are.' The rational man of the Enlightenment and of Kant's morality, who judges Christ before accepting him, is discerned in Milton's Lucifer. In a seductive version of the perennial idealist theme that the true, the good and the beautiful are what is ultimately real, the key to reality becomes not the traditional reason, but humility. Our anxious, selfish, fantasy-ridden self hides reality from us behind a veil of illusion. Pursuit of beauty and of truth are occasions for purifying our consciousness in the direction of unselfishness, objectivity and realism, requiring courage and justice. Morality is realism: 'the authority of morals is the authority of truth, that is of reality'. Reward is irrelevant. 'Mystics of all kinds have usually known this and have attempted by extremities of language to portray the nakedness and aloneness of Good, its absolute for-nothingness. One might say that true morality is a sort of unesoteric mysticism, having its source in an austere and unconsoled love of the Good.'

Without argument at this point, I should like to suggest that while a disinterested love of the Good may be possible, there is a higher virtue in expecting consolation from the Good in return for this disinterested love. The superiority is of the order of the superiority of rational requited love over passionate unrequited love. In Kant's terms we have a moral duty to seek happiness as part of the *summum bonum*, though this duty is a disinterested one. Is Miss

[1] *The Rebel*, p. 57; quoted in *The Concept of Prayer*, p. 109.

Murdoch not bringing back a version of the romanticism she earlier expelled? Has morality not become something sacred, sublime, heroic – a *Liebestod*, in fact? In this idealist connection the concept of myself as nothing is crucially important. In the un-fashionable traditional idealist terms my ego, empirical self or character – 'the avaricious tentacles of the self' in Miss Murdoch's phrase – might be thought worthless, and in the Platonic sense of degrees of reality, unreal, whereas my ideal self or Self is truly real. But the ideal self is just what I should be if I were moral. Anxious, greedy selfishness could be seen as non-being in Platonic metaphysics and existentialist anthropology; but then rational unselfishness would be not *nothing* but true being.

But rational unselfishness, as Phillips has recognised, still makes the moral demand of justice; and 'Our debtors comprise all beings and all things; they are the entire universe'.[1]

The personalist tradition of Emmanuel Mounier and Gabriel Marcel differs totally from that of Simone Weil on the legitimacy of this demand. Paul Ricœur in 'True and False Anguish'[2] accepts it fully. For him, the suffering of the innocent, of Job or the tortured child, forces us to consider that it is perhaps not we who are the origin of evil but God, that we are his victims. Every other anguish is contained in this one; anguish at our guilt, at the meaninglessness of history, at alienation, at death. The reward for justice which had traditionally been part of a rational metaphysics, which in Kant became a postulate of practical reason, has in Ricœur become only a hope:

> I shall not attempt to mask the leap that is represented in the access to the act of hope which alone would appear capable of affronting the last anguish. No apologetic, no explanatory theodicy, can take the place of hope. . . . The act of hope, to be sure, presages a good totality of being at the origin and at the end of the 'breath of creation'. But this foreboding is only the regulative idea of my metaphysical feeling; and it remains inextricably bound up with the anguish that forebodes an utterly meaningless totality . . . And then do I have hope? Thus although hope is the true contrary of anguish, I *hardly* differ from my friend who is in despair; I am riveted with silence, *like him*, before the mystery of iniquity. . . . Anguish will accompany hope until the last day.[3]

I have spoken so far as if the demand for cosmic justice were intelligible, even if unsatisfiable or illegitimate. But there are two

1 *Waiting on God*, p. 150; quoted in *The Concept of Prayer*, p. 69.
2 *History and Truth*, pp. 287-304.   3 Ibid., pp. 303 f.

possible basic objections to such a way of talking. One is that it is nonsense. The other is that it is psychologically or sociologically conditioned nonsense.

Anthony Kenny, in a review of Ladislaus Boros's *The Moment of Truth*,[1] states the following argument: 'In our volition there is to be found on the part of the volitional drive an unreflective pursuit of an end, always going further than the concrete, actual realisation of the will, the individual act of the will. This means that in every striving of the will we find as its innermost dynamism an unconscious ecstasis towards God . . .' He analyses it as follows: 'frequently, when our wishes have been gratified we are still dissatisfied. However much the will may have attained by its own power, the actual attainment never corresponds to the desire from which it issued. Nothing short of an infinite transcendent being could satisfy the perpetual demands of the will. Therefore, every act of will involves an implicit desire for God.' Of this analysis he has this to say:

> This does not follow at all. It is true that when we want one thing and get it, we frequently want another. But this does not mean that our first desire has not been satisfied . . . Even if somebody is so cross-grained that he is never satisfied no matter how many of his wishes are granted, it does not follow that he is nursing a secret desire for the infinite. There is no proof of a desire for God in the tantrums of the spoilt child.

Kenny's attack on 'grandiose rhetoric' is often deserved by existentialist writers, and what they say should be expressible in, or translatable into, simple everyday language. But, leaving aside for the moment the question of the identification of the infinite with God, is there not a valid translation into everyday language for such expressions as 'a secret desire for the infinite'? If so, perhaps other shamefaced phrases like 'cosmic justice' may be allowed to return, on condition of good behaviour, from the nursery whither they have been banished, along with 'the universal scheme of things'. Dread and boredom are existentialist themes about the totality of one's existence and the totality of one's world. Rejection and rebellion against the conditions of life – not just against one society but against the 'human condition' – are another. A deep sense of the unsatisfactoriness of the world which is the source of one basic religious attitude is another. These are all affective stances we take towards the value of the world as we totally experience it. They are attitudes we take to the real in the light of the ideal, to what is in the light of what ought to be. Must such attitudes be confined to expres-

[1] *The Listener*, 7 July 1966.

sion in art or mythology, in tragedy or sacred drama, but be inadmissible to philosophic inquiry? Winch analyses Kierkegaard's dictum that the innocent man cannot be punished as expressing 'the speaker's attitude, his realisation of the possibility of meeting the afflictions of life in a certain way'.[1] The way is that of patience:

> Kierkegaardian patience is the *voluntary* acceptance of *unavoidable* suffering . . . When we reflect on the concepts of voluntary choice and inevitability, we feel inclined to say that they are mutually exclusive . . . The concept of patience shows that this is not so. It would be a mere philosophical prejudice to argue in the opposite direction; that because inevitability excludes voluntary choice, patience is impossible. Patience clearly does exist.

Whether or not patience could be further analysed so as to remove the appearance of paradox, my concern is with the admissibility of such concepts about the totality of experience: what in France is sometimes called '*l'Être*', and in England sometimes 'the Universe', not in Hoyle's sense.

The 'philosophical elucidation' of a feeling such as *Angst*, the extraction of the philosophical meaning from symbolic language, these have been among the primary concerns of Paul Ricœur. In *Fallible Man* he examines the concepts of finitude and infinitude, perspective and totality, in human existence. He distinguishes between the *myth* of the composite soul in Plato, the 'beautiful' (not 'grandiose') *rhetoric* of Pascal, and the *confession*, the *indirect appeal* of Kierkegaard, and sets out to give a philosophical account of the reality they are expressing. The nearest to a philosophical account is Kierkegaard:

> For Kierkegaard, infinitude is the imaginary purveyor of unlimited possibilities; finitude is the achieved realisation of life in the family, the profession, the state. Despair . . . is to betray the finite in a fantastical existence without duties or obligations, or to betray the infinite in a submissive, trivial, philistine existence.[2]

In the further elaboration of this question, Ricœur compares the finitude of my body and my perspective on the world and the infinitude, the endlessness, of the intellectual determination of things which form my world, with the finitude of pleasure which rounds off a clearly delimited act and the infinitude of happiness – 'the presence to human activity, considered as a totality, of the end

---

[1] Op. cit., p. 59.

[2] Ricœur, 'The Antinomy of Human Reality and the Problem of Philosophical Anthropology', in *Il Pensiero* (1960), translated in *Readings in Existential Phenomenology*, ed. Nathaniel Lawrence and Daniel O'Connor (Englewood Cliffs, N.J., 1967) p. 393.

which will fulfil it'. Biological demands terminate in pleasure and the cessation of pain, spiritual demands in happiness. When an object of desire becomes *everything* for a man it is an object of passion; 'in this "everything" we find the mark of the desire for happiness. Life does not desire "everything"; the word "everything" has meaning not for life but for spirit. It is spirit which wills the "whole", which thinks the "whole" and does not rest except in the "whole". . . ; and it is in the indefinite demand for possession, domination, and esteem by others that the drama of the infinite and finite is played out.'

These concepts may help towards an answer to the second problem; is concern with cosmic justice psychologically or sociologically conditioned nonsense? It might be argued that the spectator of tragedy is not responding to factors in the 'universe' but in his social world; to impossible situations, conflicting values within a changing system or between a ruling class and a ruled.[1] He may think he is responding to the irrationality of the universe, but he is actually responding to the irrationality of his social world. It could be claimed that the same global sense of tragedy could be produced by psychological environment or physiological factors. Moods are fickle, and are symptoms, not diagnoses.

It seems true that depression can be cured by drugs or revolution. In reply to the Pascalian theme that man's greatness lies in the fact that he is never satisfied with his condition, one could say perhaps that theoretically it is possible that the physiological, psychological and socio-economic conditions for human happiness are ascertainable – a key tenet of the Enlightenment. But it is perhaps also and more interestingly true that an attitude to man's finitude and contingency would need to be included in the conditions for his happiness.

In contrast to a 'sociology of tragedy', Lucien Goldmann points out in *The Hidden God*:[2]

> it is the sick organ which creates awareness, and it is in periods of social and political crisis that men are most aware of the enigma of their presence in the world. In the past, this awareness has tended to find its expression in tragedy. At the present day it shows itself in existentialism.

And Goldmann's Marxist categories are sympathetic to the tragic vision:

[1] Alasdair MacIntyre gives some examples in *A Short History of Ethics* (1967) pp. 89 f.
[2] Lucien Goldmann, *The Hidden God: A Study of Tragic Vision in the Pensées of Pascal and the Tragedies of Racine* (1964) p. 48.

H

Like Kant, Pascal knows that the true demand made by man, the aspiration which alone gives him human dignity, is for a totality which – in the language of fallen man – would be the reunion of opposites, the coming together of virtue and happiness and of reason and the passions.[1]

Oenone suggests to Phèdre that since Hippolyte rejects her love, she should devote herself to something else – to ruling over Athens, for example:

This is, in fact, the most reasonable solution: in order to remain alive we must give up trying to get what we cannot have, and busy ourselves with things within our reach . . . This is precisely the course of action which no longer has any meaning for Phèdre. She was prepared, in order to obtain Totality, to fall to the lowest possible level, but she sees any attempt to use compromise merely in order to live on in the partial world of relative values as equally absurd and unworthy.[2]

It is a common objection to existentialism from advocates of common sense or positivism that it dramatises an immature wish that things should be otherwise than they are, or that it demands a clarity and rationality which just are not given and so must be done without. Is not the desire that things should be otherwise than they are a disordered passion, like Phèdre's? Ricœur speaks of the suffering arising from the rejection of necessity, from saying 'no' to what curtails and negates me; 'the rejection of the human condition expressed in man's threefold wish to be complete, without the opacity of the unconscious; and finally to be of oneself (*être par soi*) not born. Thus, the offending scandal is built into the texture of one's condition.'[3] Is this search for 'accursed lucidity' not what Merleau-Ponty inveighed against, pointing out that the human situation was necessarily ambiguous, compounded of '*sens et non-sens*', meaning and meaninglessness. Or does Goldmann have the last word: 'Merleau-Ponty says "sense and non-sense", just as Pascal did before him and as do all the dialectical thinkers who follow Pascal; but they, unlike Merleau-Ponty insist upon the fact that we must not accept such a universe but rather, if we are men, strive to transcend it.'

The answer may be speeded through the contributions of English-speaking philosophers bringing their traditional common sense to a sympathetic study of such unaccustomed themes as spirit, infinitude, totality.

[1] Ibid., p. 265.   [2] Ibid., pp. 388 f..
[3] Paul Ricœur, 'Methods and Tasks of a Phenomenology of the Will', in *Problèmes Actuels de la Phénoménologie*, trans. in *Husserl: An Analysis of his Phenomenology* (Evanston, Ill., 1967) p. 226.

16

COMMENTS ON MR DALY'S
'DOING GOOD
AND SUFFERING EVIL'

Peter Winch

In the absence of Paul Ricœur or of a paper by him my role as chairman of these proceedings obviously sits somewhat unhappily on my shoulders. I shall have to be rather more partisan than would otherwise have been the case and myself attempt some remarks in reply to Mr Daly. I have had to prepare these at very short notice, but my task has been made easier both by my belief in the great importance of the issues which Mr Daly has brought to our attention and by my profound disagreement with a large part of what he has said about these issues in his paper.

I shall not attempt the absurd task of trying to speak for Professor Ricœur – not just because I should fail miserably, but because I should not even know how to try. However, I believe I can speak in the spirit of this conference. For although the main emphasis in the proceedings so far has been on the phenomenological strain in recent European philosophy, it would of course be a great mistake to suppose that other important philosophical traditions have not been represented there. Mr Daly has concentrated a large part of his critical remarks – especially in the early part of his paper – on some writings of D. Z. Phillips, in which discussions by Simone Weil are referred to. Many of Mr Daly's criticisms are directed, either explicitly or implicitly, at positions which he takes to be Simone Weil's. I believe that Mr Daly often does not get Simone Weil quite right and in these comments I shall try to set the record straight in this respect and to see what difference these modifications make to the issues which are before us. Mr Daly's first paragraph reveals the structure of his attack: to combat the view that the suffering of the innocent cannot properly be regarded 'as a moral outrage'. As has often been pointed out, it isn't *obvious* always how the addition of the word 'moral' is to be taken in such a context. Simone Weil (and D. Z. Phillips as well as others) have certainly wanted to argue that there is something amiss with certain kinds of attitude to such suffering. But has *anyone* maintained the view under criticism by Mr Daly as he then goes on to formulate it? – 'But can the just man . . . regard with equanimity the sufferings of the innocent and the morally undeveloped: children and mental defectives?'' (p. 209) – I don't suppose he can: but who has ever maintained otherwise? Refusing to consider something a moral outrage is certainly not the same as, nor does it entail or even loosely suggest, regarding it 'with equanimity'.

The point is an obvious one, but I'm going to dwell on it, because it seems to me that to refuse to recognise elementary distinctions like this is to refuse even to begin on the sort of inquiry which Simone Weil is proposing. One of the very most important kinds of point which she is constantly making, both in the discussion of the present issue and elsewhere, is the need to make clear distinctions: this I take to be one of the main functions of the faculty of 'attention' on which she lays so much emphasis. As far as the question under discussion in Mr Daly's paper is concerned, Simone Weil opens an essay in which this receives intensive treatment as follows:

> 'Vous ne m'intéressez pas.' C'est là une parole qu'un homme ne peut pas adresser à un homme sans commettre une cruauté et blesser la justice.
> 'Votre personne ne m'intéresse pas.' Cette parole peut avoir place dans une conversation affectueuse entre amis proches sans blesser ce qu'il y a de plus délicatement ombrageuse dans l'amitié.[1]

She goes on to appeal to this feature of what can and what cannot be said without offence to criticise what she calls the 'erroneous vocabulary' of the personalist tradition, which Daly rightly places in opposition to the view expressed by Simone Weil. But it is no good just to set one view against another (common as it is to find just this being done in philosophical discussions); one needs to consider what kinds of ground one needs to appeal to in order to decide between such views. A virtue of the passage I have just quoted as well as of many other places in Simone Weil's writings is that she is doing just this: suggesting that what is needed above all else is attention to the

---

[1] 'La personne et le sacré', in *Écrits de Londres* (Paris, 1957) p. 11.

nuances of the different sorts of attitude which may be expressed towards human suffering.

Now I take it that 'regarding with equanimity the sufferings of the innocent' would be a form of saying to such people 'You do not interest me' and as such would manifest an attitude which Simone Weil would call 'cruel and unjust': not an attitude, therefore, open to 'the just man', as Mr Daly seems to think is implied by Simone Weil's view. We do not have to rely on just this passage to see that this is so; it is manifest in almost everything she wrote. Consider for instance what she says about the *Iliad* in her essay, '*l'Iliade, ou le poème de la force*'.[1] She emphasises that considerations of justice are almost completely absent from the action recounted in the poem – from the dealings of its characters with each other. Yet, she insists, the whole poem is illumined by a passionate concern with justice which radiates, as it were, from a point of view outside the events within it. I think she would have wanted to say that the *Iliad* manifests a certain sort of understanding of the war between the Greeks and the Trojans, an understanding which is internally dependent on the passion for justice which is revealed in its writing. This could be taken as an image of the kind of understanding of human life in general which she is trying to outline.

Consider the following passage from 'La personne et le sacré, (pp. 26–7):

> Il est impossible, lorsqu'on en fait un usage presque exclusif, de garder le regard fixé sur le vrai problème. Un paysan sur qui un acheteur, dans un marché, fait indiscrètement pression pour l'amener à vendre ses œufs à un prix modéré, peut très bien répondre : 'J'ai le droit de garder mes œufs si on ne m'offre pas unu assez bon prix.' Mais une jeune fille qu'on est en train de mettre de force dans une maison de prostitution ne parlera pas de ses droits. Dans une telle situation, ce mot semblerait ridicule à force d'insuffisance.
>
> C'est pourquoi le drame social, qui est analogue à la seconde situation, est apparu faussement, par l'usage de ce mot, comme analogue à la première.

There are several points to note here. First, Simone Weil does not deny that human beings *have* rights, nor even that there are many familiar human situations in which it is perfectly proper for a man to appeal to his rights, This should be set alongside Daly's insistence that 'we too have rights' (p. 211) – an insistence which he seems to think has to be made *against* Simone Weil. Of her view he says that

[1] *La Source Grècque* (Paris, 1953).

it 'seems to advocate a going not beyond but below good and evil', and he says of her emphasis on 'impersonality' in connection with love of the good that it 'transcends moral criteria'. Now I mentioned at the beginning of my remarks the difficulty there is in using the word 'moral' in this very general way. It would seem to me very odd indeed to say that Simone Weil's concern with the problems of human existence is *not* a moral concern. (That certain current 'theories of moral discourses' seem to rule this out strikes *me* as a criticism of those theories. We have to recognise that there are many different forms of genuine moral concern.) I dare say that she would not have wanted to express this concern in terms of the notion of 'criteria' – and there are very genuine difficulties in trying to use this notion in moral discussions, some of which have been brought out in Iris Murdoch's 'The Sovereignty of the Good over Other Concepts', to which Daly refers. But certainly Simone Weil insisted constantly that certain problems about human life cannot even be understood except in the light of the concept of justice – or more generally of 'the good' – and I would not understand it if someone were to suggest that this is not a moral concern. I don't think that she denies even that there are some connections in which a concern for justice will have to interest itself in people's rights; her point is that an obsessive and exclusive concern with such questions will mean that some of the most important problems are obscured from us. Incidentally, some – though by no means all – of the considerations which she thought important have been brought out in a different idiom in A. I. Melden's rather neglected book *Rights and Right Conduct*.

Part of what worries Mr Daly here is perhaps the idea that if questions about men's rights are pushed into the background we shall find ourselves in the condition of Kierkegaard's 'despair' as described in the passage from Ricœur which Daly quotes, thinking in terms of 'infinitude' as 'the imaginary purveyor of unlimited possibilities', which is 'to betray the finite in a fantastical existence without duties or obligations' (p. 216). If this is the case I should like to remind him that the notion of an obligation is right at the centre of Simone Weil's treatment of moral and social questions. To try to express the point in the terms set by Mr Daly's discussion, let me say that the 'betrayal of the infinite' (as Ricœur calls it) 'in a submissive, trivial, philistine existence' was for Simone Weil the danger of an over-exclusive concern with rights. She elaborates this point in almost Hobbesian language, when she writes:

> La notion de droit est liée à celle de partage, d'échange, de quantité. Elle a quelque chose de commercial. Elle évoque par

elle-même le procés, la plaidoirie. Le droit ne se soutient que sur un ton de revendication; et quand ce ton est adopté, c'est que la force ne'st pas loin, derrière lui, pour le confirmer, ou sans cela il est ridicule.[1]

But to recognise this is not to lapse into the 'fantastical existence without duties or obligations', for the correlative of an obligation is for her not a right but a 'need of the soul'.

This notion is elaborated in *L'Enracinement*, and if we look at that elaboration – indeed, if we even look at that title – we ought to see that Simone Weil does not by any means underrate the importance of 'a certain permanence' (a phrase which Mr Daly quotes from Phillips's exposition of her position – p.211.) Daly writes:

> The expectation of respect for our rights and just treatment from the impersonal world of nature may be deluded and greedy, but Simone Weil seems to relinquish such an expectation even from other moral agents, which would make morality unintelligible. (p.211f.)

Here as elsewhere Mr Daly puts the notion of 'respect for rights' alongside that of 'just treatment', as if they were on the same level or even more or less equivalent. We have already had an example (that of the contrast between the peasant selling eggs and the young girl being sold into a brothel) which shows that the two notions are not always applicable in the same way. It is easy enough to think of other examples in which a meticulous concern for somebody else's rights is precisely the technique I use in order to treat him with injustice. But this is *not* of course to deny that there are situations in which I could not, without injustice, deny a man his rights. The point is that the injustice which I inflict never just *consists* in the fact that I deny him his rights; it consists, Simone Weil might say, in the fact that I am intentionally doing him harm. It may indeed sometimes be that the notion of violating his rights would have to come into an account of the harm I was doing him and even occupy a central place in that account. But there are also situations, no doubt dangerously hard to identify, where I can treat a man with justice only by denying him his rights.[2]

These are some of the considerations to which Simone Weil is drawing attention. If I live in a society in which certain rights are customarily protected by the legal system or by public opinion, then

[1] 'La personne et le sacré', p. 23. Cf. Hobbes: 'The bonds of words are too weak to bridle men's ambition, avarice, anger and other passions, without the fear of some coercive power' (*Leviathan*, chap. 14).
[2] Cf. Plato's treatment in the *Republic* of the attempt to define justice in terms of 'giving to every man his own'.

I become vulnerable to the infliction of harm in ways which would not hold in a different sort of social context. *L'Enracinement* shows that Simone Weil is quite as alive to this as anyone could be. Further, her linking of the notion of rights with the exercise of force and her insistence that our understanding of human society, leaving aside the workings of grace, is an understanding of a region in which force ('gravity') is paramount[1] means that she is not very far from agreeing with Mr Daly's claim that morality would be unintelligible if we did not take account of men's rights. Indeed, the view which Mr Daly is criticising, that there is a virtue which involves relinquishing a concern with my rights, is itself unintelligible unless rights are recognised as having a certain reality. And this is something which, it seems to me, Simone Weil recognises. Only, she wants to point out a difficulty in understanding the nature of that reality.

There is much more I should like to say along these lines. I should like to emphasise, for example, the importance of 'tones of voice' in understanding what Simone Weil is saying. (Cf. 'a right can be insisted on only in the tone of voice of one making a claim'.) This is connected with her point that the cry, inseparable from human existence, 'Why are they harming me?', is 'un cri silencieux qui sonne seulement dans le secret du cœur',[2] a cry, that is, which cannot be captured in any verbal formula and which eludes the application of 'criteria' formulable in advance. But I must exercise some self-discipline and pass on to other matters.

Mr Daly's main interest in this discussion is in the propriety or otherwise of speaking of 'cosmic justice': the expectation of justice ('that every agent should be rewarded commensurately with the good he has done') not merely from men, but in the 'totality' of one's existence, from God. I have spent some time (though not enough) dwelling on the concept of justice in human affairs, because I am quite sure that we shall not be able to come to terms with the conception of 'cosmic justice' if we are unclear about that. Now one doubt which this discussion might raise is whether indeed it is a 'demand of justice', even in human affairs, that those who act well should be thus rewarded. Sometimes perhaps yes: we may think for instance that a man who, by personal self-sacrifice, contributes considerably to the prosperity of a business enterprise in which he is employed should be rewarded in some way by the management. But what should we say, for instance, of a benefactor who deliberately wishes to remain anonymous so as not to place a burden of gratitude and recompense on the beneficiary, perhaps realising how such

[1] Cf. her treatment of the *Iliad* once more.
[2] 'La personne et le sacré', p. 13.

burdens may poison human relationships and in the end be the reverse of beneficial to the recipient? *He* might say that the expectation of reward from his action was irrelevant, or even antithetical, to the nature of his action. Might it not be an insensitive impertinence for a third party to think otherwise? Mr Daly says in this connection 'that while a disinterested love of the Good may be possible, there is a higher virtue in expecting consolation from the Good in return for this disinterested love' (p. 213). Leaving aside the suspicion of incoherence in this juxtaposition of 'disinterested' with 'expecting a return', I do not myself find any inclination to speak here of a 'higher' virtue. Mr Daly concedes that he makes this point without argument and I am not altogether sure what argument there could be. Let me simply say that he has not persuaded me to think in the way he advocates on this point.

But when we transfer this suggestion to the region of 'cosmic justice' the difficulties multiply. A point on which Mr Daly places much emphasis in his criticism of Phillips is that it is incoherent to think of the natural order – in which the wicked and the good suffer affliction without distinction – as an expression of God's will, without thinking of God as an agent and in some sense a *personal* agent. He thinks Simone Weil is on his side over this and quotes from *Gravity and Grace* in his support – a passage in which she speaks of this indiscriminate distribution of affliction as 'sent by God'. But I don't think he can be allowed this support. In a passage in 'La personne et le sacré', Simone Weil writes as follows:

> Le mot de personne, il est vrai, est souvent appliqué a Dieu. Mais dans le passage où le Christ propose Dieu même aux hommes comme le modèle d'une perfection qu'il leur est commandé d'accomplir, il n'y joint pas seulement l'image d'une personne, mais surtout celle d'un ordre impersonnel: 'Devenez les fils de votre Père, celui des Cieux, en ce qu'il fait lever son soleil sur les méchants et les bons et tomber sa pluie sur les justes et les injustes.' (p. 43).

Now Daly argues that we are confronted with an exclusive alternative here: either we regard natural events as part of a system of nature 'for which God would be an unnecessary hypothesis' or else 'there is a divine agency of some sort in the world' (p. 213). But it is difficult to understand what Simone Weil is saying in terms of this dichotomy. A large part of the trouble probably lies in Mr Daly's use of the notion of a 'hypothesis'. But Simone Weil does not speak here (or elsewhere) of any hypothesis that a personal God lies behind the (presumably only apparently) impersonal order of nature. On the contrary, she seems to be saying that a certain sort of recognition of the impersonality of the order of nature is itself an acknowledgement that what happens in that order is the will of God. The difficulty is of course to understand what that 'certain sort of recognition' can amount to.

I will make a brief comment on this difficulty in a moment; but first I must draw attention to a related point on which I think Mr Daly is confused. He argues that if we do think of the natural order as God's will and if we do think that this order is unjust, then 'not to judge God would surely be to kill one's own moral being' and that the proper response to such a universe is that of Camus (p. 213). Now it is important to notice that, if we substituted for Daly's phrase 'one's own moral being' the word 'personality' ('*personne*'), his remark would exactly express Simone Weil's view; but the point is that the whole weight of her argument is against this substitution – for reasons which I have partly already indicated. It is a corollary of this argument that she would not accept Daly's characterisation of a natural order in which it rains indiscriminately on the just and the unjust as 'an unjust order': the point is that judgements about the justice *or* injustice of the natural order express a confused state of mind, a state of mind which has been nurtured by confusions concerning the notion of justice as it is applied within the world of men and society.

Let me return to the idea of recognising the impersonality of the natural order: what sort of 'recognition' is in question? We must remember that the world of men is itself to be seen as part of the natural order, ruled by 'gravity'. Recognising this is recognising that men will for the most part be concerned with obtaining what they conceive to be their 'rights'; that, as long as this is so, their relations are going to be governed by force, and obsession with 'a proper requital for good and evil' is going to make any real concern for the Good impossible.[1]

It is extremely important to notice that this statement of what is involved in recognising the impersonality of the natural (including the social) order presupposes the notion of what I called a 'real concern for the Good'. It is a recognition of what is to be expected by contrast with what is not to be expected from the natural order; and this supposes that we understand the notion of what is not to be expected. Putting the same point differently, when Simone Weil speaks of the natural order being ruled by 'gravity' this has to be understood by contrast with what she calls 'grace'; and if either term in

[1] Cf. Kleist's sombre portrayal of this sort of 'concern for justice' in *Michael Kohlhaas*.

this contrast is removed, the force of the other term is lost. However, the contrast is not between two elements to be found in the world, but between something that is to be found in the world and something that is not. The Good lies outside the world.

That is easy to say, but what does it mean? We are faced with many very serious difficulties here, most of which I know that I cannot see my way round. But I will say what I can in the brief further time which I can allow myself.

Many of the difficulties centre round the expression 'the world' and are connected with notions like those of 'infinitude' and 'totality' to which Mr Daly rightly directs our attention in the latter part of his paper. Leaving aside my own lack of confidence in having any ability to speak sensibly on this subject, the issues it raises are really too vast to be discussed directly at this point. So I will confine myself to some peripheral remarks which will still, however, be very tentative and fumbling.

A little light may be gained by returning to Simone Weil's discussion of the *Iliad* with its distinction between the (almost) universal reign of force in the events described and the passion for justice revealed in its writing:

> Pourtant une telle accumulation de violences serait froide sans un accent d'inguérissable amertume qui se fait continuellement sentir, bien qu'indiqué souvent par un seul mot, souvent même par une coupe de vers, par un rejet. C'est par là que l'Iliade est une chose unique, par cette amertume qui procède de la tendresse, et qui s'étend sur tous les humains, égale comme la clarté du soleil. Jamais le ton ne cesse d'être imprégné d'amertume, jamais non plus il ne s'abaisse à la plainte. La justice et l'amour, qui ne peuvent guère avoir de place dans ce tableau d'extrêmes et d'injustes violences, le baignent de leur lumière sans jamais être sensibles autrement que par l'accent. Rien de précieux, destiné ou non à périr, n'est méprisé, la misère de tous est exposée sans dissimulation ni dédain, aucun homme n'est placé au dessus ou au dessous de la condition commune à tous les hommes, tout ce qui est détruit est regretté. Vainqueurs et vaincus sont également proches, sont au même titre les semblables du poète et de l'auditeur.[1]

We might try to move from the distinction between the world of the poem and the mode of its portrayal by the author to a distinction between the world in which I live and the perspective from which I live it. Justice would now come in, not as something which I

[1] 'L'Iliade, ou le poème de la force', pp. 35–6.

experience in the world, nor yet as something which I am entitled
to expect from the world, but as a concept which illuminates what I
experience and makes a certain sort of understanding of it possible
for me.

Though this is a move which I think we have to make, it would
be idle to pretend that it does not raise as many difficulties as it
removes. Some of these difficulties arise from the fact that I am not
just a perspective *on* the world but also an agent and a patient *in* the
world. In more dramatic language, I am not God. So my actions and
my sufferings are as much governed by 'the law of gravity' as are any
other happenings in the world. And my thoughts and my understanding of what happens are influenced by this same gravity, since
they would not be what they are but for the situations I have been in,
the actions I have done, and the things I have suffered. This is
certainly something which Simone Weil herself insisted on: the
language of rights, for instance, her criticisms of which have been
alluded to, is thought of as subject to, and unintelligible apart from,
relations of force and therefore the 'law of gravity'. So, one might
ask, if justice is not to be found in the world, how could it be found
in my thoughts about the world?[1]

Or the point could be put the other way round and to do so will
help us to see the next step forward. The conception of justice which
makes a certain understanding of the world possible for me also
makes that understanding possible for other agents. In so far as I
can say that, I must have some conception of what would count as
a manifestation of such an understanding, of a love of justice, in the
world. And this seems as much as to say that I can understand what
it would be to find justice *in* the world. So it cannot be the case that
the law of gravity is enough for us to understand the happenings of
the world (including the actions of men); the operation of grace is
sometimes to be found in the world also.

How we are to understand this is a problem on which I must
conclude these remarks. Its extreme difficulty should not, however,
lead us to assume too quickly that the notion is incoherent. I am
myself convinced that illumination is to be won in this direction
rather than the teleological speculations about the ultimate justice of
the cosmos which Mr Daly's treatment of the problem seems to
point to.

[1] The difficulty is analogous to problems which I discussed in 'Wittgenstein's
Treatment of the Will', in *Ratio* (1968).

DISCUSSION

Mr Daly: With all due respect and thanks to Professor Winch I feel I am in a production of *Hamlet* without the Prince in the absence of Professor Ricœur. I had hoped he would have taken up some of the other themes of my paper and enlightened us on a number of questions which I merely thought I was raising. For instance, on the question whether it is proper to speak of the natural order as 'just' or 'unjust' my mind is quite open. Linguistic analysis or some other critical approach may be able to give some understanding which will remove the question as to whether it is a just or an unjust world.

My question is: Can morality be justified by reasons outside its own peculiar demand? Is the Categorical Imperative not susceptible of further explanation? Wittgenstein, in his 'Lecture on Ethics',[1] with its positivist bias – value must be reduced to 'natural' fact – nevertheless insists on the unconditional character of ethical judgements and claims that the attempt to give reasons for them involves the sublime but absurd activity of running up against the boundaries of language. Similarly Paul Tillich, in his *Morality and Beyond*,[2] says that the religious element is intrinsic to the moral demand because of its absoluteness and ultimate seriousness. The dimension of the unconditional, he says, is the religious dimension. But if morality is in the order of the sacred then the world must be accepted as sacred rather than rationally understood. Rationally speaking, the world would seem to be a very unjust order. The answer in Job and in Kafka's writing (for instance, in *The Trial* and *The Castle*) would seem to be that God and man are incommensurable and that therefore God may be an unjust tyrant whom it is impossible to question or rather who does not answer merely human questions.

Rationalist metaphysics postulated that reality could be understood by human reason. Whatever *must be*, to satisfy man's rational demands for intelligibility, *is* so – for the rationalist the 'real' is the 'rational'. This applies not only to the metaphysics of the Schools but also, as Marcuse has pointed out, to the metaphysics of Hegel and Marx. But under the dominance of a positivist idea of 'reason',

---

[1] Published in the *Philosophical Review* (1965).
[2] Fontana Books, London, 1969.

Pascal and Kierkegaard expressed an attitude of protest at the contingency and lack of rationality of existence, each in almost exactly the same way. They both asked 'Why was I born here rather than there ?', 'Why is the world as it is rather than otherwise ?' The belief in the meaningfulness of reality in any other sense than the regularity of nature is a leap for Pascal – a wager. Goldmann, in the existentialist revision of Marxism, also makes the belief in the ultimate rationality of things, which he equates with the eventual coming of socialism, not something which can itself be rationally justified, but an 'act of Faith' – a notion akin to Jaspers's 'philosophical faith'. For him as for Ricœur it is, as I have mentioned, a *hope*.

In the Book of Job the moral aspect of man's demand for intelligibility is expressed. God is seen as a person, a maker and breaker of promises – quite frequently a breaker. As Jung says, this book represents the stage when Hebrew man became aware that he was more moral than his God. The promise God broke was of earthly happiness in return for just living. If we are to speak of an unjust natural order rather than just of a capricious divine whim, such an expectation would, of course, need to be rationally justified. And this justification would, I think, be in terms of a principle of justice, that everyone should be rewarded commensurably with the good he has done.

This principle presupposes that virtue is not itself its own reward, that virtue is not the only good, as the Stoics had thought. Kant's answer to Stoicism is that it is superhuman and not therefore capable of being demanded of man. Another answer is that it leaves out the whole idea of material goods or of any hierarchy of goods – which I, for one, would like to hold on to. There are those 'goods' which we share with animals. But man has one difference from animals which Merleau-Ponty and Cassirer, following Gestalt psychologists such as Goldstein, speak of – the categorial attitude. This in turn borrows from one of phenomenology's most important contributions to philosophy – the concept of a horizon, a context within which actions and thoughts have meaning. Man's horizons are not limited to the immediate and concrete; they are in fact infinite. Man's imagination, as Kierkegaard says, points out endless possibilities. I can act within a context of the immediate satisfaction of a physical desire – for food, say, whether out of hunger or for its taste. Or I can widen my horizons, to include relationships with others – then I eat for conviviality, for friendship, or, within a different horizon, as part of a business deal. But I can widen my horizon yet further, and think outside the narrow circle of those with whom I am enjoying this meal – I can think of those who are at that moment elsewhere dying of starvation. Here again phenomenology has contributed to our understanding by its many-layered analysis of the relation of consciousness to its objects. I can be clearly or margin-ally, guiltily or perplexedly aware of my relation, as I eat in security and intimacy, to those who are starving. I can thematise this relationship on some occasions and, having either arrived at a solution of the human and moral problems it raises, or failed to do so, or decided to ignore the question, carry this attitude forward into future occasions as the marginal awareness which constitutes the structure of my relationship to this aspect of my world. But I can also move from my own horizon to the horizon of all men; and the very notion of a horizon is of something which recedes the more one approaches it. Man's horizons are limitless; and whether he the-matises them or not, whether he tries to explore them or confines his attention to a narrow range of roles, interests and desires, they are there as the ultimate boundaries of consciousness, and a man has some relationship to them, even if it is the philistine one of ignoring them. As Heidegger has shown, it requires a specific project of inauthenticity to avoid facing these ultimate horizons of being and non-being, of the infinite. But my problem is the relationship of specifically *rational* consciousness to these infinite boundaries of our condition. Man must demand that reality, which is one name for the inexhaustible dimensions of the context within which we live, should be rationally intelligible. Unless he stifles it, he must feel the need for the totality of his world to be, for instance, ordered and just. He may put his total spiritual energies into one finite sphere in absolute fanatical devotion to some cause, as to a race or nation, for instance, but he is in fact then converting the infinite to the finite. Adam Schaff said that when socialism was achieved man would be faced with one last problem – his finitude. The tendency to reject our finitude is, as Ricœur says, built into our condition. And I think this is what Sartre is referring to when he speaks of man's project to be God, which makes him into a useless passion.

I turn now to the criticisms Professor Winch has made. Firstly, he said that neither Simone Weil, nor so far as he knew, any other philosopher had spoken of the sufferings of the innocent as though they were to be regarded with equanimity. I think it would be true to say of the Stoics that all suffering was to be regarded '*aequo animo*'. This means only that such sufferings are regarded as rationally justified, not, of course, that they are to be scorned or laughed at.

Secondly, what lies behind the differences between Professor Winch and myself as regards the interpretation of Simone Weil is the meaning of the word '*personne*', as in '*votre personne ne m'intéresse*

pas'. She says that the word '*personne*' has its meaning in the 1789
talk of the rights of the human person. I am inclined to say that
'You do not interest me' can be said without great cruelty. But, in
this 1789 sense of 'person' it would seem to me cruel to say 'Your
person does not interest me'. It means 'I am not interested in your
rights'. I recognise that Simone Weil is scrupulous of the rights of
others and that she bases her ideal of the moral life on obligation.
But she seems to me to demand, as perhaps a counsel of perfection,
that we renounce the claim to our own rights, explaining rights as
psychologically conditioned. The question of the rational validity of
our rights, however, has nothing to do with how we come to feel we
have them.

The suggestion that the insistence on moral demands would be a
betrayal of the infinite by trivialisation is an interesting one. But this
would be the case only if it were true, as Simone Weil suggests, that
one can only claim a right in a contentious tone of voice. Professor
Winch backs Simone Weil here by a quotation from Hobbes in
which he says that rights are empty unless there is sufficeint force
to guarantee them. But I think this conception of 'rights' is a wrong
one. A man has rights even if he cannot, and even if he does not
want to, enforce them. I may waive a right but this is no argument
for my renouncing all my rights.

True, I did not *argue* for the superiority of rational requited love
over passionate unrequited love. This is in a fact a technical discussion, coming from Denis de Rougemont and Nygren. It is
discussed in Martin D'Arcy's *The Mind and Heart of Love*.[1] This is,
as Professor Winch points out, a key issue but I do not have time to
enter into it at present. I do not think, however, that it is incoherent
to juxtapose disinterested love of God with expectation of a return for
such love, any more than it was inconsistent of Kant to say that one
must do one's duty for duty's sake as well as believe that one will
thereby gain happiness as an immortal soul in heaven.

The notion of God as impersonal seems to me to turn on this
problem we have met already about the definition of '*personne*'. A
'person' can mean an agent and so to speak of God as 'impersonal'
might be to say that he was not an agent. Or 'impersonal' might
mean 'impartial' and so to speak of God as 'impersonal' would be
to say he was 'disinterested' – and this is the height of moral goodness. I am not sure which sense is being used here.

It is difficult to understand the notion of God if God is not thought
of as an external agent – though this Professor Winch called a
hypothesis.

[1] Fontana Books, London, 1963.

I am not sure I understand why Professor Winch says that if we substitute for my phrase 'moral being' the word 'personality' we should change my remark – that not to condemn God as unjust, would be to kill one's own moral being – into one which Simone Weil would endorse. I do not know what 'kill one's personality' means. And finally I would be glad of a further explanation of why speaking of the natural order as 'just' or 'unjust' should be thought to express a confused state of mind.

Professor Winch: I will take up only one or two of the points Mr Daly has just raised. First of all, he spoke of Stoicism in connecion with the sense in which he was using the phrase 'regarding the suffering of the innocent with equanimity'. I quite agree with him if he is saying that there are serious difficulties in the sense in which you might say that the Stoic strives to regard the condition of human suffering 'with equanimity' – though I am sure that he has a much more scholarly acquaintance with the details of the Stoic position than I have. As far as concerns the kind of view which Simone Weil is expressing, the aim is not by any means to arrive at an understanding or an attitude to the human condition which is one of 'equanimity' in any sense whatever. I think it is essential to what she is saying that the bitterness which she speaks of in the writing of the *Iliad* should continue to be the way in which we regard the suffering of humanity. And I am also quite sure – and I suppose Mr Daly agrees with this – that she would not say that we had reached a very good condition if we had come to the conclusion in the end that these sufferings were rationally justified. And this connects up with questions of how we are to understand the conception of the *will* of God if we do not think of God as an external agent. Mr Daly has raised with me privately the question whether, if we do not regard God in this way, there is any difference between saying that the sufferings which take place in the world are simply a part of the natural order and have to be seen as such and saying that they are God's will. In one sense, I would say that there is no difference at all – in the sense that the difference between using one form of expression rather than the other is not that it adds a hypothesis to the other or, in a sense, that it adds anything extra. What it does do is to mark the fact that one is inclined to raise certain questions about these sufferings (as in the Book of Job). For example, one must ask 'Why is there suffering?', 'What has he done to deserve it?', but also see that there is no answer. There is a great deal of difference between the person who thinks like this, who raises these questions in a very serious way and in the end is brought to say 'There is no answer' (or, another way of putting it would be to say 'It is the will of God'), and someone who raises the question and then says 'Yes, there is an answer, it really is rationally justified'. And there is a difference between both of these and someone who does not raise the question at all. One point that ought to be pursued in this connection is to try to get clear about what the differences are between those two sorts of people. And no doubt there are other distinctions of a similar sort one would want to make as well.

Another difficulty which Mr Daly raises concerns the phrase I quoted – *'votre personne ne m'intéresse pas'* – which I translated (like Richard Rees) 'your personality does not interest me'. This is not a happy translation but I do not see how else it could be rendered. I think Mr Daly is quite right to say that you can very well imagine many circumstances in which, as far as the words used are concerned, it might work the other way round – where someone who says 'Your personality does not interest me' is not at fault. And this is where the tones of voice come in. The importance of tones of voice and the connected importance of the context in which what is being said is being said, the kind of person who is saying what is being said, what is revealed about what is at issue for the person in the context and in the way he says it – that is the kind of thing we have to pay attention to really much more than the actual language used in an Austinian sense of the actual sentences used. And when Simone Weil criticises the language of rights, one could say that what she is criticising is talking about ethical matters in a certain tone of voice much more than using certain verbal expressions. A point I tried to make in my remarks was that someone who speaks in terms of rights may *well* be raising the sort of question about justice which Simone Weil thinks highly of. This is something you can only see by looking at the details of the discussion – what is going on there and the way in which the discussion proceeds shows something about the people who are engaged in it. This raises all sorts of questions about the distinction between saying and showing, the sort of issue that arises in discussions of Wittgenstein's work, for instance.

Finally, Mr Daly made a lot in his remarks of saying that the question of the rational validity of questions about rights has nothing to do with, or is at least quite separable from, questions about the psychological conditions of the people making claims. Whether they are inclined to make such claims and whether they have the power to enforce them are quite irrelevant to the question whether they have these rights. In a sense I agree with this. But I should also want to say that this raises other philosophical questions which have much exercised people in recent years regarding the relation between the *truth* of a claim and the *point* of making it – questions which are discussed, for instance, by Grice. The difficulty I have with the kind of move which Mr Daly makes is where he says these claims may be true *whether or not* anyone is inclined to make them. My inclination is to say '*What* claims may be true?' I do not understand what it is for which truth is being claimed unless I understand the sort of situation in which it is appropriate to make such a claim. I agree, of course, that a discussion of the sort of conditions in which it is appropriate to make a claim is not the same as a discussion of the truth of a claim. It is very difficult to get clear as to the relation between these two types of question. Only nothing is gained simply by saying that they are different questions and that we can raise questions about the truth of the claims without going into the question of the conditions under which we can understand such claims being made, and under which, therefore – as I would argue – we can understand what the claims amount to.

Mrs Pamela Moore (London): Mr Daly said in his remarks that it was difficult to accept the sufferings of the innocent as rationally justified. I would like to know whether he would make any distinction between sufferings as 'morally and rationally justified' and sufferings as 'understood and accepted'. This latter way of regarding them seems to me more that of someone like Simone Weil. Can he make this distinction in his terms?

Mr Daly: This is, I think, the key distinction. Simone Weil's view may well be true, but I do not understand it. She draws a distinction between the attitude of understanding and the acceptance of suffering. But suffering cannot be understood, so far as I can see, unless it is seen to be rationally intelligible. It seems to me that the suffering of the innocent can only be made rationally intelligible if one postulates, in the way Kant did, the existence of God and the immortality of the soul.

Mrs Moore: I should like to ask further whether there are, as one might say, 'facts of life' or conditions in the natural world which you find yourself able to accept but which cannot be rationally explained or justified at all? I find it difficult to understand how, for instance, you could hope to think of your own existence as rationally explained or justified?

Mr Daly: This was a point of Kierkegaard's – why should I have been born here rather than there? I would like to have a rational account of this. The will of a God considered as a completely rational agent would be one possible answer. Goldmann's eventual evolution of a totally rational (socialist) system would be another.

Mr G. Robinson (Southampton): This is a problem about understanding, in one sense of 'understanding'. Would you not be prepared to say that it is an increase in understanding to discover that something is, as it were, not rational? For instance, it *would* be an increase in understanding to discover that it is not rational. To discover, as when attempting to square the circle, that what one is trying to achieve is impossible – that is an increase in understanding. I take it this was the point of Mrs Moore's question. Your reply was that to see something as irrational is not to understand it. But there is a kind of second-order understanding involved here.

Mr Daly: My problem is – and this was what was, more or less, behind my paper – whether there is any point in asking the kind of 'Why?' questions which I have been asking. Is there any point in looking for intelligibility, not just in terms of natural causes and so on, but in terms of moral demands? I am not sure that there is. I said that one must be able to say that one has rights which one cannot relinquish and that the world is unintelligible if one is not treated with justice. When I said that, I expressed what I feel is an inalienable demand of rationality. But it may be that the only kind of understanding that we can achieve here is that it *is* absurd.

Professor Winch: If I could add to that, what I want to say is *not* that there is no point in asking such questions as 'Why is it?' If one does not ask that question, one is not making the move towards the sort of understanding that is expressed in, say, 'There is no reason – it is part of the natural order' or 'It is the will of God'. The difficulty is to see how one could still attach importance to that question and, at the same time, be inclined to say that it is one to which in principle there is no answer. This raises the very deep and important philosophical question whether there can be unanswerable questions.

Mrs Moore: The whole use of the word 'absurd' seems to me to pinpoint what is the matter. For it presupposes that one is still looking for a rational answer and not finding it. Hence one now sees the world in terms of the wrong question. Only by realising that it *is* the wrong question will one begin to understand, for example, the suffering of the innocent, by means which are not irrational but to which reason is not, as such, relevant.

Mr Robinson: It is important, none the less, to see that understanding has been achieved by the conclusions ('answers' is the wrong word) one comes to as a result of raising this question.

Professor J. N. Findlay (Yale): I would like to adopt the view that the question has a precise meaning, that we do know what would be an answer to it. Whether what would answer it is true, of course, is a profoundly difficult question, to which I do not know the answer at all. But it seems to me that the discrepancy between what *ought* to be and what *is* constitutes a genuine surd. It is a philosophical

surd and not a surd at the ordinary level. It is deeply discrepant that
there should be people in the world like ourselves who feel a sense of
justice and that there should be an order of things that is as utterly
unamenable to justice or injustice as anything could be. This is a
surd – *either* that we should be there *or* that the things that we
recognise as absolutely inescapable should have no influence on the
world. What would be an answer? The answer is the perfectly
simple one which has always been given. It lies in some kind of
teleological perspective. The answer is in some kind of view in which,
after long travail, the various discrepancies or unhappinesses or
injustices will somehow be shown to have been of value to something
higher. If you can provide a sufficient teleological perspective, then
this particular problem is solved. If you cannot, it cannot be.

Professor Winch: There is one final comment I would like to make
which is connected particularly with Professor Findlay's remarks
but also with other remarks that have been made. I will not now
dispute that we could form the idea of a world in which the innocent
did not suffer, in which justice did reign – although I have an idea
that difficulties of a conceptual sort might come up if one tried to
describe that in any great detail. But, leaving that aside, supposing
we accept the world as it is – in which we are all agreed that the
innocent certainly do suffer and the wicked prosper – if you now try
to clamp a teleological scheme of a Hegelian or some other sort on to
that fact, the very great difficulty I find is Dostoevsky's difficulty in
the Grand Inquisitor episode in *The Brothers Karamazov*. If somebody
says that certain sorts of suffering are going to be shown to be
necessary means to some great and wonderful end in the long run,
my reaction to this is to say, 'Well, so much the worse for that great
and wonderful end!' It seems to me that one just does not have the
right to take such a teleological view of certain sorts of thing that do
go on. And if you do take such a view, you are, it seems to me, taking
your eyes away from what has gone on. Whereas the essential thing
to do is to attend to what does go on.

PART SIX
PHILOSOPHICAL
METHODOLOGY

17

ON PHENOMENOLOGY AS A METHODOLOGY OF PHILOSOPHY[1]

Philip Pettit

THE discussion of phenomenology in the abstract is out of the question; it is only possible to discuss the phenomenology of one thinker or another. Indeed even the discussion of the phenomenology of one thinker is very difficult, because of the development which inevitably takes place in any individual's philosophy. The present discussion takes the line of least resistance, therefore, and the modest one: it is based on a single text of Edmund Husserl, the founder of phenomenology. The text is a series of five lectures delivered by Husserl in 1907 in the University of Göttingen. It was published by Walter Biemel in 1950 under the title *The Idea of Phenomenology*.[2]

In the first of the 1907 lectures Husserl says that the term 'phenomenology' 'denotes a science, a system of scientific disciplines. But it also and above all denotes a method and an attitude of mind, the specifically philosophical attitude of mind, the specifically philosophical method.'[3]

Husserl admits that phenomenology may be taken to consist in a set of philosophical doctrines; it may be taken in that sense as a

[1] The theme of this paper is developed at greater length in my short study of Husserl, *On the Idea of Phenomenology* (Dublin, 1969).

[2] Published for the first time by W. Biemel in *Husserliana*, Band II (The Hague, 1950; 2nd ed., 1958); trans. W. P. Alston and G. Nakhnikian (The Hague, 1964). The German text is referred to below as B, the translation as AN.

[3] B 23, AN 19. In this, as in other quotations, italics which seemed unnecessary have been removed. The translation of AN has in every case been accepted, as it seems satisfactory.

science, a system of scientific disciplines. He insists that what is important in a phenomenological philosophy, however, is not the set of doctrines defended, but the method used in their defence. To him phenomenology is primarily a methodology of philosophy. The methodology of any science is the account of the method of inquiry at work there. This method will often remain implicit, depending on an unexamined view of what the problems of the science are like, and what the line of their solution must be. To give a methodology of that science is to make the method explicit and, if needs be, to criticise it. To do this, of course, is to say what the method of the science should be. And this is precisely the sense in which phenomenology is concerned with the method of philosophy. It is an account of what the method of philosophy should be; as Husserl says, it denotes 'the specifically philosophical method'. Phenomenology may be regarded, therefore, as a methodology of philosophy; it is as such that we will here consider it.

What does phenomenology say, then, as a methodology? What is its specifically methodological thesis? Phenomenology, to by-pass many scholarly refinements, makes philosophy a matter of the experience and description of conscious human behaviour, in its subjective and objective aspects. It takes philosophy to be concerned, for instance, with the experience and description of the various types of perception – seeing, hearing, etc. – and their various types of objects – colour, shape, sound, and so on. On the phenomenological programme, philosophy is to be an inquiry into conscious human behaviour, and the method of the inquiry is to be experimental and descriptive.

This appears in the 1907 lectures. Husserl maintains there that philosophy has to deal with cognitive, and parallel, phenomena,[1] that is to say with the phenomena of conscious behaviour. And it has to deal with these phenomena, he says, under two aspects: as acts of the subject and as objective correlates to those acts.[2] Philosophy has to provide an experience and description of the phenomena of consciousness. For experience, or the receptivity to data, Husserl uses the term 'intuition'. He contrasts intuition with what he calls 'empty intention'. To intend something is to use a word which means it,[3] to refer to the thing symbolically,[4] to think of it.[5] It is to allow that thing assume a certain meaning for one. Every intuition involves an intention, because its object is always given with a certain meaning, as such-and-such. But the reverse does not hold. There may be an intention which is empty, which does not refer to

---

[1] B 46, AN 35–6.   [2] B 14, AN 11.   [3] B 57, AN 45.
[4] B 59, AN 47.   [5] B 61, AN 49.

anything given in intuition or experience. In his concern with the
phenomena of consciousness the philosopher should avoid empty
intention and look for intuition in each case.[1] According to Husserl,
this is meant to lead him on to description of those phenomena. In
his own idiom, it is meant to enable the philosopher to clarify and
determine the meaning of the phenomena,[2] to carry out an
elucidatory analysis of them.[3] It is quite accurate to say, therefore,
that phenomenology makes philosophy a matter of the experience
and description of conscious human behaviour.

A note must be added, however, on the sense in which Husserl
understands the experience or intuition involved in philosophy. An
intuition, as we have seen, always demands an intention which will
give its objects meaning. But an intuition may be related adequately
or inadequately to an intention. The second case is the more common
and occurs in ordinary perception. When I see a chair, for instance,
what I intuit is the chair in profile, a perspectival datum. My
intention goes beyond this, since its object is the chair as totality,
the chair as it may be seen from any particular angle. The intuition
in such a case is inadequate to the intention. Husserl maintains that
a cognition is possible, however, in which intuition and intention are
adequately correlated. In this cognition, which Husserl calls 'pure
seeing',[4] 'things are given in just exactly the sense in which they are
thought of, and moreover are self-given in the strictest sense – in
such a way that nothing which is meant fails to be given'.[5] The
object of intention coincides in pure seeing with the object of
intuition; the object of such cognition is at once, and in its entirety,
given and meaningful.

Pure seeing is involved, according to Husserl, in the philosophical
experience of the phenomena of consciousness. 'The thought processes which I really perform are given to me insofar as I reflect
upon them, receive them and set them up in a pure "seeing".'[6]
Because it is a case of pure seeing, philosophical experience is not
questionable. Husserl argues that it is possible to doubt the validity
of an experience in which there is something intended which is not
strictly given. 'But to see and to intend absolutely nothing more than
what is grasped in seeing, and then still to question and doubt, that
is nonsense'.[7] Philosophical experience is fit to underpin an absolutely
certain science; its objects are beyond all doubt. But the fact that
this experience involves pure seeing also means that it is has uni-

---

[1] B 30-1, AN 23-4.   [2] B 58, AN 46.   [3] B 13, AN 10.
[4] B 30, AN 23. AN puts the word 'seeing' in double quotes where it is used in a
broad sense for the German *schauen*; this convention does not seem necessary,
however, and has not been adopted.
[5] B 61, AN 49.   [6] B 30, AN 23.   [7] B 49-50, AN 39.

versals or essences for its objects, that it is, in Husserl's phrase, a
Wesenschau. Husserl argues that in the intuition of a particular there
is always the intention of a universal in terms of which the particular
is seen as a such-and-such; that is to say, there is always something
invoked in the intuition of particulars which is not strictly given.
When Husserl says that philosophical experience is a matter of pure
seeing, therefore, he suggests that its objects are not particulars. He
maintains, in fact, that they are universals: the essential types among
phenomena of consciousness and the essential relations between
them.[1] As a pure seeing, therefore, philosophical experience is such
that it enables philosophy to be an absolutely certain science and
an analysis of essences.

There are two lines which the critique of phenomenology might
take. It might question the area of concern assigned to philosophy –
man in his conscious behaviour – or might question the way in
which philosophy is supposed to master this area – by experience and
description. The present discussion takes the less radical line of
criticism. It is assumed that philosophy is in fact concerned with
man in his conscious behaviour. But it is argued that philosophy
cannot be merely a matter of experience and description. The
criticism, therefore, which is presented here of Husserlian phenomenology is made from a standpoint which, in a loose sense, is
itself phenomenological.

What we need for our critique of Husserl is a theory of the relation
of experience and description. There may obviously be an experience
which is never described or a description for which there is no
experience. I may look at the fireplace opposite without ever feeling
the need to give a description of it. And I may describe an imaginary
object which neither I, nor anybody else, have ever experienced. But
yet there is a very close tie between experience and description.
Every experience anticipates a possible description. Every description
relates to a conceivable experience, even though it be one which is
impossible in practice. The relation betwen experience and description, of course, varies a great deal. It varies from the simple relation,
at one extreme, between my experience and description of the fireplace to the relation, at the other extreme, between a description of
the state of the nation's economy and the particular experiences
which lead to it. The simpler the relation, obviously, the easier it is
to provide the required description of an experience. The relation
is simple in the case of low-level description, where to describe is to
give an account of how the data appear in a particular experience.
The relation is naturally more complex in high-level description,

[1] B 50, AN 40.

where the description synthesises the data of many different experiences in terms of some overall pattern. In phenomenological philosophy it is clearly low-level description which is meant to be involved, description based in each case on a particular experience. This is description in the proper sense. High-level description is really a matter of processing data which, in the strict sense, have already been described. What we now require is a theory of the relation between any experience and its description, where description is understood in the proper sense of the word.

A common theory of this relation is that which John Stuart Mill provides in his *System of Logic*.[1] In Mill's theory description enriches experience beyond measure. Before description there is only the experience of objects as particular, irreducible data, available here and now. With description these data are related to the data of other possible experiences and classified according to type. 'The perception is only of one individual thing; but to describe it is to affirm a connection between it and every other thing which is either denoted or connoted by any of the terms used. . . . It is inherent in a description, to be the statement of a resemblance or resemblances.'[2] Now it may be true that in the high-level processing of data there is active comparison of the data of different experiences and the classification of these data according to type. It is completely mistaken, however, to think that description in the proper sense involves a similar process. It is not description, as Mill thought, which gives meaningfulness to the data of experience. The data of normal experience are meaningful to a human subject whether or not he chooses to give a description of them. To see an object, as the contemporary truism goes, is always to see it as something. What I see before me as I write, I see as a page; I do not see a particular *this* which I interpret on reflective classification as a page. There is no pure experience in human life, no mere receptivity to a this and a that, here and now. Mill's theory of the relation between experience and description, therefore, must be rejected.

There must be a theory put in its place which allows for the meaningfulness of the data in ordinary experience. An explanatory correlation must be set up between these data and the description which may be given of them. If we start with the meaningfulness of any set of data, we may invoke an element in the experience to explain why the data appear as already meaningful, and not in brute fashion. The receptivity of experience does not explain this meaningfulness; on the other hand, there is no evidence of active interpretation in experience. It is necessary to postulate a filter, as we

[1] J. S. Mill, *A System of Logic*, 8th ed. (1893) pp. 420 ff.   [2] Ibid., p. 422.

may call it, in experience, as an *a priori* element in virtue of which the data of experience assume certain meanings for the subject. This filter must be be regarded as linguistic because the meaningfulness of experiential data is normally articulated in words. To posit the filter, in fact, is to do no more than generalise Wittgenstein's point that an object appears as of the same type with other objects, and achieves meaningfulness in terms of that relation, only because of the use of a word involving a rule which says that *the object* shall count as of a certain type. Ordinary experience is filtered, and its data are meaningful, only because man has the use of language.

Its linguistic character gives the filter of an experience a special relation to a description of that experience. The filter is the implicit linguistic function in virtue of which the data of an experience assume a particular meaning. The description is an explicit linguistic function, that which articulates the meaning of the experiential data. But this is to suggest that the description of an experience is related to the filter as explicit to implicit, actual to potential. To say that an experience is filtered is to say that it is capable of being described, no more and no less. The description in simply the explication, the explicit version, of the filter in terms of which data assume meaning. Put another way, the filter of an experience is a subjective determinant which is objectified in the description. We are left with a triadic structure, therefore, in every experience. There is the meaningfulness of the data, the filter which explains that meaningfulness, and the possible description which is related to both: as that which articulates the meaningfulness of the data and explicates the filter of the experience. We have a theory here of the relation between experience and description which provides us with a standpoint for the criticism of Husserl's phenomenology.

Husserl maintains that philosophy is a matter of experience and description. He argues that philosophy should avail itself of a special experienc eof conscious phenomena, and then described them.

The question which now arises is that of the relative importance of experience and description in Husserl's programme for philosophy. Is experience primary, and philosophy a sort of experiential discipline? Or is description the more important, and philosophy a descriptive science? If Husserl reduces philosophy to an experiential discipline, then this methodology must be put in question. He would admit this himself. For he wants to say that philosophy is a science of phenomena which is primarily 'supposed to make assertions, indeed objectively valid assertions'.[1] It would be wholly unacceptable to

---

[1] B 47, AN 37.

Husserl that philosophy should be regarded as an experiential discipline akin to yoga. Indeed it seems quite absurd to regard it in that way. We will argue, however, that philosophy cannot be taken as a descriptive science and, on Husserl's account, is reduced to an experiential discipline.

Of what value can description be to the philosopher? On an account such as that given by Mill it might be attributed intrinsic value. For on that account it is description which first gives the data of an experience meaningfulness by presenting them in terms of their universal significance. On our account, however, every normal experience is of the already meaningful, or intelligible; it does not stand in need of description to have its data appear in terms of their universal, or repeatable, features. No description, except perhaps the one which carries an artistic dimension, is of intrinsic worth. There seems to be no intrinsic reason, therefore, why the philosopher should want to describe what he experiences. He should be content on Husserl's programme to have the phenomena of consciousness present themselves to him. To describe the phenomena would be merely to make the words explicit which give the phenomena meaning for the subject. It would be to perform a task which seems superfluous from the point of view of the subject.

If philosophical description has no intrinsic worth, however, perhaps it has some functional value? This may be Husserl's way of escape from the charge that he makes philosophy an experiential discipline. Description normally serves to represent an experience, but such representation does not seem to be of any use to the philosopher. Descriptive representation is necessary when a person wants to recall a past experience, anticipate a future one, or indicate one which is impossible in practice. It may also be necessary to communicate an experience to one who has never had it; a description may provide such a person with the means of imagining the experience. On Husserl's premisses, however, none of these cases holds in philosophy. The philosopher is concerned with the experience of his own conscious processes. This experience is available to every human being, and on any occasion. There seems to be no good reason, then, why the philosopher should want to represent any of his experiences in a description. We are led back to the conclusion that to try to make philosophy a descriptive science is in fact to reduce it to an experiential discipline.

There is one valid objection to this conclusion, but it only demands a refinement of it. The objection is that description, besides serving a representative function is useful for improving the quality of an experience, and may be needed in philosophy. Description improves the quality of an experience by making the filter of the experience explicit, and focusing attention on important factors. In the objection to our conclusion it is said that philosophers may find it useful to describe their experiences for themselves, compare notes, and so give the experiences stable form. The point is a good one, but Husserl is still not saved from the charge of making philosophy an experiential discipline. In fact he is more certainly incriminated, for description is now recognised as no more than an element in the technique of philosophical experience. The objection, made in the cause of the defence, is its final condemnation. It is the very admission that description is secondary, and philosophy a matter of experience, on Husserl's programme. The programme itself is therefore put in question.

There is one last line of defence open to Husserl, however, and this must now be considered. Husserl might well argue that description is necessary in philosophy because of the privileged and novel experience which underlies it. He might say that this description is gleaned from a very special type of experience, and for that reason is capable of throwing light on various problems. He does in fact maintain this in *The Idea of Phenomenology*. He holds that there is a special philosophical experience in which I can intuit the phenomena of consciousness in their very essence. Now this experience is meant to be such that a description of it will serve to make the particular, external activities of consciousness intelligible. The philosophical description of cognition, for instance, is meant to explain how individual acts of cognition are realised. It is held to be capable of this because it is the description of the cognition as internal to the subject, and in its very essence. According to Husserl, then, philosophy 'sets out to be a science and a method which will explain possibilities – possibilities of cognition and possibilities or valuation – and will explain them in terms of their fundamental essence'.[1] On Husserl's last line of defence, philosophical description is necessary because it serves an explanatory function. This line of defence breaks down because of the weakness of the claim that philosophy supplies a novel type of experience.

We challenge that claim at a general and at a particular level. At the general level we argue that the concept of a privileged and novel experience is a fiction, or an absurdity. Experience normally has the character, as we have seen, of being experience of the meaningful, being capable of description, or being filtered. The filter of experience is provided by language, and common experience is a type in so far as it is filtered by ordinary language. The data of

[1] B 51, AN 41.

common experience are meaningful in terms of that language and may be described in terms of it. A radically new experience, then, such as that with which Husserl credits the philosopher, would have to break with ordinary language to qualify as radically new. It would demand an original language of its own, therefore, or would be left without any. In the first case it becomes a fiction. In the second case it becomes an absurdity, a mere passivity before data. There is no point in talking of an experience with a language of its own. There is no sense in talking of one without any language. We must reject the concept, therefore, of a radically new experience. And this means that we must dismiss Husserl's argument that philosophical description serves an explanatory function. For there is no sense in which the experience of everyday could explain human behaviour. The most it can do is present the data which need explanation.

Besides the general argument against Husserl's case, however, we may argue at a more particular level that the radical philosophical experience to which he appeals does not exist. He speaks of the internal experience of the phenomena of consciousness in their very essence. There are two aspects under which this supposed experience is radically new, and in virtue of which philosophical description is given explanatory value. Under neither aspect is there evidence for the experience; under each in fact it is problematic, if not absurd. The experience is supposed to be internal, first of all, the experience by an individual of a private sphere of data unavailable to anyone else. And, secondly, it is supposed to be an eidetic experience, the experience of phenomena as universals. As internal, the experience should yield a description which would explain conscious activities as external; as eidetic, it should yield a description which would explain these activities as particular. But an examination will show that under each aspect the experience is a myth.

Philosophical experience is meant to be internal experience, first of all, experience of a sphere of data private to the subject. It is supposed to be the experience of objects the like of which may not be assumed to be experienced by anyone else, or at least the like of which are not experienced in common with anyone else. There is no evidence for such an experience; I see nothing when I close my eyelids. Certainly there is consciousness; I am normally aware of what I am doing. But consciousness is a quality of my behaviour, that in virtue of which I can consciously write, or eat, or feel panic. It is not a second activity of looking at my writing, or eating, or feeling panic. As P. T. Geach says, to use one of our examples, 'there is no "inner" sensation in which I see or feel the panic and discriminate its panicky quality – there is only the feeling of panic itself'.[1] There is no evidence whatsoever for the sort of internal experience to which Husserl appeals.

But the concept of such experience is at any rate problematic. The experience is meant to be the experience of private objects, objects which are never shared with anyone else. How are the objects of such an experience, however, to assume meaning? In terms of what filter are they to appear to the subject? There is no language original to the subject which could filter such an experience. The only language to supply the need, therefore, is ordinary language. But ordinary language is essentially public. It has meaning only when it is used systematically in a context shared by a community of individuals. This is a point of Wittgenstein. To use a word meaningfully is to follow a rule, and to follow a rule is to establish the possibility for communication and society. Ordinary language is the product of society realised and can never filter a purely private experience. Any supposed private experience, then, and in particular the internal experience of Husserl, is a fiction, or if it is held to do without language, an absurdity, a meaningless receptivity.

There is a second aspect to Husserl's philosophical experience; it is supposed to be an eidetic experience, an experience of essences. There is no more evidence for such an experience, however, than there is for an internal one. I may certainly be said to experience this thing and that, this chair and that table. But in what possible sense could I be said to experience what it means to be a chair, or a table? Husserl himself distinguishes between intuition and intention. The one is the receptive process in experience which yields me the data to which my words refer. The other is a postulated correlative process, that which yields me the supposed meanings or universals in terms of which experiential data are said to be interpreted. We may not want to speak in terms of such hypostasised universals. But even if we do, there seems to be no evidence for saying that we experience them. The universal is a postulate, not a datum.

There does not seem to be any sense in saying that we can experience universals. Intention and intuition, if we allow Husserl his terms, are two entirely different activities of consciousness. They may both perhaps be said to have objects, but the one has hard data, the other has ideal objects, as they are sometimes called. There is no sense in saying that the ideal objects have a status parallel to that of hard data, that redness as such is in some way correlative to this patch of red. And yet this is precisely what Husserl says when he speaks of

---

[1] P. T. Geach, *Mental Acts* (1960) p. 123.

eidetic experience. He maintains that I can experience universals, the correlates of intention, in the same way as I experience particulars, the data of intuition. He falls into the absurdity of holding that intuition and intention, and likewise their corresponding objects, differ in degree rather than in quality. Like his internal experience, therefore, Husserl's eidetic experience is at best non-existent, and at worst absurd.

Husserl's claim that philosophical description can serve an explanatory function breaks down once it is realised that there is no radical experience to make such description possible. It is worth noting that what leads him to that claim, and ultimately what leads him to his descriptive notion of philosophy, is his peculiar theory of language.[1] Husserl's problems are very often the same as those as Wittgenstein. Each can ask what it means, for instance, to know. What distinguishes the two is their theories of language. With the problem of knowledge his theory of language would lead Wittgenstein to ask how we use the word 'know' in our ordinary discourse. For to him the meaning of a word is its use in a language. To Husserl, however, the meaning of a word is normally a universal which is intended in the use of the word; this is the universal of which the particular objects denoted by the word are instances. To answer the problem of what it means to know, therefore, it is only necessary to examine the essence of knowing, to bring the universal intended in the word to givenness. And this is precisely the task which Husserl assigns to a descriptive philosophy. It is basically because we reject his theory of language that we dismiss his notion of a descriptive science. Philosophy cannot be merely a matter of description.

This is to argue not only against Husserl, but also against Wittgenstein. For Wittgenstein makes philosophy descriptive in a different sense; he makes it the description of conceptual usage. This does not seem to be an adequate statement of what philosophy should, and does, try to achieve. It makes philosophy a discussion of the way in which we talk about man. That is important, but preparatory, work. Philosophy seems to be better presented as the discussion itself of man. Husserl does seem to be justified in holding that the area of philosophical investigation is conscious human behaviour. This is an assumption which we make in the present paper.[2] The point which we will now argue is that the nature of philosophical investigation is explanatory and not descriptive, as

---

[1] This point is developed at length in J. Derrids, *La Voix et le Phénomène* (Paris 1967).
[2] The assumption is defended in the last part of the work quoted above: *On the Idea of Phenomenology* (Dublin, 1969).

Husserl thought. We will maintain that philosophy is the attempt to explain conscious human behaviour. That is to say, we will present a position which may be described as a refined phenomenology.

To regard philosophy as explanatory is not to deny experience and description a place in philosophy. They are now given a place as preparatory to explanation. In other words they are both given functional value. It is only if data have been experienced, and are taken to be described in a certain way, that they can be put up for explanation. The experience involved in philosophy is the non-observational experience of consciousness. It is described when the subject gives an account of his activities. This experience and description are involved, at least implicitly, in most philosophising. Take Gilbert Ryle's discussion in *The Concept of Mind*, for instance, of what it means to understand an argument. 'It should be noticed', he says, 'that there is no single nuclear performance, overt or in your head, which would determine that you had understood the argument.'[1] In saying this, Ryle appeals to the subject's consciousness and to the description which this would force him to give of what it means to understood an argument. This appeal is common in philosophy and shows the philosophical relevance of experience and description. What we maintain is that this experience and description only have point in so far as they lead to explanation.

'Explanation' is an unpopular word in philosophy. It is usually understood in a reductive sense as the process of making an object intelligible in terms of something else, such as its cause. In this sense Wittgenstein maintains in his *Blue Book* that 'it can never be our job to reduce anything to anything, or to explain anything. Philosophy really is "purely descriptive".'[2] And in the same way Husserl maintains in *The Idea of Phenomenology* that philosophy does not theorise or carry out mathematical operations; that is to say, it carries through no explanations in the sense of deductive theory.[3] The bias of phenomenologists against an explanatory view of philosophy is so strong that Herbert Spiegelberg can say that 'on all levels the phenomenological approach is opposed to explanatory hypothesis; it confines itself to the direct evidence of intuitive seeing'.[4] It is against significant opposition that we present the main task of philosophy as explanation.

The argument which encourages us to provoke this opposition is the purely negative one that, since philosophy cannot be exclusively

[1] G. Ryle, *The Concept of Mind*, Peregrine ed. (1958) p. 163.
[2] L. Wittgenstein, *The Blue and Brown Books* (Oxford, 1958) p. 18.
[3] B 58, AN 46.
[4] H. Spiegelberg, *The Phenomenological Movement*, 2nd ed. (The Hague, 1965).

descriptive without becoming merely experiential, it must be primarily a matter of explanation. The only positive defence for this argument is the non-reductive account which we offer of explanation. To explain something is always to presuppose a description, in the proper low-level sense or in the high-level sense, of what is to be explained. We may take the case of proper description only, as there is no difficulty in extending what is said to the case of the high-level processing of data. The description of any set of data gives an account of how they appear in a filtered or intelligent experience. The description makes the data intelligible, or meaningful, as they appear in that experience. The explanation of that set of data, however, serves an entirely different purpose. It is the attempt to make intelligible the fact that the data are such that they appear as they are described. To describe is to say how data do, or perhaps could, appear. To explain is to say why they are such that they appear in that way.

A simple example may bring out the difference between description and explanation. Say that I now hear a noise in the room. I describe it, if I am stupid or pedantic enough, as a hollow sound coming from the door. That is to say, I make the datum intelligible as it appears to me. Taken under this description, however, I might explain the datum in terms of someone knocking on the door. In that case, I make intelligible the fact that the datum is such that it appears as a hollow sound coming from the door. This example is very simple and suffers from the defect that the explanation offered might be assumed within a new description of the phenomenon as a knock on the door. This does not seem to be the case with the more important, scientific sort of explanation. In such explanation the terms are very often non-experiential, most obviously so when they are mathematical functions, and cannot become elements in the revised filter for the experience of the phenomenon explained. Consider the physicist's explanation of the sound which I hear, for instance, in terms of a certain frequency of sound vibrations. This explanation involves non-experiential terms and cannot be assumed within a new description. If it is used descriptively, then it is not with the same value that it has as an explanation.

Explanation of conscious human behaviour seems to be the primary task of philosophy. Like any explanation, the philosophical sort is the attempt to make intelligible the fact that a set of data appear in a certain way. It is not explanation in terms of factors which might be given in a special experience, and cannot therefore be assumed within any form of description. To recall our example of the knock, there is no door on conscious behaviour which might conceivably be opened. This, in a way, is precisely the point missed by Husserl. Philosophical explanation forms hypotheses which establish correlations between data sufficient to explain why the data are such that they appear as they do. There is no suggestion of a hidden world behind the data, a covert mechanism, which might be brought to light in a privileged experience. There is no room left for the possibility, to which Husserl clings, that such an experience could be made available, and a description with explanatory dimensions achieved.

The most important point about philosophical explanation, however, is that it is not reductive. Philosophers presume that explanation is reductive, that it always makes an object intelligible in terms of something other than itself, and are led for that reason to regard philosophy as descriptive. To describe water, some of them would say, is to leave it as it is found in experience. To explain water in terms of molecules in each of which, to use an unrefined idiom, there is an atom of oxygen and two atoms of hydrogen is to reduce it to something other than itself. This way of looking at the matter, however, is quite mistaken. The chemist's explanation is not reductive. It does not reduce, but rather is meant to guarantee, that chemical set of data which is water to us. A reductive explanation would not respect that specific set of data but would treat it as no more than the generic set of data implicit in the specific. Thus the physicist might give a reductive explanation of water by treating it simply as a formation of matter, and explaining it, let us say, as the function of a certain quantisation of energy levels. Philosophical explanation is not reductive in this sense. It is explanation, and that means it has not the warmth of description, but to deplore this would be silly. Far from making any set of data intelligible in terms of something else, philosophical explanation guarantees every set of data with which it deals.

Philosophy is here taken to be the explanation of conscious human behaviour. The experience and description of conscious life are the concern of philosophy only in so far as they prepare the way for this explanation. The question immediately arises of the relation between other types of explanation of conscious life, that of a physiologist, for instance, or a psychoanalyst, and philosophical explanation. On the typical phenomenological view, philosophy is a matter of description, as distinct from physiology and psycho-analysis, which may indeed involve explanation. We maintain, however, that physiology and psychoanalysis give reductive explanations of what philosophy tries to explain non-reductively. The physiologist will treat any human activity in so far as it constitutes a limited set of data, say a pattern of neuro-muscular excitation; the psychoanalyst will treat it in parallel fashion as the sublimation, for instance, of repressed infantile desires. Neither of them will take the activity in the full human meaning with which it appears in consciousness, and try to make sense of it. This is the job of the philosopher. The philosopher must take every form of human behaviour and give an account of it which makes intelligible the fact that it appears with its own peculiar meaning in consciousness. Examples of philosophical explanation are ready to hand, even in the writings of those who regard philosophy as descriptive. When Husserl talks of constitution, for instance, or intentionality, it can be argued that he does not describe any nuclear performance to be found on reflection, but postulates a correlation of consciousness and its object which, unlike the spatial model, will make knowing intelligible. Again it can be said that Wittgenstein performs an explanatory task when he argues that for a referential word to be meaningful, it must embody a rule of sameness which will mark off the objects to which the word is to apply.

The theory of philosophy which emerges from this paper is a modification of Husserl's phenomenology. It seems that philosophy cannot be regarded as a descriptive science without being reduced to an experiential discipline. There is no sense in crediting philosophy, as Husserl does, with a special description capable of explaining human behaviour. And yet it does seem reasonable to make the explanation of conscious human behaviour the primary end of philosophy. What must be understood, and what this paper has attempted to argue, is that this philosophical explanation can only be achieved through postulating correlations between the data of consciousness. Philosophy must go the hard road of hypothesis and theory. Man has no privileged access to himself.

18

DESCRIPTION AS THE METHOD OF PHILOSOPHY: A REPLY TO MR PETTIT

Ernst Tugendhat

WHETHER, in a symposium on philosophical methodology, it is a good idea to concentrate on Husserl, I do not know. The upshot of Mr Pettit's paper is that it is not. He has done so, nevertheless, and I must follow suit.

Schematically, Mr Pettit's criticism of Husserl may be outlined as follows: You believe in d (description) as philosophical method, don't you? But by d you must mean either d_1 or d_2 (p. 246). Now d_1 you think yourself to be 'unacceptable' (pp. 246f.). And d_2 would be 'superfluous' (p. 247). I give you as a 'last line of defence', d_3 (p. 248). but this can be shown to be 'a fiction or . . . an absurdity' (p. 250). And that is the end of d.

This is, of course, the good old Socratic method, with the difference, however, that Mr Pettit has not given the interlocutor much of a chance to explain himself. This gap, or a part of it, I shall try to fill up, not in order to save phenomenology from the grave, but to contribute to a fair funeral which, as is customary on such occasions, should provide a lesson and a challenge for the living.

THE PHENOMENOLOGICAL ASSUMPTION OF A MENTAL EYE

If a discussion of Husserl is to be of profit to contemporary philosophy, it seems to me important to distinguish between the broad philosophical and methodological conceptions from which Husserl started out and the particular philosophical system and method which he developed. I agree with Mr Pettit that the two fundamental assumptions which underlie Husserl's developed method do not withstand scrutiny (pp. 249f.) : (*a*) there is no 'inner sense' with which we could 'look at' what Husserl calls 'acts'; nobody has yet solved the riddles of inner consciousness, but so much we can be sure of: it is not an internal experience. And (*b*), there is no eidetic intuition; Husserl's assumption that we can 'see' universals (in some very strained sense of the word 'see') cannot be proved and seems to be a chimera.[1] This second point is the more important one, because it concerns not only Husserl, but all phenomenology. The assumption that you can somehow see with a mental eye essences and their interrelations is, explicitly or implicitly, of the essence of phenomenology. Wittgenstein has shown that we do not have such a mental eye and that even if we had one it would be of no use to philosophy as a communicative enterprise. This demonstration is very simple and also very devastating. The explicit or implicit assumption of a mental eye has been common to the whole of traditional philosophy since Plato, and with his doctrine of eidetic intuition Husserl has only provided this assumption with a theoretical foundation. With the refutation of Husserl's theory of intuition, therefore, not only phenomenology but a much longer philosophical tradition comes to an end. It is not, as some have feared and others have hoped, the end of philosophy, but the beginning of a new one. Whereas the philosophical tradition from Descartes to Husserl has followed the methodical principle 'Claim only what you can see clearly', the principle of the new philosophy is 'Claim only what you can show clearly'. The difference between the new philosophy and the old is not, to quote the title of a well-known book, a difference between 'words and things', but rather between the assumption that you can deal with all things from the point of view of an isolated, pure subjectivity and the postulate that you must deal with all things from the point of view of intersubjective communication, this being the original and genuine medium of our understanding.

TWO SENSES OF PHENOMENOLOGY

I have said that we have to distinguish the broad assumptions concerning philosophical methodology with which Husserl started out from the particular methods which he actually developed. Accordingly, we can now distinguish between a strict and a wide sense of phenomenology. Phenomenology in the strict sense I

[1] In my book *Der Wahrheitsbegriff bei Husserl und Heidegger* (1967) I tried to make sense of Husserl's notions of *kategoriale Anschauung* and *Wesensschau* (§§6–7). I now believe that this attempt was a failure, and I hope to show this in detail in the near future. ('Phänomenologie und Sprachanalyse', in Bubner, Cramer, Wiehl eds., *Hermeneutik und Dialektik*, ii (Tübingen, 1970) pp. 3–23.)

propose to call a descriptive philosophy to which the assumption
of a mental eye is essential. Phenomenology in the wide sense may
be taken as the general title for the idea of a descriptive philosophy.
This wide sense corresponds to what I meant by the broad conception from which Husserl started out. In this sense also Wittgenstein
and J. L. Austin used the term 'phenomenology' for what they were
doing, and it could be so used for most of what goes under the label
of analytical or linguistic philosophy, or at least for that part of it
which is called ordinary-language philosophy. It is therefore this
wide sense which is of primary interest for contemporary philosophy.

This is the point at which I wish to quarrel with Mr Pettit. For
he turns what he has to say against Husserl's method of eidetic
intuition against the idea of a descriptive philosophy in general
(p. 255). And it is against this broad aspect of Husserl's position that
his main argument, which I have schematically outlined above, is
directed. It is here where I believe that Mr Pettit is not really
arguing with Husserl, but using his terms in a way other than that in
which Husserl used them. Both his characterisation of the *subject-
matter* of philosophy and his interpretation of Husserl's basic
conception of philosophical *method* I believe to be erroneous. Let me
consider these two points in order.

THE SUBJECT-MATTER OF PHILOSOPHY

The subject-matter of philosophy, says Mr Pettit, is for Husserl
'conscious human behaviour' (p. 242), and Mr Pettit himself
agrees with this (p. 251). I shall not quarrel about the term 'behaviour'. Husserl would not have used it, of course, and would have
spoken of consciousness *simpliciter*. But this is not to be our problem.
I am in sympathy with the behaviouristic turn which Mr Pettit
gives to the concept of consciousness. What is really troublesome is
something else. When we speak either of human consciousness or of
conscious human behaviour without further qualification, would we
not rather say that this is the subject-matter of a particular empirical
science, namely psychology? I believe that most contemporary
philosophers would say this, and certainly Husserl would have.
Surely we cannot say what philosophy is about by delimiting any
one region of objects. Philosophy always has been·characterised by
distinguishing it from the sciences in some way. And this is also what
Husserl does. To give a full account of the way Husserl distinguishes
philosophy from the sciences would lead us too far afield in the
present context.[1] Let it suffice that at the beginning of the text

[1] Cf. my *Wahrheitsbegriff . . .* (§§ 8–9).

which Mr Pettit uses as his point of departure,[1] Husserl stresses the reflective character of philosophy in contrast to the 'direct' unreflective character of our understanding in the sciences and in ordinary life.

What is the basis of such a distinction? Perhaps I can put it like this. In all our understanding there is something which we understand but to which we pay no attention. The most straightforward example is the meaning of the words we use. In science or ordinary life our attention is directed to what we say, not to the meaning of what we say. This unheeded penumbra of our understanding is something we may be said to know, whereas that to which our attention is normally directed, we may sometimes be said to know, sometimes not. (We may or may not know that *p*, but, in doubting that, we know what '*p*' means.) However, when we are asked to say what we thus know, we usually find if difficult to answer, and that because of the difficulty of focusing our attention on something to which our attention is not directed normally. So here is an aspect of all understanding, of which we may say that everything which belongs to it we know already ('*a priori*'), even though this knowledge is not explicit and therefore seems susceptible to some sort of further illumination. According to Husserl, as according to many earlier as well as contemporary philosophers, this knowledge is the domain of philosophy.

Yet Husserl would insist that such an account is still too general. In order to characterise philosophy this domain has to be restricted in a certain way. What are the specifically philosophical problems? I shall try to lead up to Husserl's answer by way of a discussion of contemporary linguistic philosophy.

In the above account, I deliberately chose the meaning of words as an example. Let us now, as is customary in linguistic philosophy, restrict the realm of understanding to the understanding of linguistic expressions. The domain of philosophy then seems to be that of the meaning of words. But shall we say that it is the task of philosophy to deal with the meaning of all words? Or only of the more important ones? But which are the more important words?

From some of the writings of those called ordinary-language philosophers, for example J. L. Austin, one might get the impression

[1] I do not quite understand why Mr Pettit picked out just this little book for a discussion of Husserl's philosophical method. This book has become famous for containing the first statement of the method of 'phenomenological reduction', but it is precisely this aspect of Husserl's method which Mr Pettit leaves entirely out of consideration. I shall do likewise, because this aspect of Husserl's method presupposes an egological conception of meaning and justification, and is therefore of least interest to contemporary philosophy with its intersubjective conception of meaning and justification. But it should at least be remarked that Husserl himself considered the 'reduction' to be the most important aspect of his method.

that in principle all words are considered worthy of philosophical reflection, and there seems to be no criterion for the important ones. A remarkable advance was made in my opinion by P. F. Strawson. He requires for philosophy proper, which he calls 'metaphysics', a certain 'level of generality'. With this he does not mean words of greater generality, but the 'general structure' of our 'conceptual apparatus'.[1] By such a characterisation, Strawson only gave expression to what analytical philosophers have been doing, more or less, all along. They were interested not so much in the meaning of particular expressions but rather in the general structure of linguistic understanding. And this redefinition of the philosophical enterprise provides us also with a criterion for distinguishing the philosophically important words (e.g. the word 'meaning' itself is such a word, while the meaning of 'bachelor' is of no philosophical interest except as an example).

It is important to notice that the step from the analysis of word meaning to the analysis of the structure of linguistic understanding is not just a step from the less to the more general. The structure which is being analysed is, although linguistic, not given in words at all. On the contrary, philosophers have to invent new words (or new meanings for old words) in order to describe the structural aspects they are interested in (e.g. 'reference', 'illocutionary act'). What is being investigated is not, or at least not primarily, the meaning of linguistic expressions, yet it fits into the general account of philosophy given above. The general structure and functioning of our linguistic expressions is something we understand as well as the meanings of the expressions themselves; and of it, as well as of the meaning of the expressions, we may be said to have a specifically inexplicit knowledge.

And now a further step seems required. The description of the structure of linguistic understanding leads us to aspects of understanding or experience which, although connected with language, are not in themselves linguistic. If all understanding were an understanding of sentences, we could never understand a connection between a number of sentences save by construing them as one complex sentence. But not only the connection between the primary elements of understanding may be non-linguistic, the primary elements themselves may be non-linguistic. As an example, consider actions. The person who does something consciously understands and even knows what he is doing, yet neither he nor anybody else

---

[1] 'Analyse, science et métaphysique', in *La Philosophie Analytique*, Cahiers de Royaumont, IV (1962) p. 115 (English translation in R. Rorty, *The Linguistic Turn* (1967) pp. 312–20).

may be able to express in words what he is doing (making just this grimace, playing precisely that tune). We have therefore to redefine the philosophical enterprise once more: its subject-matter seems to be our knowledge of the structure of all conscious experience, of the structure of understanding in general, not merely of linguistic understanding. Accordingly, the criterion given above for philosophically important words has to be extended: not only those words are philosophically interesting which describe semantic structure, but all those which describe any structural aspects of our understanding.

This redefinition of philosophy in its turn corresponds to the general account of philosophy given above and it also seems to be applicable to what analytical philosophers actually do. Yet I presume that many of them would protest against my claim that what they are doing is analysing non-linguistic experience. Perhaps they would insist that what they are doing is analysing the meaning of certain words. This is true enough. But does it explain why they are concentrating on just these words and not on others? Besides, here too new words have to be invented, new verbal distinctions have to be drawn. We can only analyse the structure of our non-linguistic understanding by analysing the way we speak about it or in connection with it, yet when we do that we are not just analysing the meaning of certain words nor are we analysing the structure of our speech.

With this characterisation of the subject-matter of philosophy as the structure of our understanding, we have arrived at Husserl's fundamental conception of philosophy. According to Husserl, the aim of philosophy is to clarify our inexplicit knowledge of the structure of our experience and of the different types of our experience.[1] This conception of philosophy might contain a challenge to contemporary analytical philosophy, because (if the account I have given is correct) such a description of philosophy (even though in a new linguistic dress) seems to be applicable to what analytical philosophers are doing, although they are not aware of it. One reason why this is so may be that in England far more than on the Continent the traditional division of philosophy into disciplines continues to be taken for granted. Now these disciplines are simply the result of the distinctions among different types of experience and understanding as they were being drawn by earlier philosophers, according to criteria which may, at least in part, appear obsolete to us. Instead of taking these divisions for granted, we should therefore try to find our own, contemporary answer to the question of what

[1] Cf. my *Wahrheitsbegriff* ... (§ 8).

fundamental types of understanding ought to be distinguished and how they are interrelated. Such a programme presupposes, of course, that we revive (not as a dogma, but as a problem) the old idea, shared by Husserl, that philosophy is one and universal. And this idea must be revived if it is true that our understanding is somehow one and all-embracing and not just a chest of many drawers. As far as I can see, such a programme would not contradict any essential tenet of linguistic philosophy, and some recent work like that of Strawson and Hampshire seems to me to lead in this very direction.

With the above redefinition of philosophy – and this is Husserl's definition – I have come very close to the characterisation of philosophy given by Mr Pettit; however, a qualification has now been added. To use Mr Pettit's terms, the subject-matter of philosophy is not simply conscious human behaviour, but our inexplicit knowledge of the structure of our conscious behaviour. This qualification will prove important for determining what is the method of philosophy.

THE METHOD OF PHILOSOPHY

The subject-matter of philosophy must somehow determine the methods which are to be applied to it. I have claimed that the domain of philosophy is that penumbra of our understanding which contains what we know already though inexplicitly, and that it is this inexplicitness which makes it open to some form of illumination. The illumination that is being called for is therefore a method for converting inexplicit knowledge into explicit knowledge, and nothing more. When we begin to reflect on our inexplicit knowledge, we become aware of being confused about what we know. Accordingly, the process of illumination that is in question must consist in a transition from confused knowledge to clear knowledge. The method that is being called for must have the character of clarification. How this is to be achieved we shall have to ask later. At any rate, it is clarification that philosophers like Husserl or Wittgenstein mean when they speak of description as the only adequate philosophical method.[1]

What is being called for, then, is clarification, and nothing more, since the kind of knowledge with which we are concerned in philosophy does not seem to allow of anything else. It is hard to see that anything like 'explanation' can have a place in philosophy. The

[1] Husserl himself often uses such expressions as '*zur Klarheit bringen*', '*aufklären*'. The word '*aufklären*', and not '*erklären*', is also used by Husserl in the sentence which Mr Pettit cites on p. 248, where it is quite erroneously rendered as 'explain'. This mistake of the translators had induced Mr Pettit to claim that Husserl gives philosophical description an 'explanatory function' (pp. 248f).

kind of knowledge that is susceptible to, and may call for, explanation is synthetic. Here and only here does it make sense to say: 'Thus it is, but why?' The knowledge with which philosophy is concerned is analytic, and here it does not make sense to say 'Thus it is, but why?' What does make sense is to ask for the relation in which something that we understand stands to other things that we understand; but this is part of what we understand and its discovery is again descriptive.

How is it possible that Mr Pettit should have come to the contrary conclusion, namely that 'the nature of philosophical investigation is explanatory and not descriptive' (p. 251)? As he himself admits (pp. 252f.), his only reason is a negative one, the belief that an exclusively descriptive method in philosophy would lead to nothing. This conclusion depends in turn on his assumption, criticised above, that the subject-matter of philosophy is 'conscious human behaviour'. From this assumption Mr Pettit is led to the assertion that philosophical description would be 'superfluous', since it would only repeat what is contained in our experience (p. 247). 'Description' merely 'serves to represent an experience', and 'such representation does not seem to be of any use to the philosopher' (p. 247). Indeed it is not, if description is nothing but the description of concrete experience. That Mr Pettit should assume this is the result of his failure to distinguish between the experience itself and the implicit knowledge within experience; more specifically, between the experience and the structure of experience. When we describe the structure of some experience, we do not just repeat what somebody who has the experience would say to describe it.

Mr Pettit finally considers as a 'last line of defence' open to the descriptivist the claim that there is an especially privileged and novel description, and that this is the philosophical one (p. 248). Now this is no last line of defence. The descriptivist would claim from the start that, whether privileged or not, philosophical description is indeed a novel one, and this simply because it is different. According to Mr Pettit this is an 'absurdity'; in particular, this novel kind of description would demand a 'language of its own' (p. 248f.). But that is in fact the case, as has been shown above: philosophers have to invent new words to describe structural aspects which have not found articulation in ordinary language.

From Mr Pettit's characterisation of the subject-matter of philosophy as conscious human behaviour it follows consistently that the only method which we can employ without repetition on this subject-matter is to form 'hypotheses' to 'explain why the data' of conscious human behaviour 'appear as they do' p. (254). Having characterised the subject-matter of philosophy as that which one would normally call the subject-matter of psychology, it appears reasonable that Mr Pettit should also describe the method of philosophy as that which one would normally attribute to empirical psychology. As far as I can see, no difference between philosophy and psychology remains. Mr Pettit's distinction between reductive and non-reductive explanation (p. 254), which is not clear to me, does not help, since a non-reductive empirical psychology is equally conceivable.

One reason why Mr Pettit attacks the descriptive conception of philosophy is that it led Husserl to the idea of a special kind of philosophical 'experience' (p. 248). This brings us back to the question that was left open: how is clarification to be achieved, what does it mean concretely? Until this question is answered, we have not refuted Mr Pettit's contention that the assumption of a special philosophical 'description' is unwarranted.

Husserl was guided in his extensive thinking on this question by the concepts 'intention' and 'intuition'. Although I consider Husserl's notion of intuition untenable, I believe that this pair of concepts contains a fundamental insight that can be freed from that idea. Mr Pettit does not describe Husserl's conception quite correctly: what Husserl calls intuition is not a 'receptivity to data', to which the intention adds a meaning (p. 242). The intuition is for Husserl always dependent on, and functionally related to, the intention (meaning). The intuition is called the realisation (*Erfüllung*)[1] of the intention, and it is better to dispense with the word 'intuition' altogether and retain only the more formal term. What Husserl wants to say is this: When we turn our attention to the meaning of a word, it usually remains at first unclear to us, we do not really 'grasp' the meaning and this is what Husserl calls the 'mere intention'. To understand the meaning clearly, to grasp it, would be the 'realisation' of the intention. 'Intention' and 'realisation' are therefore simply Husserl's terms for the beginning and end of the process of clarification.[2]

We can now understand what Husserl considers to be the supreme methodological rule for all philosophy. It is this: never be content with mere intentions but always bring them to realisation.[3] This rule obviously remains valid for every descriptive philosophy. But

[1] This may be the most satisfactory translation. Husserl himself used the expression '*realisieren*' synonymously with '*erfüllen*'; cf. *Logische Untersuchungen*, 2nd ed., II 1, pp. 37–8.
[2] Husserl's theory is actually more complicated, since it covers not only clarification but also verification, but we can safely overlook this in the present context.
[3] Cf. *Logische Untersuchungen*, II, Einleitung, §2.

what does 'realisation' consist in? It is here that Husserl's conception of an intuition of essences comes in. That the realisation should come about by way of an intuition appeared to him self-evident, but must be taken by us as only one possible answer. If we refuse to accept the assumption of a mental eye and if we insist that meanings are something essentially intersubjective, then the realisation of the intention of a meaning must be, at least potentially, an intersubjective process. This process I should like to call with Paul Lorenzen the 'methodical introduction' of the meaning.[1] The idea is well known and goes back to Wittgenstein. The (or a) meaning of a term is methodically introduced by presenting all the steps that would have to be taken to teach or show somebody the use of the term in this meaning, without presupposing that he already knows a synonymous term. From this point of view, the idea that the realisation of the 'intention' of a meaning consists in an intuition appears as an attempt to avoid the efforts of methodical introduction. It is obviously far simpler to imagine having an intuition of the (or a) meaning of the word 'good' than to present a methodical introduction of it.

With the concept of methodical introduction the vague idea of the clarification of meaning has acquired a definite sense. Husserl's methodological rule can be reformulated thus: give a methodical introduction of the meaning of all the words with which you deal. This rule obviously applies both to the case where we wish to clarify meanings already in use and to the introduction of new terms.[2]

At this point a note may be in order about what is often considered to be the most important methodological controversy in contemporary linguistic philosophy, the controversy between constructivists of ideal languages and ordinary-language philosophers. Two different distinctions which are often confused appear to me to be involved in this controversy. On the one hand, there is the distinction between (*a*) the analysis of linguistic expressions already in use and (*b*) the introduction of new expressions or of new (or newly delimited) meanings. On the other hand, we have two different conceptions of the object of philosophy: (i) the clarification of the structure of our understanding, and (ii) the construction of new languages which can serve certain functions (for example, clarity) better than our given language. Ordinary-language philosophy is often attacked as if it simply consisted in (*a*). But the programme of this philosophy is or, if not, should be, (i), and (i) does not contradict (*b*), indeed it

[1] Lorenzen, 'Methodisches Denken', *Ratio*, VII (1965) 1–23.
[2] To speak both of 'the introduction of a term' and of 'the introduction of a meaning' seems to me innocuous, because both expressions are to be understood as abbreviations for 'the introduction of a term in a certain meaning'.

includes (*b*), as was shown above. Therefore (ii) cannot be recommended by simply assimilating (i) to (*a*). Besides, (ii) is no real
alternative to (i), since its relation to (i) is that of part to whole.
The proposal of a new language does not dispense one from the
task of philosophical clarification, and this now includes in addition
the demonstrating of the relation in which the new language stands
to ordinary language. It is a mistake to confuse clarity in the use of a
language with philosophical clarity about the language.[1]

Ordinary-language philosophy therefore will have to follow the
rule of the methodical introduction of meanings in both senses: the
methodical reintroduction of meanings already in use and the
introduction of new meanings.

With the concept of methodical introduction of meanings the
general idea of clarification has acquired a definite sense only in one
of its two aspects, namely, where we speak of the clarification of the
meaning of a term. If philosophy is understood, as was suggested
above, as the clarification of the structure of our understanding, this
clarification is not just a clarification of meanings: the structure ot
understanding has not yet been clearly described when all the terms
which are used in this description have been methodically introduced. Of this second aspect of the concept of clarification, which
appears to me to be fundamental for an adequate methodical
conception of a descriptive philosophy, I shall not attempt to give
an exposition here. I wish I had one to give.

[1] This mistake has led many linguistic philosophers to believe that as soon as we
no longer stumble over our language when using it, philosophy will become
superfluous. It is true that the ambiguities and paradoxes which we hit upon in the
use of language often serve as the occasions for philosophical reflection, but that
penumbra of our understanding, to which our attention is normally not directed, is
there anyway and can be reflected upon just as well for the sake of perspicuity alone.

19

THE CASE FOR EXPLANATION CONTINUED: A REPLY TO PROFESSOR TUGENDHAT

Philip Pettit

THE attempt to reply to a reply may seem inelegant; in the present case, however, I see it as necessary. Professor Tugendhat has presented his view of philosophy with great clarity, and related it to mine by criticism. I wish in turn to present my view through the criticism of his; if you like, I wish to complete the circle of debate.

Professor Tugendhat argues that the subject-matter of philosophy is not quite conscious human behaviour, but something that is known implicitly in that behaviour, much as the meaning of words is known implicitly in speech; its structure (pp. 260–2; I presume that Professor Tugendhat is speaking somewhat imprecisely when he says that the subject-matter of philosophy is the knowledge of this structure, rather than the structure itself). The method whereby philosophy is to investigate the structure of conscious behaviour is descriptive (p. 262f.). More precisely, it is a form of clarification akin to the clarification of our words which we can achieve by the method-ical introduction of their meaning (p. 265). But what precisely it involves is a question left open by Professor Tugendhat at the end of his paper (p. 266).

To put the two views of philosophical methodology in dialogue, it is necessary to return to the fundamental concepts of description and explanation and give a more thorough account of them.

A description in the proper or low-level sense is a proposition or series of propositions which is capable of being directly verified in one experience, or in the report of one experience. In this sense a description is always the description of a concrete experience. Professor Tugendhat suggests that it is not, when he speaks of the description of the structure of an experience (p. 263). This description is supposed to be based on our implicit knowledge of that structure. But surely this implicit knowledge – the more so since it is something capable of being brought to attention (p. 259) – is a form of experience which has the structure for its object? And in the case the description is a description of the concrete experience of the structure. Or are we brought back to some form of experience with a non-concrete object, a new intuition of essences? We will return later to this question.

On the scheme presented in my paper, high-level description is contrasted with the proper low-level form. This high-level description would have collective entities for its objects, such as the economy of the nation; it is meant to be verified directly, but in a number of experiences or reports I am no longer so sure of this high-level description; a proposition which seems to be of this form may often be an explanation of one of the types discussed below. In any case, we may include it within our scheme.

There is a further form of description, however, which does not receive discussion in my paper. Unlike low-level description, it is verified in a number of experiences. Unlike both low-level and high-level, it is verified indirectly: there is a process of argument involved. This description is not particular but generalised. It takes the form 'Every X is Y', where 'X is Y' is a particular description. The experiences in which the generalised description is verified are the experiences to which its part particularisations refer. The argument through which it is verified is the process of inference which Lukasiewicz called 'reduction'. This process is opposed to deduction: it involves the strictly improper inference from the consequent of a conditional proposition to its antecedent rather than the other way around. In generalisation we argue as follows: if A then B, B, therefore A, where A is the generalisation and B the series of particular descriptions, or perhaps one of them, which it generalises.

The reductive process of inference may serve here as our criterion for an explanation. Deduction only seems to base explanation on axiomatic systems; it is involved too in explanation where the antecedent is capable of independent verification, but in this case reduction is also involved. Sometimes reduction may ground the useless generalisation which explains nothing. But in most cases the reductive argument grounds what may be called an explanation: the proposition or series of propositions which makes sense of some problematic set of data or descriptions.

On our criterion, then, the generalised description is also a form of explanation: let us call it the 'generalising explanation'. It makes sense of the facts recorded in the particular descriptions which it generalises. What enables us to call it a generalising explanation is that no non-logical variables occur in it which do not appear in the descriptions which it explains.

And this brings us to the concept of the non-generalising explanation which explains a certain description or set of descriptions – particular or generalised – but contains some non-logical variable or variables that do not appear in the descriptions. This is the explanation which is perhaps of most importance to us. It is exemplified in the common-sense explanation of the sound from the door and the physicist's explanation of the noise.

But non-generalising explanations divide into two further types because one class among them contain some non-logical variables – most notoriously the physical explanations that use terms like 'anti-matter' – which could not conceivably occur in a description. These words are defined by a process of 'implicit definition', as the German mathematician Hilbert called it, and not in terms of descriptive data or further descriptive words. In implicit definition a set of terms define one another by each delimiting the use which the other has. Thus the concepts of point and line implicitly define one another in Euclidian geometry.[1]

We are left with a scheme of the following sort:

$$\text{Description} \begin{cases} \text{particular: low-level} \\ \qquad\qquad\text{high-level} \\ \text{generalised} = \text{generalising} \\ \qquad \text{non-generalising: descriptive} \\ \qquad\qquad\qquad\text{non-descriptive} \end{cases} \Bigg\} \text{Explanation}$$

This scheme will enable us to articulate the argument between Professor Tugendhat's view of philosophy and mine.

Of what kind, then, are the typical philosophical propositions? On the view defended in my paper they are mainly particular low-level descriptions and non-generalising explanations which often involve non-descriptive terms. There are also generalisations of course, more or less akin to those which predominate in the sciences, though of little explanatory value.[2] But what does Professor Tugendhat say?

---

[1] Cf. E. Nagel, *The Structure of Science* (1961) pp. 91–3.

[2] On the difference between the generalisation which does have explanatory power and that which does not, between the explanation which makes intelligible the fact that data appear in the way they do and that which fails to make this intelligible, cf. Nagel, op. cit., pp. 49–52. The 'useless' generalisation, also mentioned above, shows that the reductive argument as a criterion of explanation does need refinement.

He maintains that philosophical propositions are clarificatory or, as he also says, descriptive in a sense in which description need not be the description of a concrete experience (pp. 262f.). Where then can such propositions fit into our scheme?

The clue to classifying them may be found in the remark of a contemporary logician, I. M. Bochenski:

> It is one of the most important insights of exact methodology that the truth of a sentence must be either apprehended directly (or inferred); there is not, and furthermore there cannot be, any other way.[1]

We may ask whether Professor Tugendhat's clarificatory propositions are to be verified by direct experience or by inference.

If they are to be verified by inference, then they must be verified by deduction since this only seems to be significant in axiomatic systems. The inference must be reductive. But if philosophical propositions are reductively established, then on the criterion offered above they are explanatory. This would mean that the argument between Professor Tugendhat and me is primarily a terminological one.

Despite what he says about 'showing' and 'seeing' (p. 257), it is more likely that Professor Tugendhat holds that philosophical propositions are verified directly in experience. In that case they are particular descriptions in the strict sense suggested by our scheme. The protest that they are descriptions of another sort does not make sense to me. If they are based on an implicit knowledge which can be transformed into direct attention (p. 259), then they seem to be nothing other than particular descriptions of what is found in an experience normally called 'consciousness'.

Or does Professor Tugendhat suggest, in an idiom that is not altogether unfamiliar, that the experience on which philosophy relies is of a special type? It is to be the experience of a structure or structures in conscious behaviour (pp. 260f.). But there is no definition of a structure offered. Is the structure a particular thing such as might be the object of any experience? Hardly, since philosophical description is not supposed to be the description of a concrete experience (p. 263). The structure or structures with which philosophy concerns itself must be abstract entities of some sort. But in that case how are they to be distinguished from the essences of which

[1] I. M. Bochenski, *The Methods of Contemporary Thought* (Dordrecht, 1965) p. 65.

[2] Professor Tugendhat might perhaps argue that they are collective entities which are the objects of high-level description. Fairly or not, this possibility has not been considered here because of the difficulties noted above with the identification of the high-level description.

Husserl spoke?[2] Is Professor Tugendhat driven back to admit an experience which differs in no significant way from Husserl's intuition of essences? He explicitly rejects the idea of such an intuition (p. 265), but fails to put anything in its place (p. 266). It is difficult not to think that his assertions are out of line with the real movement of his thought.

We have forced a dilemma of Professor Tugendhat. If the clarificatory propositions, to which he limits philosophy, are based on inference, then, on our scheme, they are explanatory and the debate is terminological. If they are not based on inference, then they must be particular descriptions and, granted the tenor of Professor Tugendhat's remarks, must be based on a special type of experience not unlike Husserl's intuition. On the argument of my paper, such an experience is a fiction. Where is the philosophical language which could carry a special experience? There is only the ordinary language, the language of concrete things and qualities. To suggest, as Professor Tugendhat does (p. 263), that the technical terms of philosophy constitute such a language is to miss the point at issue. These terms are certainly new but it is only in a patently equivocal sense that they constitute a new type of language.

To sum up, then, Professor Tugendhat says that the work of philosophy is to describe the structure of conscious human behaviour. It seems plain to me that in doing so he falls into the fallacy of introducing a metaphysical entity to get rid of a methodological problem. He falls into the same mistake as the one who would say that physics describes the structure of matter and feels that he has sketched an adequate methodology of the science. For what is the structure of which Professor Tugendhat speaks? And in what possible sense can it become the object of a description? So far as I can see, he offers no definition of his two central terms: 'structure' and 'description'. The claim that philosophy describes the structure of conscious human behaviour hardly seems to have any more content than a metaphorical commonplace.

But what validity has the opposed claim that philosophy attempts to describe and explain conscious human behaviour? Professor Tugendhat offers one serious objection to this claim which is independent of his own position. It is the objection that on my account philosophy and psychology become indistinguishable (pp. 258, 263-4). This we must now consider.

There are two sciences or, better perhaps, two groups of sciences which deal with human behaviour: the social sciences and the psychological ones. The one group studies patterns in the behaviour of society, the other patterns in individual behaviour. Each begins from particular descriptions and, in articulating patterns, offers generalisations of these. They both go on then, or at least attempt to go on, to present non-generalising explanations which make sense of the intermediary generalisations. Marx attempts a sociological explanation of this type with his theory of the unconscious.

If philosophy is the attempt to explain conscious human behaviour, how is it to be distinguished from these sciences? It is distinguished in the fact that it takes behaviour from the non-observational standpoint of consciousness – from the point of view of Professor Tugendhat's implicit knowledge – and tries to explain that behaviour in the merely human characteristics with which it appears there, not in the variations which it manifests at the individual and social levels to an observer. This is to say, for instance, that philosophy tries to explain the social relations as such and not the actual pattern of those relations, the motive and not the pattern in the sources of motive. The social and psychological sciences will often involve themselves in philosophy, of course – witness Marx and Freud – but the disciplines are quite distinct from one another. They have a common explanatory method but each a subject-matter which is at least formally unique: the social science studies behaviour in its social variations, the psychological one behaviour in its individual variations; philosophy studies behaviour simply, behaviour in the fundamental status which it has for consciousness.

A final reflection on what it means for philosophy to explain conscious behaviour will reveal why I find Professor Tugendhat's view that it describes the structure of that behaviour no more than a metaphorical account of philosophy. On the methodology defended in my paper, philosophy must attempt to explain perception, for instance, or emotion. In such an attempt it will define a number of terms, some of which must undoubtedly be descriptive, and construct a system with them which it offers as the model for emotion or perception. This system is an explanatory success when it makes sense of the descriptive data from which it originates by a reductive process of argument. It is easy to see that in the version which imagination will give of this method, the theoretical philosophical construct or system must appear as the picture of the internal structure or make-up of the phenomena explained. For that reason it becomes perfectly plausible to speak, in a metaphorical idiom of philosophy describing the structure of conscious human behaviour. It remains nevertheless methodologically unhelpful.

PHENOMENOLOGY AS THE METHOD OF PHILOSOPHY

Anthony Manser

THE title of this conference is 'Philosophers into Europe'; I am not sure precisely what the organisers had in mind, but I presume they wanted to demonstrate that some form of 'common market-place' or forum was possible for English and European philosophy. If this is a correct account of their aims, then it seems to me that it will best be achieved by English philosophers endeavouring to show their colleagues across the Channel that the kind of researches which we are engaged in in this country are in fact relevant, and importantly so, to what is being done in Europe. And this means not trying to produce philosophy in the idiom that is currently employed in Continental schools, but producing it in our own current idiom and trying to show how this is relevant to questions asked or problems raised by Husserl, Heidegger or Merleau-Ponty and their disciples and colleagues. Hence I here make no attempt to speak in the language of phenomenology, though I will often draw attention to things that phenomenologists have said.

Both Mr Pettit and Professor Tugendhat attend mainly to Husserl, as the first 'phenomenologist', though both also refer to many other contemporary philosophers. Like them, I will centre my remarks on Husserl, but, again like them, I shall not be concerned with a detailed analysis of his writings: this is a symposium of philosophical method, to which Husserl and phenomenology are thought to have made important contributions. Hence I think it would be a pity if discussion were to concentrate on the meaning of a particular remark of Husserl's rather than on the general theme of the papers presented. It is clear the Husserl regarded phenomenology as above all a *method* of philosophy, if, indeed, not the only possible method, and he connected this with another fundamental idea, that of 'philosophy as a strict or rigorous science'. (*Philosophie als strenge Wissenschaft*), an idea which seems to run through all his works. And this point is again connected with his idea of philosophy as something which forms a foundation for all other branches of knowledge, so that they cannot really be satisfactorily pursued if it has not properly laid their foundations. This means that philosophy cannot have anything uncertain about it. The scandal is that so far it had not succeeded in reaching this necessary certainty. Husserl even bizarrely envisaged the possibility that, once the foundations had been truly laid by his own work, generations of phenomenologists could each perform his descriptive task, confident that the validity of the method would guarantee the certainty of their results. Such descriptive activity would presumably not need great philosophical skill, any more than the research students of a great scientist need any such. The application of the method to the problem at hand is all that is required.

That Husserl did mean something like this is, I think, fairly clear. In his *Philosophy as a Rigorous Science* (1911) he remarks: 'Kant was fond of saying that one could not learn philosophy, only to philosophise. What is this but an admission of philosophy's unscientific character? As far as science, real science, extends, so far can one teach and learn, and this everywhere in the same sense'. His contrast is with the sciences of mathematics and physics and his aim was to make philosophy like them. I mention this point here because neither symposiast says much about this aspect of Husserl's work, but it seems to me necessarily connected with the idea of a method in philosophy. The right method will produce agreed results, and, just as most physicists most of the time can rely on what is published in their journals without checking them in detail, so, if Husserl's programme were carried out, he thinks future philosophers will do the same. (It is perhaps worth remarking in parenthesis that it is not altogether clear that it is just a method that enables physicists to agree. More would need to be said about this point than can be discussed here).

It is a curious feature of this symposium that both writers apparently destroy their ostensible subject-matter, phenomenology, though in very different ways. Mr Pettit does this by making the aim of philosophy explanation, not description, as Husserl insisted. One thing is clear: if Mr Pettit insists on explanation in the ordinary sense as the aim of philosophy, then he is no phenomenologist.

Professor Tugendhat demolishes a central idea of Husserl's phenomenology by his rejection of 'eidetic intuition' and the 'seeing' of universals (p. 257). And he thinks that this also destroys most of pre-Husserlian philosophy, which equally depended on the notion of the 'mental eye'. He further claims that Wittgenstein showed all such talk to be nonsense. Certainly Husserl and other philosophers before him have made use of the idea of a 'mental eye' to explain the way in which we understand arguments or recognise *a priori* truths, but one of the dangers of talking about philosophy, rather than actually doing it, is that there is a tendency to misrepresent what actually goes on in philosophical works. Husserl often talked about 'seeing' universals, but in his writings he relied on the kinds of argumentation that philosophers have always used, was in fact concerned to 'show' others what he was talking about. He did not merely chronicle his 'eidetic intuitions' and expect others to accept them, as a glance at his work will show. Indeed, if he had not proceeded in this way, had not striven to convince his readers of the truth of his remarks, he would hardly be entitled to be called a 'philosopher'. The very fact that he was writing in a public language might be said to compel such an approach. Given this, I wonder if the relative paucity of actual phenomenological descriptions in the writings of Husserl, compared with the amount of discussion of what is involved in giving such a description, is not due to the fact that philosophy must undertake to be public, to convince. If a philosopher talks of a 'mental eye' then he has to assume that this is the same in all of us. Descartes, for example, did not think of the *cogito* as a peculiar act which only he could perform, but as something that should be evident to anyone who approached without prejudices. And these 'prejudices' were removed by a process of argument. The *cogito* might be an 'internal' act, but it was necessarily the same in all men; if it were not, there would be little point in discussing it. And much the same, I think, can be said of Husserl's 'mental eye'.

But although both symposiasts seem in different ways to destroy central ideas of Husserl's phenomenology, there is much on which they agree. The basic agreement, then, between the two symposiasts is that they both accept the idea of a particular subject-matter of philosophy and that of a method of doing it. These two things are closely connected and, it seems to me, serious philosophical errors. If the end of a philosophical tradition came with Wittgenstein, then this is the one he destroyed.

Professor Tugendhat explicitly makes the connection between method and subject-matter, e.g. 'The subject-matter of philosophy must somehow determine the methods which are to be applied to it' (p. 262). But, by entitling the section in which this sentence occurs

'The Method of Philosophy' he makes it clear that he expects there to be only one real method. At first sight it seems reasonable to say that the nature of the subject-matter determines the method of investigating it, though even in the case of the natural sciences I am not sure how helpful this remark is. For it does not seem to be obvious *a priori* that the investigation of nature demands the hypothetico-deductive method – this surely came to be seen appropriate as the result of unmethodical prior investigations. And even if a case can be made out for a clear sense of method in the natural sciences, the case of philosophy might well seem to be different. It is surprising that neither Professor Tugendhat nor Mr Pettit find anything problematical in the idea of a philosophical method, though I think it is clear that their belief in a particular subject-matter of philosophy helps to conceal the difficulty from them. Part of the trouble is that the subject-matter of philosophy is thought to be something especially important – in some sense philosophy is felt to be a foundation for everything else. This seems to involve generality, or at least width of scope, and so the method must be similarly wide and at the same time give the air of profundity.

This is connected with the widespread feeling that there is something trivial about much contemporary English philosophy. Because, for example, Austin suggests dealing not with the nature of beauty, but rather with the difference between the dainty and the dumpy, it is felt that something has been lost. Professor Tugendhat certainly feels this way (cf. pp. 259–60). I must add one minor point about his remarks on 'linguistic philosophy'; he says, 'Let us now, as is customary in linguistic philosophy, restrict the realm of understanding to the understanding of linguistic expressions' (p. 259). I know of no one who has made such a demand. He wants linguistic philosophers to deal with the important words in their studies. But Austin's point was that there was no *a priori* method of determining which words were the important ones. Attempting to construct a genuinely 'presuppositionless' philosophy (though he probably would not have put it in this way), he left it an open question, one to be dealt with by detailed work, which words were the ones that mattered. And very often he showed that the kind of term on which philosophers had hitherto concentrated their attention was an artificial philosophic construction, not the name for a genuine problem. The central point here is that to start, as Husserl did, with a belief in the traditional subject-matter of philosophy is already to be saddled with a mass of unnoticed presuppositions.

It is because Professor Tugendhat feels like this that he regards Strawson's aim of 'laying bare the most general features of our

conceptual structure' as an important advance (p. 260). The first
point that can be made here is Austin's; there is no reason to suppose
that we have a 'conceptual structure', that, in his words, 'The
various models used in creating our vocabulary, primitive or recent,
should all fit together neatly as parts into one single, total model or
scheme. . . .'[1] If one starts an investigation with a belief in some
underlying scheme, then one is liable to distort the facts to make
them fit, and it seems that this is what Strawson in fact does in
Individuals. I cannot here demonstrate this in detail, though in fairness
to Strawson I must add that I do not think he intends 'descriptive
metaphysics' to replace philosophy, but rather to constitute one
section of it.

There is a common philosophical confusion here which it is
important to get clear about. Certainly many philosophical problems have an air of depth about them, and this need not be an
illusion. But this is not to say that they are very general or fundamental in the sense of underlying the rest of our knowledge. As if
philosophy were needed to make us certain of everyday facts. But
talk in terms of 'method' and 'subject-matter' may lead to confusions. For example, Professor Tugendhat speaks of the 'methodical
introduction' of a meaning, which he explains by saying that the
meaning of a term is methodically introduced by presenting all the
steps which would have to be taken to teach (show) somebody the
use of the term in this meaning, without presupposing that he already knew a synonymous term (cf. pp. 265–6). He attributes this
notion to Wittgenstein, and also suggests that linguistic philosophers
will have to follow this rule. Now Wittgenstein certainly discusses the
way in which a child learns the word 'pain', though it is to be noted
that he does not attempt anything like a complete account of this
complex process. The point of the example is to get rid of problems
that philosophers have raised about knowing the meaning of such a
word only from one's own case. For if the kind of account which
Wittgenstein is criticising were correct, then it is difficult to see how
we could be sure that the child had learnt the word correctly, or how
we could attempt to teach it to him. In the face of some common
philosophical arguments, the technique succeeds. But it does not
follow, nor did Wittgenstein think it did, that the same technique
would be of use in other cases.

Here the craving for generality has misled philosophers in a way
that they would not be misled in ordinary life. Because Dr X's medicine
was good for my stomach-ache, it does not follow that it will be good
for my cold, not even for your stomach-ache. We must be clear about

[1] *Philosophical Papers* (Oxford, 1961) p. 151.

the disease before we can discuss the remedy. Wittgenstein's central point in his later works was that there are many different philosophical problems, and hence many different remedies. Compare *Philosophical Investigations* 133: 'There is not *a* philosophical method, though there are indeed methods, like different therapies'. And: 'Think of the tools in a tool-box: there is a hammer, pliers, a saw, a screw-driver, a rule, a glue-pot, glue, nails and screws . . .' (ibid. 11). I believe that Wittgenstein has shown the 'right method in philosophy', but this is not one way of handling all cases, any more than the carpenter's tools are all for one task. The 'method' of carpentry, as it were, is to employ all the tools in the correct manner, appropriate to the job in hand. And it should be remembered that there is no given set of tools; the carpenter may improvise new ones to deal with new situations, or construct a jig for one particular job and throw it away afterwards.

These last two cases are important, for there is a tendency to think that if there is not *one* method, then there must be some finite set of them. And there have been philosophers who have used *Philosophical Investigations* in this way, as a kind of 'storehouse' of philosophical methods. It seems to me clear that Wittgenstein was opposed to any attempt to look upon philosophy as a subject to be learnt; what philosophers have to do is to philosophise. Any method which could be applied automatically to the problem in hand would remove the need for philosophising, would be an easy way out. It seems to me that this latter was Husserl's aim. If philosophy could become a rigorous science, something which could be taught and learnt like other sciences, then it would not have the kind of difficulty that it in fact does. I must add, in fairness to Husserl, that his attitude to his own philosophising was certainly not one of making it easier for himself, however much he talked of making philosophy easier.

But the 'craving for generality' is hard for philosophers to resist, and there are two ways (at least) in which those who claim to be following Wittgenstein can go astray. One is by taking the fact that what is pointed to in much of his work is not new facts but something which we all know as some kind of general characterisation of philosophy. Professor Tugendhat mentions a point very like this in talking of Husserl: 'So here is an aspect of all understanding, of which we may say that everything which belongs to it we know already (*'a priori'*), even though this knowledge is not explicit and therefore seems susceptible to some sort of further enlightenment. According to Husserl, as according to many earlier as well as contemporary philosophers, this knowledge is the domain of philosophy' (p. 259). But Wittgenstein's point is a negative one; there is no special realm of deep facts with which only philosophers are acquainted. 'What we all know but fail to realise' is not meant to mark off a special area, but to be part of a denial that there is any area to be marked off.

In many cases philosophers have set up a metaphysical system (a subject-matter for philosophy) and have from this determined what seems the appropriate way of studying it. It is also possible to work in the reverse manner, to decide on the right method and hence to discover a subject-matter. It might be argued that philosophy must be descriptive because being the fundamental study there is nothing in terms of which explanation could be given. (Or, by another route, a philosopher might come to believe that description was the right and only method because of the failure of all others.) But what is to be described must be of a special nature, not the subject of one of the special sciences. So we find such topics as 'general features of human consciousness' or 'the use of words' or 'the structure of our conceptual apparatus'.

The second possible mistake in reading Wittgenstein is very like this. He says:

> We must do away with all *explanation*, and description alone must take its place. And this description gets its power of illumination – i.e. its purpose – from the philosophical problems. These are, of course, not empirical problems: they are solved, rather, by looking into the workings of our language, and that in such a way as to make us recognise those workings: in despite of an urge to misunderstand them. The problems are solved, not by giving new information, but by arranging what we have always known. Philosophy is a battle against the bewitchment of our intelligence by means of language.[1]

This certainly sounds like a 'programme' for philosophy and it has been read as such. (It even sounds rather like some things that Husserl said transcribed into the linguistic mode). But the point being made in the quoted passage is that it is the problems which are primary, which determine what is to be described and what sort of description is necessary. And there can be no *a priori* way of deciding how to deal with any problem that does arise, nor even what problems will arise.

In conclusion I want to make two points: first, it is hard to adopt this kind of 'negative' view of philosophy, for the whole training of

[1] *Philosophical Investigations* 109.

philosophers works against it. Crudely, in most matters our normal (and normally successful) way of proceeding is to try and find some general method which will save us the trouble of thinking about what we are dealing with. Genius may be required for this, but once found the method can often be put into a form in which it can be taught to and practised by ordinary men. If philosophy were like this, then the lack of agreed results would indeed be a scandal, as so many innovating philosophers have thought. When Wittgenstein said, 'Go the bloody *hard* way',[1] he meant that there couldn't be any 'short cuts', any general methods that would help us out.

The second point is that the kind of discussion in this symposium is almost bound to be misleading, for it tempts us to generalise, as do all discussions of the nature of philosophy. To avoid this, the only sure way, not 'method', is to get on with the job in detail. And so far as this has been the practice, whatever the theories, of many great philosophers, we can find value in their work.

[1] Quoted in Rhees, *Without Answers* (1969) p. 169.

DISCUSSION

Professor Tugendhat: Both Mr Pettit in his reply to my reply and Mr Manser in his comments have characterised what I tried to say in my paper as a rather strange position to take, although they have done so from quite opposite points of view. For my part, I thought that what I wrote was rather trivial and certainly unoriginal, while I feel that both Mr Manser's and Mr Pettit's position are quite remarkable and extraordinary.

Let me first make a few remarks on the comments of Mr Manser. In the first part of his comments, he seems to imply that I have misrepresented Husserl. I believe that he is mistaken, but I shall not go into this since I do not want to yield again to the tendency to Husserlian scholasticism which has appeared already several times during this conference, and which, I believe, could only lead us away from the questions that are at stake. Let me only mention one point. Mr Manser does not distinguish between the method which Husserl actually followed and his explicit theory of philosophical method. I had primarily his explicit theory in mind, as it is developed in his 2nd, 3rd and 6th *Logical Investigations*, in the first chapter of his *Ideas* and in some other texts. Husserl never reflected about the methodical problems of how to bring what he thought he saw across to some-body else. That he tried to do this is, of course, true, as it is true for anybody who writes a book. However, his explicit methodological convictions had a decisive bearing on his manner of exposition. To show something to somebody else meant for him to help the other person to see in his own mind what Husserl saw in his mind, and it is this seeing in one's mind which I believe to be a naïveté, although I am not going to demonstrate this here any more than I have demonstrated it in my paper. I thought that this had become a commonplace in England. We might come back to it in the discussion if it is desired.

Let me now turn to the second and important part of Mr Manser's comments. And here I propose to be no more concerned with Wittgensteinian and Austinian scholarship than with Husserlian scholarship. I think we all are not so much concerned with what is true about Wittgenstein or somebody else as with what is true simply. Now the very remarkable suggestion which Mr Manser

K

makes is this. It is a prejudice, he said, to believe that there is any definite subject-matter of philosophy, and it is equally a prejudice to believe that there is any method or even any number of methods of philosophy. 'Any method', he said, 'which could be applied automatically, . . . would remove the need for philosophising.' This would be true enough, but, I ask, does the belief in methods imply that these are methods that can be applied automatically? I would call this a technique rather than a method. Take, for example, what I have said in my paper about the descriptive method. Is this something that could be applied automatically? Surely not, since at the end of the paper I confess I don't even know its full concrete significance, and even if I did, this method stands not for a technique, but for a general approach, to be adjusted to the different problems to which it is applied. Specifications are called for, but precisely in order to specify you have to have some idea of that which you wish to specify. To use the Wittgensteinian example which Mr Manser cited; of course, you need different tools for different problems; but why not say what these tools are? Every one of them calls for clarification and all of them belong somehow together. They are, for example, the tools of a carpenter, and the tools a carpenter uses depends on what he is supposed to do. If there is no definite, although certainly very varied domain of what he is setting out to do, then he has no use for any tools whatsoever.

This brings me to the question of the domain, the subject-matter of philosophy. Mr Manser says it is a prejudice to speak of one. Now I wonder whether Mr Manser would be prepared to call any discourse whatsoever a philosophical discourse? If not, what reasons would he give? But once agreed that one kind of discourse is philosophical and another is not, is he not conceding a definite subject-matter of philosophy? I agree with him that we should remain open-minded for changes in what we consider philosophy to be about, but surely we cannot anticipate changes in something the existence of which we do not admit in the first place. People who believe they don't have to think about the subject-matter of philosophy, actually rely, in my opinion, on some philosophical tradition which has done the work for them. Mr Manser claims that those who talk about a subject-matter and methods of philosophy are taking the easy way. I wonder if it is not he who is proposing the easy way, since it may be easier to leave everything open and say nothing than to say something and then try to revise it.

So I now turn to Mr Pettit, who criticises me, not for having a view about method, but for not having the right one. In my opinion the argument in his second paper is vitiated by the same mistake as in his first paper, and this is his neglect to distinguish between the empirical and the *a priori*. He makes a series of distinctions which may perhaps be summarised thus: (*a*) a particular description, (*b*) an inductive generalisation, (*c*) an explanation of an inductive generalisation by theory. From this, he claims, a dilemma arises for my conception of philosophical propositions. They would, he thinks, have to fall under one of these three headings, and he rightly feels that I would not be happy with any one of them. But the dilemma does not arise since philosophical propositions are not empirical and hence cannot fall under one of these types of empirical propositions. Philosophical propositions are neither descriptions of something particular, nor are they inductive generalisations, nor explanations of inductive generalisations. But, says Mr Pettit, then they would have to be somehow general and non-inductive, which he thinks does not make sense. But surely it does make sense: any analytical statement about the meaning of a word has just this character. We do not arrive at it by inference, but indeed by direct verification, which is yet general and not particular. This, Mr Pettit thinks, would lead me back to Husserl's essences. But this much of Husserl is, of course, irrevocable, that in philosophy we deal with non-inductive generalities. My criticism of Husserl referred only to his supposition that these generalities consist in something that you can see intuitively rather than in a rule of usage of words.

Finally, I wish to make an attempt at reconciliation with Mr Pettit. I should first like to call attention to the fact that we can use the word 'explanation', which he cherishes, in two quite different ways. We use it in one sense when we say, e.g., 'Explain to me why *a* is *b*', and we use it in another sense when we say, e.g., 'Explain to me what *x* is'. I shall call these the explanation *why* and the explanation *what*, respectively. Now what Mr Pettit affirms, and what I deny, is that what philosophy is dealing with are explanations *why*. An explanation *what*, on the other hand, is a sort of description, and what I mean by philosophical description is of just this sort. For example, we can introduce any clarification of the meaning of a word by asking, 'Explain what that means'. I have already said in my paper that I don't believe that the word 'description' is really a happy one. And this is why I preferred to speak of clarification, since the word 'explanation' is out because of its ambiguity.

Modern philosophers from Brentano onwards have used the word 'descriptive' as a characterisation of their method in a primarily negative polemical sense. It was used to rule out what one did not want, the regressive method of the Kantians and the constructivist method of the Hegelians. What we can do in philosophy is only the clarification of what we understand. The question *why* seems to be inapplicable. In this basic methodological conception, phenomenology and British philosophy seem to me to agree.

Now the fact that this conception is primarily a negative one is the reason for what is justly deplored by Mr Pettit: that I have not given a satisfactory positive account of this descriptive method, nor has anyone else as far as I know. It may even be that a fully satisfactory account of the descriptive method would find itself forced to include some elements of explanation *why*. This might come in where we wish to understand the connection between different elements of our understanding. We might be forced to establish general propositions which can no longer be justified directly, but only by means of the conclusions which follow from them. This would be a sort of *a priori* inductive method, where a general feature not directly accessible serves as an explanation *why* for several less general features of our understanding. It seems to be this that Mr Pettit has in mind. But this aspect of philosophical method, if it really is one, can surely only be worked out after having taken a firm stand in the specific domain of philosophy, which is an *a priori* domain in which the first if not also the last task is clarification.

Mr Pettit: Before discussing Mr Manser's objections to my position and Professor Tugendhat's further comments on it, I propose to be personal – without, I hope, seeming pretentious – and give an account of my 'conversion' to that position.

The problems which troubled me most when I first began to think about the method of philosophy were problems in the 'new realism' of the early Moore and Russell, in particular the problems which led to the theory of descriptions and the theory of types. At the time, I was reading Sartre and other phenomenological writers. I became convinced that a radical solution to the problems of Moore and Russell could be developed with the use of the Husserlian method. That method would make philosophy descriptive, it would bring philosophy back to the experience of such structures of consciousness as perception, conceptualisation, judgement, and so on. I felt that it would reveal the false assumptions of the 'new realism' and make it possible to go beyond theories like the theory of descriptions; this theory I say was an *ad hoc* solution to a derivative problem.

I did not remain happy, however, with a view of philosophy as experiential and descriptive. The idea of a presuppositionless description, a description of essences, seemed absurd to me. Phenomenology, it then appeared, made of philosophy an experiential discipline, an attempt to deepen one's experience of oneself; description was merely a by-product. This did not satisfy me.

But the analytic view of philosophy as it had been developed by Wittgenstein did not offer me an acceptable alternative. I admired the work done in contemporary analytic philosophy but did not think that the analytic methodology did justice to it – or indeed to the work of any school of philosophy. That methodology, it appeared to me, made philosophy a study in the nuances of describing human activity – an important study perhaps, since the nuances are so often overlooked, but not one to claim the title of philosophy.

I turned then to classical philosophy – ancient, medieval and modern – and put my methodological questions to it. What was Aristotle at, when he argued that the material thing was a composite of *hyle* and *morphe*? Aquinas, when he distinguished essence and existence in the contingent thing and called them separate principles? Descartes, when he constructed a theory about man which divided him into a body and a soul? Berkeley, when he claimed that one could do away with the concept of matter and be an idealist, without denying any of the facts of common experience? Kant, when he argued that there were *a priori* forms to the sensibility, forms of space and time?

These questions led me to think of philosophy in terms very different to those of Husserl or Wittgenstein. The classical practice of philosophy led me to reject the contemporary theory. I began to think of philosophy as a matter of reason rather than inspection, theory rather than experience, explanation rather than description. Certainly inspection as well as reason was involved in philosophy, experience and description as well as theory and explanation. But I saw the aspects unstressed in contemporary philosophy as the more important. I regarded philosophy as the attempt, not to record data as they intelligibly appear, but to reconstruct what, metaphorically speaking, is their hidden intelligibility: the structure which makes them appear as they do.

I used the term 'explanation' to characterise philosophy because it was the term with which both Husserl and Wittgenstein had contrasted their own 'description'. But I did feel it was necessary to insist, and I did insist in the first paper, that this explanation was non-reductive. I must now clarify the concept of non-reductive explanation, since both Professor Tugendhat and Mr Manser have complained that they do not understand it fully.

An explanation must always be based on a description or set of descriptions of data, or on generalisations from such descriptions. Now a description may be proper or improper, it may or it may not provide a sufficient criterion for identifying the data described. If it is improper and fails to provide such a criterion, then the explanation based on it is a reductive one. If it is proper, the explanation is non-reductive or, as it may also be called, reconstructive. To take an example, I may describe a salute as the movement of an arm from point *A* to point *B*. This is an improper description as it does not provide a sufficient criterion for identifying a salute; it does not distinguish it, for instance, from a wave or a gesture of recognition. Hence the explanation of a salute in physiological terms, which is based on such a description, is a reductive explanation.

The concept of reductive explanation is a familiar one in the philosophy of science. One level of explanation is reduced to another and a set of phenomena reductively explained when the proper description of those phenomena is replaced by an improper one to which it is systematically related; a chemical description might be replaced, for instance, by a physical one and an attempt made to explain the chemical data in physical terms. The problem, of course, with any reductive attempt is that of elaborating the relation between the two descriptions; on this elaboration depends the success of the reduction.

My present claim that philosophical explanation is non-reductive may be linked with the phenomenological thesis that philosophy must avoid treating man naturalistically and consider him as a conscious subject. I have always presumed that the data with which philosophy is concerned are the data of human experience, in a broad sense, or human behaviour. To take those data naturalistically, it may be argued, is precisely to take them under an improper description. The only proper description of them is that which is given from the point of view of the subject. When I say, therefore, that philosophical explanation is non-reductive, I am taking the phenomenological point about the true approach to human experience, even if I maintain that this approach need not restrict itself to description.

The logic of explanation I have worked out in my reply to Professor Tugendhat and I need only mention it here. Particular description may be directly verified in experience, but not so the generalisation from it, which in fact normally serves as a generalising explanation. That generalising explanation is paralleled by a non-generalising form. The difference between the two is that some non-logical variables occur in the non-generalising form, which do not occur in the descriptions to be explained. The most common form of verification for any explanation, generalising or non-generalising, is – in a sense of the term different to that used above – the reductive argument. This argument is logically vulnerable: it takes the form, 'If A, then B; B; therefore A.' 'A' is the explanatory hypothesis, of course, 'B' the series of descriptions which it is to explain.

When I say that philosophy is explanatory, I mean to say that it is concerned with formulating non-generalising hypotheses which explain human experience taken under certain descriptions. Those descriptions must be true to consciousness and respect the demands of ordinary linguistic usage. They will cover in a very abstract way the varieties of human experience and behaviour, giving an account of what it is to work in general or to recognise beauty, to ask questions or to understand another mind and so on. (The question of the relation of psychology to philosophy, which arises at this point, may be left for the discussion.) Philosophical explanation, as I conceive of it, will take these descriptions and work out, by reductive argument, the hypotheses which would make sense of them. These hypotheses will articulate the conditions under which the descriptions may hold. As those descriptions are general and must hold of man in any cultural context, the philosophical hypotheses may be said to frame the invariable conditions for the possibility of man being man, doing the things mentioned in the descriptions.[1]

To come to the objections, Mr Manser argues that there are many methods to philosophy and that any view of philosophy such as mine is therefore radically unsound. He says that Husserl uses many methods himself, many different types of argument, and he quotes Wittgenstein's comparison between the philosopher and the carpenter with his bag of tools. If there are many methods to philosophy of course, then there is a fundamental misconception in speaking of *the* method of philosophy, as I have done, and indeed, Professor Tugendhat too.

It should first be pointed out that if Mr Manser's objection holds, then the two philosophers whom he invokes, Husserl and

[1] Note (May 1970): Perhaps it is misleading to say that philosophy tries to explain human experience taken under certain descriptions. It suggests too close a parallel with natural science which, in classic fashion, seeks the sufficient conditions for the truth of certain descriptions, the conditions under which the described facts are inevitable. Philosophy seeks the necessary conditions for the truth of other descriptions, the only conditions under which the described facts are possible. Hence the impossibility of falsifying a philosophical hypothesis is not a radical methodological defect. The distinction between explanation by sufficient conditions (which may of course also be necessary, a possibility not considered here) and explanation by necessary conditions now seems very important to me and crucial in the distinction between natural and human science. Explanation by necessary conditions is not verified in a reductive argument but in an argument of the form: 'If not A, not B; B; therefore A', where 'A' is a hypothesis and 'B' a series of descriptions.

Wittgenstein, must be an embarrassment to him. Husserl did speak of the one true method of philosophy so he must be accused of misinterpreting his own work. Wittgenstein did characterise philosophy as descriptive and he too must be accused, if not of a misinterpretation, at least of a misleading way of speaking.

Mr Manser seems to me to be guilty of a conceptual mistake. When I speak of 'method', he takes me at my word, points out that there is another way of using it and then insists that this is the only correct way. Where he speaks of the many methods of philosophy, however, I would speak of techniques. The question of method is the question of what an inquiry is attempting, at least on my use of the term, and the question of technique is the question of how the inquiry is attempting it. For me, philosophy has one method: it is the inquiry which seeks the invariable conditions for the possibility of man being man. But it has many techniques: techniques of description, which would include reflection and linguistic analysis, and techniques of hypothesis-formulation, among them, for instance, the study of historical systems of thought. When I speak to you of the method of philosophy, I am not presuming to give you advice on how to pursue your questions; I am merely trying to articulate the direction of those questions. With this made explicit, I think that Mr Manser's objection may be taken as answered.

Professor Tugendhat answers Mr Manser in much the same way as I do but still continues to insist, of course, on his criticism of my position. Instead of explanation, he speaks of descriptive clarification.

I would argue against him that either clarificatory propositions in philosophy are argued and explanatory, so that the difference between us is terminological, or they are directly verifiable and of no more value than reports on consciousness.

Professor Tugendhat says that I do not allow for the *a priori* nature of philosophy. This is a charge which I do not understand fully. I think that the answer to it may be that the conditions which explanatory philosophy invokes are invariable, and precisely *a priori*. Indeed Kant, the philosopher *par excellence* of the *a priori*, is the historical figure who is most amenable to my methodological scheme.

I have not had a chance to study Professor Tugendhat's remarks but, on first hearing, I cannot see the usefulness of his distinction between explanation *why* and explanation *what*. When he allows that there may be explanation *why* in philosophy, it does seem that our positions are similar, but it is hard to say.

Let me say finally against Professor Tugendhat that I still feel he is hypostasising the concept of structure. For me, an explanatory theory which accounts for certain phenomena may be said to reveal their structure. Taken in this way, structure is defined at a second remove as the objective of explanatory theory; if explanation means intelligence at work, structure means intelligibility. Professor Tugendhat seems to me to make a thing of this structure. He speaks of the structure of conscious behaviour, with which philosophy is concerned, as an object of experience that can be descriptively explicated. This way of speaking, however, makes no literal sense. At best, it is metaphorical; at worst, it is very misleading.

Professor Hartmann (Bonn): I would like to make two points. One point refers to Husserl's method. There seems to be agreement between the two symposiasts that Husserl's method is descriptive, but I wonder whether in this way his method isn't sold short. I agree that the *Logical Investigations* are strictly descriptive. But let me focus on *Ideas I* and later writings and, in these, on chapters dealing with constitution. Constitution theory is the attempt to account for *noemas*, and the peculiar case of Husserl's method seems to be that this account which is clearly explanatory is at the same time descriptive. So we should be able to inspect stages antecedent of concreteness, at least if we are proper phenomenologists. I draw your attention to analyses in the phenomenology of internal time-consciousness where a very different kind of time from what we are used to, a more primary stage of time, is described as an explanans of objective time. So, clearly, the method is descriptive and explanatory. I wonder whether or not the symposiasts would call this method, with its reference to constituting acts, a 'reductive' method?

Now my second point. I wonder whether in the two papers sufficient attention has been given to other possible positions? One may hold that there is a complete disjunction as between description and explanation. Or, if you will, explanation must be reductive or non-reductive, and if non-reductive, it is descriptive, a case I wouldn't call 'explanation' at all. But as for explanation proper: if non-descriptive, would it have to be 'reductive'? I am thinking here of positions Mr Pettit wouldn't subscribe to, positions like the Aristotelean one or, more generally, the categorial position where ontological principles are invoked to govern the sciences. Or I am thinking of more refined schemes like the Hegelian and, possibly, the Kantian, where categories are themselves rationalised in a system. The idea is that thought can be unfolded so as to result in explanation. Again, I wonder whether the symposiasts would call this 'reductive' explanation? I can see that they would rule it out as non-descriptive. But is it 'reductive'?

Apparently, the attempt to invoke principles is precisely not to 'reduce' something concrete to some impoverished other thing, but to relate it to a stance somehow continuous with the concrete and yet other. This method of devising principiation, or of invoking principles, has been glossed over in a cavalier way, and I wonder whether this method isn't really the main source of inspiration in the matter of explanation, and whether we shouldn't bring it in?

Mr Pettit: I would like to comment first of all, Professor Hartmann, on your claim that Husserl in cases is doing explanatory work. We must distinguish, of course, between practice and theory. Both Professor Tugendhat and I were dealing with Husserl's theory of his method rather than with his actual method in practice. At least, that is certainly what I was dealing with. I can accept therefore what Mr Manser said, that Husserl uses various types of argument which may not be descriptive, and I can certainly accept what you say, that in cases he is doing explanatory work. I quote from my own paper (p. 255):

> When Husserl talks of constitution, for instance, or intentionality it can be argued that he does not describe any nuclear performance to be found on reflection, but postulates a correlation of consciousness and its object which, unlike the spatial model, will make knowing intelligible.

To take up your second point, you say that you would not call non-reductive explanation, explanation at all. If that is the case, then what are you saying Husserl is giving, when you say that Husserl is offering explanation? On the question of principles, I still feel that these can be assimilated to the explanatory view of philosophy.

Hartmann: On the same level?

Pettit: Well, I'm not sure, I think they can; you offered no evidence which would convince me that they cannot.

Hartmann: A principle on the same level as a principiatum?

Pettit: What sort of a principle have you in mind?

Hartmann: Any.

Pettit: Could you mention one in particular?

Hartmann: Substance.

Pettit: But substance is a concept.

Hartmann: And a principle.

Pettit: Well, I think that substance is a concept occurring within a system of explanatory concepts with which we attempt to make sense of certain ranges of data, taken under certain descriptions.

Hartmann: You deny principles.

Pettit: No. For me, your principle is an explanatory concept defined, as I suggested, in the way mathematical concepts are sometimes defined, by implicit definition.

Tugendhat: I don't agree with Professor Hartmann that what Husserl means by 'constitution' is an explanatory method. The phenomenological theory of constitution must be distinguished from constructivist theories of the sort developed in German Idealism. For Husserl, the need for a theory of constitution arises because he is undertaking to analyse descriptively the way in which things are given. Now the way things are given refers back, according to Husserl, to an elaborate synthetic process which he calls 'constitution'. But this process is to be described intuitively, it is not a theoretical construction. Husserl's constitutional questions do not start out from the question 'why?' but from the question 'how?' ('How are objects, and objects of such and such a kind, given?')

Concerning the second point of Professor Hartmann, I agree that there is no complete disjunction between description and explanation, at least as long as we understand 'explanation' in the empirical way suggested by Mr Pettit. Constructivist methods of the Hegelian kind have indeed been neglected by us both. They are, I think, explanatory as well, but explanatory in an *a priori* sense. I agree with Professor Hartmann that it would be more worth while to confront the descriptivist position with the *a priori* explanatory position of the constructivists. But I don't understand why he cites the Aristotelean position as an example of some kind of explanatory method. Aristotle seems to me to be the paradigm case of a descriptivist.

James Daly (Belfast): Would it help our understanding of this problem to situate it historically, by saying that Husserl's first use of the distinction between explanatory and descriptive arose out of the need to refute psychologism, which is the theory that our ideas can and must be explained by their origin in psychological fashion, as Hume and Mill did. Husserl's theory of descriptive psychology was intended to enable him to classify and analyse each level of experience, perception, concept, or theory without having to *explain* it reductively in terms of prior mental entities such as 'impressions', as Hume had done. And this brings me back to a question which I was going to ask earlier. Mr Pettit said that the question would undoubtedly arise in the discussion of how to separate philosophy from psychology. I would like to bear out this prediction by raising it now. But I do so to ask Mr Pettit what problem he sees here. Perhaps he can explain why he sees any difficulty in separating psychology and philosophy, which for most of us are now regarded as pretty well clearly distinct, though perhaps they were not for Husserl in 1911?

Pettit: In my view, psychology in practice often contains a good deal of strictly philosophical argument. Leaving that aside, however, psychology proper begins like any science from a series of descriptions. In its case, these are observational descriptions of human behaviour; animal psychology we need not consider here. The goal of psychology is to make these descriptions intelligible, to explain them. It does so normally by looking for generalisations of them. Such generalisations are to be found in the universal statements which industrial psychology may make about break-periods, learning-theory about the usefulness of teaching methods and psychoanalysis about the effect of childhood experiences on adult behaviour. In an area such as psychoanalysis, there is a further movement towards non-generalising explanation with the introduction of theoretical terms like 'id' and 'ego'.

Philosophy contrasts with psychology first of all in the standpoint of its descriptions. This is the standpoint of consciousness, not that of observation. It is my standpoint as subject, the standpoint which any one of us takes up when he answers a question put to him about his perception or activity. In philosophy, I begin from descriptions about forms of human experience which are made from this standpoint. I then go on to try to make those descriptions intelligible within a theoretical framework. I may try, for instance, to develop a theory of emotion, a theory which would have to counter various established views, such as that of Descartes.

My view of the relation between philosophical and psychological explanation is very much that of Sartre in his *Sketch for a Theory of the Emotions*. In the case of emotion, philosophy offers a theory about the nature of emotion as such, while psychology takes such a theory for granted and deals with particular patterns among emotions. In his *Action, Emotion and the Will*, for instance, Anthony Kenny shows how many psychologies take a Cartesian philosophy of emotion for granted.

Daly: But is there any danger of confusing philosophy and psychology, and is there therefore any particular problem of a separation between philosophy and psychology, any more than there is a problem of a separation between philosophy and physics? What has psychology got to do with philosophy, in fact?

Pettit: There is a danger of confusing philosophy and psychology, for the obvious reason that each is a study of man. The danger, however, must affect any methodology. It is not a peculiar weakness of the one which I defend, that it does not eliminate the danger.

Dr S. Raschid (London): It seems to me that this question of the 'mental eye' is a very crucial issue, not only in relation to Husserlian phenomenology but also in its wider implication. For the moment I would just like to make some preliminary points, even at the risk of being charged with what Professor Tugendhat referred to as 'Husserl scholasticism'. I find it a bit odd that Mr Pettit should choose *The Idea of Phenomenology* in order to discuss Husserl, because it is well recognised that his mature works are *Ideas I* and *II*, and the *Cartesian Meditations*. Also Mr Pettit betrayed tremendous prejudice in talking about 'conscious human behaviour'. This is, of course, an absolute travesty of Husserl.

To get on to the question of the 'mental eye'. Professor Tugendhat very easily assumes that this relates to the eidetic intuition of essences, and he refers to the *Logical Investigations* and Chapter I of *Ideas*; again this is rather the earlier phase of Husserl in which the whole theory of consciousness, reduction, and so forth, has not yet been developed. It has been argued that the 'essences' are the most dispensable part of Husserlian phenomenology. Certainly Gurwitsch maintains that Scheler made the great mistake of confusing the eidetic with the transcendental reduction. The eidetic reduction is simply the discussion of universals, and this can be carried on in the ordinary natural attitude, e.g. when we talk about objects in general, chairs, tables, concepts, etc., and this is all it implies. We are then left with the question of what the 'mental eye' is. I suggest that it refers to the role of reflection, which is one of the vital things in, if not the centre of, the Husserlian method. Here we go on to this very dogmatic assertion that Wittgenstein had made some 'devastating observations', etc.

This word 'devastating' was also used by George Nakhnikian in his Introduction to the 1964 (Nijhoff) edition of Husserl's *The Idea of Phenomenology;* and he gave a number of references to Wittgenstein. On careful examination we find that Wittgenstein makes various points about the nature of mental processes, reflection, etc., with characteristic superficiality . . . (*Uproar*) . . . . Contrast this with the discussion of reflection in Husserl's *Ideas*, section 77 onwards, and *Cartesian Meditations*, section 15; we find that all the points made by Wittgenstein have been made in great detail, depth and rigour by Husserl. Therefore I think the burden of proof is on you to show, firstly, what you meant by the 'mental eye', and secondly, what were these 'devastating observations'. I would simply add that reflection, as Husserl says, is the direction of consciousness on to an already conscious act. Take a very simple example: I am looking at the blackboard and I am, as it were, immersed in this experience. I then sit back and reflect on the fact that I'm looking at the blackboard; of course this involves various differences.

Tugendhat: Dr Raschid is, of course, right about the difference between the eidetic reduction and the transcendental reduction in Husserl, and I myself called attention to this in a note to my paper. However, I don't think that Dr Raschid is right in claiming that the eidetic reduction, the method of intuitive analysis of essential connections, lost importance for the later Husserl. At no stage of his development did Husserl cease to insist that, even on the transcendental level, the proper method of philosophy was intuitive. But however that may be, the starting-point of Husserl's transcendental method – the reflecting inner eye (inner sense) – is no less problematic than the starting-point of his eidetic method – the mental (intellectual) eye. You take it for granted, Dr Raschid, that we can 'reflect' on 'acts'. But is not the burden of proof on you? Are you sure we can find and observe such things as mental acts in ourselves? What are they? Husserl thought of them somehow as arrows of consciousness directed at objects. But this is a metaphor, and the question is: how can we give an unmetaphorical account of what is meant? According to Husserl, by looking at something internally given. According to the analytic philosophers, by analysing certain uses of language. This is a real difference, and whichever side we may take, we should not minimise it by saying that one part is doing the same thing as the other, only more superficially. The trouble with Husserl's claim that everybody must be able to see their acts is that some people just don't, and what can you do in such a situation?

Raschid: Well, obviously the answer is that we cannot deal with the 'acts' in isolation without considering the whole problem of reduction, constitution and the intentional theory of consciousness. I doubt whether you can 'see' in the sense you have been suggesting.

Tugendhat: But surely, the theory of reduction is already based on the assumption of acts. The reduction starts out from the structure *cogito – cogitatum* and is accomplished by bracketing the *cogitatum*.

Raschid: You don't bracket the *cogitatum;* the *cogitatum* is the *noema*.

Tugendhat: What is bracketed is, strictly speaking, the thetic character of the *cogitatum*, and this makes it possible, according to Husserl, to analyse the *cogitatum qua cogitatum*.

Michael Stant (Durham): I'd like to get back to the actual subject of the paper on description and explanation in philosophy. It seems to me that both symposiasts have missed out certain kinds of statements that sometimes appear in physics and the natural sciences, which may well appear in fact in philosophy. An example of this would be the statement that light travels in a straight line. Now this sort of statement is not a summary of laboratory findings or observations, or whatever. And it doesn't seem to me to be apparent that this is an *a priori* statement either. Nor is it one of Mr Pettit's non-generalising statements. The point is that such statements, if you like, introduce a language for talking about phenomena. And it strikes one that it is remarkable in some respects, that, e.g., when we're talking about object lines, we're talking about them as angles and lines. Now there's nothing *a priori* about this that we should talk about objects or phenomena in this sort of way. It seems to me important that this class of statements at least is introduced.

Pettit: I would like to comment on the example that you use: the statement that light travels in straight lines. I am not sure, on first reflection, what type of statement this is. It is worth considering, however, that it may be a non-generalising explanation, rather than a description. It may be taken as the explanation of phenomena in the description of which the term 'line' does not occur. The concept of straight line, while it may certainly have a descriptive usage, is very probably used in the statement in the implicit definition which Euclid gives of it, as a function of the concept of point: the shortest distance between two points. In that case, the statement would seem to be explanatory in intent.

Stant: No, I'm not sure about this issue whether one can start with Euclidean lines in ordinary language – not defined in terms of Euclidean geometry . . .

Dr Wightman (Oxford): May I add a rider here? The explication of the proposition 'light travels in straight lines' is ambiguous, because there is no independent definition of a straight line, and it is very likely that the notion that Euclid applied in his *Optics* arose out of the natural observation of shadows and eclipses, and this became incorporated in Euclidean geometry. Now you know that in principle there is great difficulty in defining a straight line, which Archimedes, for instance, defined as 'the shortest distance between two points'. But you have no idea how to find the shortest distance between two points except by the use of an optical instrument; so the circle is complete. In this issue, fundamental to natural philosophy, as Whitehead said of all philosophical discussion, 'the merest hint of dogmatic certainty as to finality of statement is an exhibition of folly'.

Dr Harry Lewis (Leeds): I have more hope for the classification of judgements, in spite of what the last two speakers have said, than I have for the classification of disciplines, which is what we seem to be about tonight. I'd like to make two comments, one about a distinction between what philosophers ought to do and what they in fact do; and the other about a distinction between seeing that philosophers do something special and being able to say what it is that they do. Mr Pettit's remarks about psychology suggest sceptical reflections about what has just been said about philosophical method. Philosophers may be no better than anybody else – although perhaps they ought to be – at saying what they are doing.

Mr Pettit was quite happy to tell us what psychology really is. He was quite prepared to say that what psychologists are (as a matter of empirical fact) doing is not what psychology really is. But perhaps philosophers likewise don't do what philosophy really is. It seems to me that this evening's discussion leads to a question, because neither the symposiasts nor anybody else have paid much attention to empirical evidence, that is, actual philosophical argumentation. Their method has been to use their philosophical intuition to say what philosophy is or what philosophical method is. That is something like saying what philosophers ought to do.

The second point is this: even assuming that there is some special kind of activity or discourse rightly said to be philosophical, I would question whether it follows that there is any saying, or indeed any use in asking what is special about it. Professor Tugendhat made use of an argument here: as soon as we identify – or Mr Manser is prepared to identify – a pattern of discussion as philosophical, then its subject-matter could be said to be at least part of the subject-matter of philosophy. But this is a questionable argument, because the assumption that any passage of discourse has at least one, and only one, subject-matter is open to question. Moreover, it might not be the subject-matter – let us say some entities which are being talked about – which determines the special character of the passage: it might be something else. For example, I might while doing aesthetics discuss the pattern of a passage of music, and I might be discussing printing while considering the same pattern; but the subject-matter would be the same. More generally, I doubt whether a discussion about philosophical method has more than heuristic value – just because of the evidence of philosophers who have made such confident statements about philosophical method.

The case has to be made, even if there is something special about philosophical discourse, that there's a hope of saying what it is. I think in this connection of Wittgenstein: merely because we collect a number of different passages of discourse under one term, that does not give us the right to say that there must be something you can mention that they have in common. And for this reason I would like to support what Mr Manser said, and say that we should start here with problems or with what perplexes us as philosophers, rather than worry too much – except perhaps in the bath or on Sunday afternoons – about what sort of activity it is.

Professor G. N. A. Vesey (Open University) : I want to be clear about Mr Manser's position here. I thought that Mr Manser said that there is not a method or a technique of doing philosophy, and that Mr Pettit, talking about what Mr Manser said, said that Mr Manser says there are many techniques of doing philosophy. Could we be clear as to whether Mr Manser said there is no method or whether there are many methods?

Manser: I claimed there is no method. There may be a number of different ways or techniques. One may in fact solve a particular problem in a particular way but this does not mean that there is a method here which one can then apply to any other problem. I mean, in other words, there may be philosophical problems for which solutions can be found, but these solutions cannot be generalised.

Vesey: Would I be correct, then, in saying that if someone were to ask you what the methods of philosophy were or what the techniques of philosophy were, you would say, 'You shouldn't start by asking that question. You should start by looking at some problem which I'll show you and then we'll go into them together and see what we can do with them'?

Manser: Yes.

Pettit: But suppose somebody asks you to explain why what you are doing is not physics?

Guy Robinson (Southampton) : Dismiss him as a student!

Anthony Palmer (Southampton): Mr Manser says that delineating philosophy or the subject-matter of philosophy is a mistake. The general reaction to this is that if you didn't then pretty well anything would count as philosophy. Those who believe this do so because they seem to think that if there are ways of ruling something out as philosophy or anything else, then there must be some rule that brings philosophy, or whatever else, in. Now I don't think that the one follows from the other. For example, I think that some philosophers do sometimes know what they are doing, but that when they do, this does not necessarily mean that there is something that they are doing (and then a delineation is produced) and they know what it is, any more than 'I know what I want' needs to be translated into 'There is something that I want and I know what it is'. If I am doing something intentionally I can know when I go wrong without being able to say what going right would be. For example, when I am doing a bit of stage acting I may feel that I am going wrong, that *that's* not how I wanted it, when there is no specific delineable way in which I want to do it. Not that that is not sensible, because, of course, there are such cases – cases in which you want to do something in a particular way, e.g. I want to act it in the way in which

Gielgud acted it, to produce a piece of Gielgud tremulo. But all cases of doing something intentionally are not like that, and when they are not it does not follow that one doesn't know what one wants or is doing.

I took Professor Tugendhat as saying something like this in the earlier part of his paper when he talked about implicit knowledge, but in effect denying it later on when he talked about the 'implicit structure of consciousness'. Once you start talking about structure the point is denied and you are led to suppose that 'I know what I'm doing' must always mean 'There is something that I am doing and I know what it is'.

Pettit: Before concluding, I would like to mention two points of criticism which Professor Tugendhat makes against me in his initial paper. The first he makes on p. 264; he says that I suggest that for Husserl intuition is separable from intention. It is true that I do not make clear that intuition is necessarily related to intention in Husserl's thought. However, I had never meant to suggest that they were separable for him, and I do say explicitly in my paper that Husserl does not consider the possibility of an intuition without an intention (p. 242).

Professor Tugendhat makes a second point against me on p. 262, note 1, where he suggests that I am misled by the standard translation, when I take Husserl's *aufklären* as 'explain' rather than 'clarify'. It is true that I was hasty in my translation of *aufklären*, because of the standard version. However, I do not see that the matter is of more than verbal importance. In the context, Husserl is speaking of possibilities, and in English there is no significant difference between clarifying possibilities and explaining them.

In conclusion, then, I remain convinced that the methodology of philosophy is an important subject. I take Dr Lewis's point that it may often be normative rather than descriptive. It is so, because it is based, not only on the philosophical work recorded in historical texts, but on the philosophical work of which the methodologist has experience in himself. As a methodologist, the philosopher takes a certain definition of philosophical question for granted and tries to show the pattern and direction of such questions; in doing so, he must rely on his own performance and not just on that of others. Hence he must sometimes make judgements on where others go wrong. Yet I do not think this is to say that the methodologist assumes the role of consultant to other philosophers, as he would do if he began to offer advice on techniques of inquiry.

There certainly are difficulties in the concept of a methodology of philosophy: these have been raised by Mr Manser and others. I can only say now that they do not seem to me to be insurmountable. I do so in the awareness of further difficulties which seem to me quite genuine, the difficulties in the actual working out of a methodology. It is with these that I have been mainly concerned in the present discussion. If I could ever have felt that I had cleared up many of them, I can certainly do so no longer. There, for me, lies the value of that discussion.

Tugendhat: I would only like to make a few comments on the last remarks that were made.

Mr Palmer has been speaking about something that the philosopher may be knowing only implicitly. But this should not be confused with what I meant, in my paper, by implicit knowledge, since this was not an implicit knowledge of the philosopher *qua* philosopher, but the implicit knowledge of anybody, which the philosopher undertakes to analyse. And I don't see why we should not say that, in particular, we also have an implicit knowledge of the structure of our understanding. Mr Pettit, at the beginning of his second paper, suggests that I was speaking 'somewhat imprecisely' when I said that the subject-matter of philosophy was the knowledge of this structure rather than the structure itself. But if the object of philosophy is to clarify, its subject-matter seems to be implicit knowledge. To stress this seems to me important in order to distinguish the kind of structure which interests philosophers from the kinds of structure which interest, e.g., psychologists or linguists. Not any structure of our understanding or behaviour or language is a structure which we implicitly know.

I agree with Dr Lewis that we should pay more attention to actual philosophical argumentation to arrive at a more definite conception of philosophical method. Such general remarks as I have made in my paper do not lead us very far. But the method of analysing method which Dr Lewis recommends cannot be as empirical as he suggests. We shall have to analyse actual argumentation, but shall we not proceed selectively, calling some arguments bad, for some reason or other, and others good? We shall choose certain paradigm cases and reject others (somebody may choose a piece of Wittgenstein as a paradigm case and reject a piece of Hegel, or vice versa). The question 'What is the method of philosophy?' is not an empirical but a normative question.

In his second point, Dr Lewis claims that we cannot identify a piece of philosophic discourse by means of the subject-matter which it is about. What determines it as philosophical may be some other characteristic than its subject-matter. I agree, if we take 'subject-matter' to be the 'entities' we talk about. But if I say that the subject-matter of philosophy is implicit knowledge, this is not a subject-matter in this narrow sense and refers not just to the object but to the object in a specific approach. I admit that this shows that the expression 'subject-matter' is rather misleading.

Finally, Dr Lewis claims, like Mr Manser, that there is really no need to worry about philosophical method at all. This worry amounts to an unfruitful reflection, and what we should rather do is go ahead with the philosophical problems themselves. But, I should ask, which problems, and how should we go ahead with them? At this point we can remark a fundamental difference between the philosophical situation in Britain and on the Continent. In England, philosophy appears at present still as a going 'concern'. You seem to know what the problems are and you seem to know what the methods are (e.g. you would not hesitate whether to choose Wittgenstein or Hegel as a paradigm case). In such a situation the question about method may well appear superfluous. On the Continent, there have been periods of similar confidence. But at present we are not so sure what the problems are and we are not so sure how to deal with them. In such a situation of bewilderment the question of method appears urgent. It is not a very dignified situation, but perhaps a truly philosophical one. The places and times to which Dr Lewis wants to restrict the apparently idle question of philosophical method, are precisely the places and times to which most people ever since Socrates always wanted to restrict the whole of philosophy anyway.

INDEX OF NAMES

INDEX OF SUBJECTS